Ecocritics and Ecoskeptics
A Humanist Reading of Recent French Ecofiction

Studies in Modern and Contemporary France 5

Studies in Modern and Contemporary France

Series Editors
Professor Gill Allwood, Nottingham Trent University
Professor Denis M. Provencher, University of Arizona
Professor Martin O'Shaughnessy, Nottingham Trent University

The Studies in Modern and Contemporary France book series is a new collaboration between the Association for the Study of Modern and Contemporary France (ASMCF) and Liverpool University Press (LUP). Submissions are encouraged focusing on French politics, history, society, media and culture. The series will serve as an important focus for all those whose engagement with France is not restricted to the more classically literary, and can be seen as a long-form companion to the Association's journal, *Modern and Contemporary France,* and to *Contemporary French Civilization*, published by Liverpool University Press.

Ecocritics and Ecoskeptics

A Humanist Reading of Recent French Ecofiction

JONATHAN F. KRELL

Liverpool University Press

First published 2020 by
Liverpool University Press
4 Cambridge Street
Liverpool
L69 7ZU

Copyright © 2020 Jonathan F. Krell

The right of Jonathan F. Krell to be identified as the author of this book has been asserted by him in accordance with the Copyright, Designs and Patents Act 1988.

All rights reserved. No part of this book may be reproduced, stored in a retrieval system, or transmitted, in any form or by any means, electronic, mechanical, photocopying, recording, or otherwise, without the prior written permission of the publisher.

British Library Cataloguing-in-Publication data
A British Library CIP record is available

ISBN 978-1-78962-205-8 cased

Typeset by Carnegie Book Production, Lancaster
Printed and bound by CPI Group (UK) Ltd, Croydon CR0 4YY

To Kristin
and
In memory of Michel Tournier

Contents

List of Illustrations — ix

Acknowledgments — xi

Introduction: The Fundamental Debate: Michel Serres the Ecocritic vs. Luc Ferry the Ecoskeptic — 1

Part 1: Three French Ecofictions

1. Time, Weather, and Waste: Michel Tournier's *Gemini* (*Les Météores*) — 23

2. Cloud Erotica: Stéphane Audeguy's *The Theory of Clouds* (*La Théorie des nuages*) — 53

3. A Fairy in the Age of Prometheus: Chantal Chawaf's *Mélusine des détritus* — 77

Part 2: The Animal Question

4. Ethical Humanism and the Animal Question: Vercors's *You Shall Know Them* (*Les Animaux dénaturés*) — 95

5. Marginality and Animality: Olivia Rosenthal's *Que font les rennes après Noël?* — 123

Part 3: Two Ecoskeptics: The Humanist and the Humorist

6. Deep Ecology Gone Wrong: J.-C. Rufin's *Globalia* and *Le Parfum d'Adam*   151

7. From Ecohumor to Ecohumanism: Iegor Gran's *O.N.G!* and *L'Écologie en bas de chez moi*   175

Conclusion: Environmentalism Is a Humanism   193

Appendix: Interviews with Stéphane Audeguy and Iegor Gran   217

Bibliography   239

Index   255

Illustrations

1. Marseille landfill at Entressen, Istres, France, 1997. Photograph by Franck Pourcel.   22

2. Grazing reindeer in snowstorm. iStock.com/SeppFriedhuber.   94

3. Liberty under a globe. iStock.com/Vadmary.   150

Acknowledgments

Some chapters have appeared elsewhere in various forms. The Introduction is partially based on "Michel Serres, Luc Ferry, and the Possibility of a Natural Contract," *The Environment in French and Francophone Literature and Film*, French Literature Series 39, Rodopi, 2012, pp. 1–13. Chapter 2 is based on "Ecoerotica in Stéphane Audeguy's *La Théorie des nuages*," *French Ecocriticism: From the Early Modern Period to the Twenty-First Century*, Peter Lang, 2017, pp. 175–93. Portions of Chapter 3 were published in French in "*Mélusine des détritus ou les cris de la Terre*," *Écriture et réécriture du merveilleux féerique. Autour de Mélusine*, Classiques Garnier, 2012, pp. 245–54. The bulk of Chapter 4 appeared in "When Ecocriticism Meets Existentialism: Vercors's *You Shall Know Them*," *Interdisciplinary Studies in Literature and Environment*, vol. 24, no. 1, 2017, pp. 22–46. A shorter version of Chapter 7 was given as a talk in French titled "Iegor Gran: un rare cas d'écohumour," at l'Université d'Angers, France, in 2016, to be published in the forthcoming *Écocritique: nouvelles territorialités*, Classiques Garnier. The interview with Iegor Gran in the Appendix is a translation of an interview that appeared in *The French Review*, vol. 91, no. 3, 2018, pp. 182–91.

I would like to thank The American College of the Mediterranean in Aix-en-Provence, France, for their generous resident fellowships during spring 2017 and summer 2019 that gave me precious time to work on this book. Dana Bultman, Catherine Jones, and Jan Pendergrass, colleagues in the Department of Romance Languages at the University of Georgia, provided precious advice on humanism. I am very grateful to my brother David for his thorough reading and philosophical knowledge, and to my wife Kristin for her research expertise, patience, and encouragement. The various editors at Liverpool University Press and Carnegie Book Production who saw the manuscript through to completion have been models of efficiency and helpfulness, especially during the trying days of spring and summer 2020. Finally, I thank Zola, Pastis, and Colette for their sage and silent advice on the animal question.

Introduction
The Fundamental Debate: Michel Serres the Ecocritic vs. Luc Ferry the Ecoskeptic

> Love our two fathers, natural and human, the land and the neighbor; love humanity, our human mother, and our natural mother, the Earth.
>
> —Serres, *The Natural Contract* 49

> Our present behaviors, even our sensibility now take into consideration the fragility of things, and so presuppose that Nature is slowly becoming a legal subject.
>
> —Serres, "Revisiting the Natural Contract"

In 1755, when he published his *Second Discourse*, the *Discourse on the Origin and Foundations of Inequality Among Men*, Jean-Jacques Rousseau seemingly righted many wrongs of that philosophical enemy number one of ecocritics: Descartes. Rousseau's nostalgic depiction of the state of nature, his esteem for animals, and his identification of society and laws as the foundation of inequality among human beings clearly separate him from Descartes, who, in his *Second Meditation* (*Philosophical Works* 149–57), suggests that humans are superior to the rest of nature, since we possess an animus (mind; later named "cogito") that gives us the ability to think, whereas other living beings have at most an anima (soul), which might permit them to move and to feel, but never to think.

The Descartes-Rousseau dichotomy is important for ecocritics because it brings into focus two fundamental ways of viewing humans' place in nature: the classical anthropocentric model and the romantic ecocentric (biocentric) model. Michel Serres made an important contribution to the discussion with *The Natural Contract* (*Le Contrat naturel*, 1990). After examining Serres's concept of the natural contract and the scathing critique of it written by Luc Ferry in his *New Ecological Order* (*Le Nouvel Ordre écologique*, 1992), we will ponder—if not answer—this question: could Serres's natural contract ever come to fruition, or will it remain a wistful metaphor from the pen of this brilliant and poetic philosopher?

The Natural Contract begins with an analysis of one of Goya's black paintings, *Two Men Fighting with Clubs* (1819–23). The men are knee-deep in mud, and the viewer can imagine that as they beat each other, their efforts will only force them deeper into the quagmire as they fight to the death. Serres advises that if placing a bet on this fight, we would do well to put our money on the mud, rather than either of the two combatants. Serres interprets this painting as an illustration of the current standing of our relationship to nature. Long a victim of human aggression,[1] nature will soon be unable to endure any more, and will swallow us up, just as the mud inevitably will engulf Goya's fighters. We are about to pay for our history of abusing and ignoring nature.

What is history but an endless recurrence of violence? In a brief essay in *The Mirror of Ideas*, entitled "History and Geography," Michel Tournier contrasts the historical novel genre with what he calls the "geographical novel," which concerns not time, but space, in which authors might express a nomadic "ardor of exploration" (like Jules Verne or Pierre Loti) or a sedentary "love of the native land" (like Pierre Jakez Hélias from Brittany, or Jean Giono from Provence). They are "writers for whom the earth, the shores, the waters and the forests, the rain and the light play as vital a role as men and women" (54).[2] Tournier sees historical time as measured by a linear succession of mostly tragic events, written "in letters of blood" (55), while

---

1 Serres differentiates between "subjective wars" (wars between people or nations), neatly defined as "Violence plus some contract") and "objective violence" (violence against the world) (*Natural Contract* 14).
2 Citations of French authors are based on published translations, where

geography "is inscribed in the regular cycle of the seasons," and is thus "fundamentally optimistic" (54), linked to the constant renewal of seasonal time. For Tournier, geography suggests gentleness, and history evokes hate.

Michel Serres makes a similar distinction in *The Natural Contract*. For this philosopher, history celebrates the warrior "whose valor comes from laurels won in limitless, endlessly renewed war. Violence, with its morbid luster, glorifies the victors for propelling the motor of history" (2). Serres draws a sharp contrast between the dark events of history and "essential and exquisite" geography (6). "[N]othing is as beautiful as the world; nothing beautiful comes forth without this gracious giver of all splendor" (24). History, unfortunately, "[i]n its burning heat, ... remains blind to nature" (7).

But Serres warns that gentle space and terrible time are converging in the environmental crisis: "Global history enters nature; global nature enters history: this is something utterly new in philosophy" (4). The current ecological crisis has blurred the boundaries between history and geography, and between subject (humanity) and object (nature). "Subjective wars" between nations or peoples have long been the stuff of our history, but the "objective violence" (10) that humans wage against the environment has only recently entered our consciousness. And this war might well strike back against humanity, as ecological degradation threatens the world. Nature could soon be at war with nations: "At stake is the Earth in its totality, and humanity, collectively" (4).

Geography shapes history: witness the harsh historical destiny of the war-ravaged peoples of the flat steppes of Western Asia contrasted with that of the relatively wealthy Swiss, protected by the natural fortress of the Alps. Nevertheless, as the above quotations from Tournier and Serres show, the two disciplines have more often been contrasted than compared. Admitting the current confluence of history and geography is a necessary step to readmitting historical humans to nature, from which they have long been separated in Western thought, formed by texts like Genesis 1.28 ("Be fruitful, and multiply, and replenish the earth, and subdue it: and have dominion over the fish of the sea, and over the fowl of the air, and over every living thing that moveth upon

---

available, as listed in the bibliography. Otherwise, translations from French sources are my own.

the earth") and Descartes's *Discourse on the Method*, Part 6 (1637), which deems humans to be "masters and possessors of nature" (*Philosophical Works* 119). Ecologists now perceive humans, long denatured, as an integral part of a new hybrid nature. And fiction writers contribute to the renaturing of humanity; the ambitious "New Story" called for by the ecotheologian Thomas Berry (that is, a new way of understanding how we fit into the universe) is being built on the modest stories of novelists.

We find ourselves in an environmental predicament in which nature—were it capable of acting like a human—would seem to be taking its revenge. Blizzards, hurricanes, and tornadoes are more severe than ever, both droughts and floods appear to be on the rise, poison ivy and bedbugs are stronger and angrier than ever. For all this we can thank Descartes, among others. Serres summarizes the Cartesian attitude towards nature in two words, mastery and possession:

> Mastery and possession: these are the master words launched by Descartes at the dawn of the scientific and technological age, when our Western reason went off to conquer the universe. We dominate and appropriate it: such is the shared philosophy underlying industrial enterprise as well as so-called disinterested science, which are indistinguishable in this respect. (*Natural Contract* 32)

Mastery and possession have also led to pollution, as Serres explains in a more recent essay, *Malfeasance: Appropriation through Pollution?* (*Le Mal propre*, 2008). In this entertaining albeit serious book, Serres delves into "urine," "manure," "blood," "sperm," and "garbage" (see chapter titles in the table of contents), playing on the etymological similarity between *propriété* (property) and *propreté* (cleanliness), both derived from *propre* (an adjective that can signify "clean" or "own") and thus linking the concepts of cleanliness and ownership. We know how people pollute, but do we know why? Of course, pollution has economic causes, but it is also part of our animal—and human—nature. Polluting something claims it as ours: if I spit in a bowl of soup, writes Serres, it's mine; if a tiger, a lion, or a dog urinates around the perimeter of an area, it has marked that territory as its own. Thus, Descartes's call for thinking humans to master and possess nature ironically assimilates us to animals acting on instinct: "Poor Descartes ratified our animal customs" (*Malfeasance* 84).

Introduction: Michel Serres the Ecocritic vs. Luc Ferry the Ecoskeptic

It is high time, claims Serres, that a natural contract supplement Rousseau's famous social contract. Serres laments that Rousseau abandons all consideration of nature as soon as his interest passes from humans in the state of nature, in *The Second Discourse*, to humans under the laws of civil society, in *The Social Contract*, written seven years later:

> We keep forgetting about meteors; we're always attributing human causality to thousands of events that are actually determined by climate. Our ancestors the Gauls, like myself, would have preferred geography, which is so serene, to history, so chaotic, and preferred Montesquieu to Rousseau. The latter must be taken literally when he says that, after the contract, there is no more nature except for the solitary dreamer, whom society has forgotten. Meteors vanish in political philosophies, which are every bit as a-cosmic as social science, after a few initial moments that are indeed evoked or thought of as originary, the better to eliminate the world. (*Natural Contract* 73)

The Social Contract (1762) and *The Declaration of the Rights of Man and of the Citizen* (1789) are derived from natural law, human reason, and human nature, but they are blind to nonhuman nature, declares Serres. These two documents, fruits of the Enlightenment and the French Revolution, were

> closed upon [themselves], leaving the world on the sidelines, an enormous collection of things reduced to the status of passive objects to be appropriated. Human reason was of age, external nature a minor. The subject of knowledge and action enjoys all rights and its objects none. They have not yet attained any legal dignity. (*Natural Contract* 36)

Legal dignity, then, is what Serres aspires to confer upon nature. The following passage succinctly summarizes his concept of a natural contract. Serres denounces the stercoraceous, "excremental" quality of the Cartesian concept of mastery over nature, an idea that will later form the thesis of *Malfeasance*. Human beings have been living off nature like parasites, polluting and slowly destroying their host. A natural contract would replace this parasitic relationship with a symbiotic one, essential for the survival of both humans and the world, thus ending the "objective war" against nature:

Back to nature, then! That means we must add to the exclusively social contract a natural contract of symbiosis and reciprocity in which our relationship to things would set aside mastery and possession in favor of admiring attention, reciprocity, contemplation, and respect; where knowledge would no longer imply property, nor action mastery, nor would property and mastery imply their excremental results and origins. An armistice contract in the objective war, a contract of symbiosis, for a symbiont recognizes the host's rights, whereas a parasite—which is what we are now—condemns to death the one he pillages and inhabits, not realizing that in the long run he's condemning himself to death too. (*Natural Contract* 38)

Michel Serres's world view is ecocentric rather than anthropocentric: he avoids the word "environment" in *The Natural Contract* (33), because it implies that humans are superior, at the center of creation, surrounded (*environnés*) by an inferior world. For him, humans—who could not exist without the earth—are peripheral, and the earth—which could get along just fine without humans—is central. For this reason, Luc Ferry, one of Serres's strongest critics, brands him as a "deep ecologist."[3]

Ferry's *New Ecological Order* is essentially a denunciation of deep ecology, ecofeminism, and any ecological movement that Ferry considers "radical" or "fundamentalist," two adjectives that recur over and over in the essay. Ferry's main critique is the antihumanist spirit of deep ecology, which values nonhuman life as much as human life. This attitude, as we have seen in Serres's analysis of Rousseau's *Social Contract*, runs counter to Enlightenment thought. Ferry would seem to favor the human-centered "shallow" environmentalism option—which is concerned only about environmental problems that pose a

---

[3] The Norwegian philosopher Arne Naess is considered the founder of deep ecology. In *Ecocriticism* (21), Greg Garrard quotes two crucial points of Naess's "deep ecology platform":
The well-being and flourishing of human and non-human life on Earth have value in themselves ... . These values are independent of the usefulness of the non-human world for human purposes. ... The flourishing of human life and cultures is compatible with a substantial smaller human population. The flourishing of non-human life *requires* a smaller human population. See all eight points of the platform at www.deepecology.org/platform.htm.

threat to human welfare—over deep ecology, which he considers a new and dangerous fundamentalist religion:

> [T]he first preserves the heritage of modern humanism intact (it is in man's interest to respect the earth), while the second implies the most radical questioning of it. Humanism is not the answer to the crisis of the modern industrial world but rather an original sin, the primary cause of evil. (60)

Chris Cuomo, in her review of the English translation, points out many inadequacies in Ferry's book. She criticizes the "sweeping generalizations and mischaracterizations of work in environmental ethics," and Ferry's apparent view that deep ecology and ecofeminism "are pure and utter nonsense" (768). His "offhanded dismissal" of ecofeminism is based "on work that has been widely criticized by feminists and ecological feminists and entirely ignores the more sophisticated and comprehensive work that has been published in the 1990s" (769).

Bruno Latour, in "Arrachement ou attachement à la nature?," also finds many faults with Ferry's essay. He thinks that Ferry's ideas on nature are mired in modernism, especially the philosophy of Kant. Nature is important for Kant, but largely because "the living world reminds us of the freedom that we as humans enjoy. ... Animals and trees, ecosystems and biotopes are not worthy of respect in themselves, but because each one serves as an *analogon* of freedom" (16–17). Humanism, for Ferry, necessitates a tearing away (*arrachement*) from nature, whereas for Latour—and his mentor Serres—humans are a part (*attachement*) of nature: "We see now the serious conflict of a culture of *arrachement* and one of *attachement*, between Ferry, a humanist in the tradition of Kant, and Serres, a genuine humanist" (23).

Despite the serious shortcomings pointed out by Cuomo and Latour, Ferry does make some valid points about the potential dangers of deep ecology, most controversially its "moralizing power" (*New Ecological Order* 63) that can be transformed into a utopian, totalizing ideology whose pure ambitions and fervent love for the "fatherland" (*terroir*) (xxi) bear troubling similarities to the *Blut und Boden* (blood and soil) creed of the Third Reich. Like Nazism, with its roots in Teutonic mythology and its millennial dream of a new world to come after the terrible apocalyptic battle that was World War II (Eliade, *Mythes, rêves et mystères* 25), deep ecology, in the eyes of Ferry, is obsessed with the past and the future at the expense of the present: "[T]he deep ecologist is guided by a hatred of modernity, by hostility toward the present. ... The ideal of deep ecology would be a world in which lost epochs and distant horizons take precedence over the present" (*New Ecological Order* 89–90).[4]

Cuomo asserts—and I agree with her—that Ferry's most interesting chapter discusses the ecological positions of Germany's Nazi party in the early 1930s. Hitler personally recommended and had passed three important environmental laws: the first protected animals (*Tierschutzgesetz*, 1933), the second imposed limits on hunting (*Reichsjagdgesetz*, 1934), and the third, a "landmark of modern ecology," according to Ferry (91), concerned the protection of nature (*Reichsnaturschutzgesetz*, 1935). Now Ferry does not equate deep ecologists and Nazis because they share a love of nature, but he does want to point out that the Nazi example demonstrates that "an utterly sincere zoophilia" does not obviate "the most ruthless hatred of men history has ever known" (93). Deep ecology and Nazism share affinities with the love of unspoiled nature that characterized sentimental Romanticism and the Rousseau of the *Second Discourse*. This view contradicts Cartesian and Enlightenment thought, for which there was no nature except that perceived and ordered by human intellect (95), as exemplified by the formal and geometrical French garden: "[T]he French garden, crafted, pruned, designed, calculated, overly subtle, artificial, and forced is ultimately, if we want to get at the bottom of things, *more natural* than a wild forest. ... What is presented for aesthetic contemplation is a cultivated, controlled nature" (95).[5] Before Rousseau and Romanticism, "real" nature was, Ferry adds, not wild and unspoiled, but "polished" and "humanized" (96).[6]

---

4   In Chapter 6 we will examine Jean-Christophe Rufin's novel *Le Parfum d'Adam* (2007), an ecological thriller that explores the potential threat posed by radical ecologists. Their obsession with the past is described in the plot summary on the back cover: "The quest for a lost Paradise, nostalgia for a time when man was in harmony with nature, can lead to the most deadly fanaticism."
5   Ferry quotes Catherine Kinzler's *Jean-Philippe Rameau, splendeur et naufrage de l'esthétique du plaisir à l'âge classique*, Minerve, 1983.
6   Ferry's link of Romanticism and deep ecology to German National Socialism is well-founded. Serres reminds us, however, that the Enlightenment's social contract also has a troubling affinity with totalitarianism. The "general will" under which Rousseau's ideal society would be organized could lead to the

Introduction: Michel Serres the Ecocritic vs. Luc Ferry the Ecoskeptic

Ferry concedes that Descartes's "metaphysical humanism," which considers humanity the "masters and possessors of nature," has led to a "an unprecedented colonization of nature" (xxii). He suggests that Cartesianism should yield to a new and improved type of humanism, "nontyrannical, nonmetaphysical" (xxii), which would make possible a human-centered "democratic ecology" (127–46), preserving humanist and democratic values while resisting the authoritarian tendencies of deep ecology. For Ferry, love of nature consists largely of "democratic passions shared by the immense majority of individuals who wish to avoid a degradation in their quality of life" (143).

Serres's vision of a contract between humans and nature is impossible, insists Ferry, for three reasons. First, nature is made up of objects, unable to express values or interests, which inevitably must emanate from humans. A natural object could never become a subject with legal rights. Attempting to make it so would be a return to a "premodern," "prehumanistic" era (xiii), when beetles, leeches, rats, and other destructive creatures were actually brought to trial and threatened with excommunication if they did not mend their ways.[7] Deep ecologists who believe in the intrinsic value of nature forget that "all valorization, including that of nature, is the deed of man and that, consequently, all normative ethic is in some sense humanist and anthropocentrist" (131).

Second, even if parts of nature hold intrinsic value, nature in its entirety does not. The biosphere contains many good things, but it also contains horrific organisms: can anyone seriously believe, asks Ferry, that the plague and cholera bacteria or the HIV virus should possess a legal status on the same level as humans (140)?

Third, if a natural contract were agreed upon, who would be the signatories of the pact? How could an unthinking concept or a collection of objects—nature—sign a legal document? Ferry suggests that Serres does not "seriously" consider that a literal contract is possible; perhaps he is merely exercising "poetic license," and "the idea of a law of nature is just a literary metaphor, destined to arrest the attention of a public sunk in lethargy" (132). Why would Serres do this,

---

suppression of individualism and a "fine totalizing" (Serres, *Natural Contract* 67–68) where neighbors would spy on neighbors in order to ensure their obedience to the state.
7   Ferry cites several such trials that took place in France between the fifteenth and seventeenth centuries.

wonders Ferry, since such lyricism surely reduces the "philosophical weight" (132) of his argument.[8]

How have ecologists countered Ferry's objections, some of which are not entirely unreasonable? Is a natural contract, recognizing nature as a legal entity, feasible? A key refutation of Ferry actually appeared 20 years before *The New Ecological Order*. Back in 1972, Christopher D. Stone, a law professor at the University of Southern California, published a landmark essay on environmental ethics in the *Southern California Law Review* entitled "Should Trees Have Standing? Toward Legal Rights for Natural Objects." Writing in defense of the Sierra Club's efforts to block Walt Disney's plans for a massive ski resort in the Mineral King Valley of Sequoia National Park,[9] Stone declares that, just as it was once "unthinkable" (459) for inanimate objects such as corporations, trusts, and nation-states to possess legal rights, the time has come for the unthinkable to happen again: for the environment to have legal standing.[10] Land, water, wildlife, and trees cannot speak

---

8   I find this comment especially puzzling. Do philosophers not use metaphors? Do talented writers make flawed philosophers? Rousseau and Nietzsche, among others, might disagree. So would Serres, who remarked in a conversation with Bruno Latour: "Philosophy is profound enough to make us understand that literature is even more profound" (Serres and Latour, *Conversations* 25).

9   This case went all the way to the Supreme Court, which ruled in Disney's favor. However, the outcry from environmentalists was so intense that Disney abandoned the project, and the Mineral King Valley was eventually annexed to Sequoia National Park, protecting it from development.

10   "Throughout legal history, each successive extension of rights to some new entity has been, theretofore, a bit unthinkable. We are inclined to suppose the rightlessness of rightless 'things' to be a decree of Nature, not a legal convention acting in support of some status quo. ... The fact is, that each time there is a movement to confer rights onto some new 'entity,' the proposal is bound to sound odd or frightening or laughable" (Stone, "Should Trees Have Standing?" 459). Ethics also develop in ways that might be considered "unthinkable" to some. Decades before Stone's essay, Aldo Leopold, in the opening pages of his "Land Ethic," recounted how the ethics of ancient Greece would have permitted Odysseus, upon his return from war, to hang a dozen slave-girls merely because he suspected them of "misbehavior" (201). What would be murder today was at the time merely a man disposing of his property as he saw fit. Leopold notes that since Homer's time ethics have evolved dramatically, covering relationships between individuals (the first ethics), and later those between the individual and society (the second ethics). Leopold calls for a third, a land ethic, which would include nature as well as humans: "There is as yet no ethic dealing with man's relation to land and to the animals and plants which grow upon it.

for themselves, but this is no reason for them to be denied rights. Stone proposes a "guardianship approach" (462–63), similar to that in place for humans who are no longer competent to make legal decisions for themselves. In their introduction to the reprint of Stone's essay cited here, the editors of the *Encyclopedia of Environmental Ethics and Philosophy*, J. Baird Callicott and Robert Frodeman, define the guardianship approach as follows: "an appointed guardian represents the interests of natural objects themselves, not as their degradation impacts human interests, and where monetary remedies would run to the benefit of the natural objects directly" (458).

Stone is of course an object of derision in Ferry's book, which devotes a section called "Trees on Trial" (*New Ecological Order* xvii–xx) to Stone and the Disney-Mineral King case. I do not find Ferry convincing, however, when he equates Stone's attempt to give natural objects legal standing to the "pre-modern," comical trials of beetles and leeches. Ferry asks his reader to ponder "postmodern" ecologists' attempts, through the legal process, to prevent humans from damaging nature because it has intrinsic value:

> For can it not be said that these thinkers, who claim to be "postmodern" in the literal sense of the world—philosophers or jurists of "posthumanism"—are in communion with a *premodern* vision of the world, *in which beings of nature recover their status as legal subjects?* Is it not also strange to us, insofar as we are still Moderns, that trees or insects can win or lose a trial? (xix; emphasis original)

Ferry earlier used the same adjective—"strange"—to describe the insect trials of long ago (xvi). He is obviously implying that when environmentalists thwart Disney's plans to construct a huge resort in a pristine valley or challenge an industry's right to pollute in areas that will not affect human populations, they are performing some "strange" ritual akin to excommunicating leeches and rats. The connection is tenuous at best.

Another weak point in Ferry's argument is his claim that deep

---

Land, like Odysseus' slave-girls, is still property. The land relation is still strictly economic, entailing privileges but no obligations. The extension of ethics to this third element in human environment is, if I read the evidence correctly, an evolutionary possibility and an ecological necessity" (203).

ecologists are demanding the same rights for nature that human beings possess, or that all natural objects should have the same rights. Stone makes no such claims. As if predicting Ferry's objection concerning the granting of rights to deadly bacteria and viruses, Stone writes:

> [T]o say that the environment should have rights is not to say that it should have every right we can imagine, or even the same body of rights as human beings have. Nor is it to say that everything in the environment should have the same rights as every other thing in the environment. (460)[11]

As for Ferry's objection that nature is incapable of signing a contract with humanity, Serres himself replies that no, nature would not sign a natural contract, just as no humans ever signed Rousseau's social contract:

> I am neither so dumb nor so animistic to think that Nature is a person. I could also answer that the same objection was leveled at Rousseau's social contract; no one has ever signed this contract in a ceremony the date and circumstances of which could be documented. The General Will has as few hands as nature. ("Revisiting the Natural Contract" n. pag.)

No, both the social and natural contracts are "conditions," under which humans must act "as if" a contract had been signed.

At the beginning of this introduction I said that would not answer the question about the possibility of a natural contract: I will not break my promise. If Serres's proposal is viable for the philosopher or the ethicist, it poses many problems for the lawyer. In an article entitled "Environmental Law," the distinguished law professor Joseph L. Sax is not totally pessimistic regarding future legislation that could better manage and protect the environment, but he foresees at least three

---

[11] Peter Singer, the leading philosopher behind the animal liberation movement, similarly insists on the need to nuance the granting of equal rights to animals. In "All Animals Are Equal," he writes: "The extension of the basic principle of equality from [humans to other animals] does not imply that we must treat both groups in exactly the same way, or grant exactly the same rights to both groups. Whether we should do so will depend on the nature of the members of the two groups. The basic principle of equality, I should argue, is equality of consideration; and equal consideration for different beings may lead to different treatment and different rights" (28).

obstacles. First, it will be difficult to change "centuries of legal and economic development in which protecting natural systems was not a societal priority" (352). The law has long protected humans' perceived need to domesticate nature, and "thus has been the intentionally efficient cause of ecological destruction" (352). Second, the unmanaged global commons—territory unclaimed by any nation-state[12]—has and will continue to be "subject to unrestricted exploitation and to unrestricted use for waste disposal" (352). Third, political divisions and boundaries "bear no relation to ecologically rational divisions such as watersheds or habitat requirements for animal populations, the boundaries that reflect what is required for natural systems to flourish" (352). Philosophers like Serres and Ferry will continue to debate the relative merits of anthropocentric and ecocentric environmental ethics; nevertheless, if a shift is ever made from the first to the second, legal recognition of such concepts as a natural contract, the intrinsic value of nature, and the perception of nature as a living organism will require a "vast leap" (352) by environmental legislators.[13]

Specifically regarding animals, the philosopher Élisabeth de Fontenay, citing the law professor Jean-Pierre Marguénaud, reminds us of the difference between *personne juridique* (legal person) and *sujet de droit* (subject of law) ("Les animaux considérés" 147). In French law, animals are legal persons, and are thus protected from abuse. However, they cannot be subjects of law, and so "the border between humanity and animality" (147) holds firm. Fontenay concludes that "like the legal entity [*personne morale*], the animal is thus a legal person without being a subject of law, and this legal reality must be brought to light for debates on the matter to make sense" (148).

Some progress has been made since Fontenay wrote these words. In January 2015, a historic law was passed in France which declares that animals are "sentient living beings" (*être vivants doués de sensibilité*), where

---

12 Protecting the global commons has been a particular concern of Christopher Stone. Nations would first have to accept responsibility for polluting these areas, and then an immense amount of funding through a Global Commons Trust Fund would be required. See Stone's *The Gnat Is Older than Man* and "Defending the Global Commons."
13 The "Gaia Hypothesis," developed by James Lovelock in *Gaia: A New Look at Life on Earth*, considers the entire earth to be one living super-organism. Like Serres's natural contract, Lovelock's hypothesis has been ridiculed by some as a "charming metaphor" (Garrard 174).

up to then animals had essentially the legal status of furniture (*meubles*). The new law will "unlock the legal debate" about animal rights and makes France one of the more progressive European countries in this matter (Hutin and Marguénaud n. pag.). Animal advocates Reha Hutin and Jean-Pierre Marguénaud summarize thus the importance of the law:

> Since everyone is now convinced that animals, sentient living beings, are no longer legally considered goods, innovative solutions will emerge to solve—progressively and one by one—the different questions that come up every day in animal law: intensive animal farming, transportation, experimentation, bullfighting, and the serious cruelty inflicted on wild animals. (n. pag.)

Michel Serres and Luc Ferry have set the stage for the environmental debate in the twenty-first century. The crux of the problem is which world view must humanity adopt: ecocentric or anthropocentric? Which is more important, the health of the human species or the health of all species? And is the human species, because of its superior intelligence, irremediably torn from nature (the modern viewpoint), or an integral part of nature (the postmodern viewpoint)? What is the place of humans and humanism in the environmental discussion? Jean-Christophe Rufin describes the debate as a struggle between revolutionaries like Serres and reformers like Ferry (*La Dictature libérale* 205), or again between Serres's "utopian" and Ferry's "realist" position (204):

> The opposition of realist ecology and deep ecology essentially involves how each side views the planet. Realists are exclusively concerned with the industrial North. They claim to be able to solve environmental problems without questioning the principles of industrial civilization. Deep ecologists, in the name of a global vision of the planet, remain attached to the idea that a sustainable development entails a break with the growth models of free-market economies. ... [Radicals] like Michel Serres exalt a "mother nature" betrayed by industrial society and dying of sorrow. The others, like Luc Ferry, think that radical ecology is just a new totalitarianism that could result in a human as well as natural apocalypse, that is, a return to barbarism. (206–08)[14]

14   In *La société écologique et ses ennemis* (The Ecological Society and its Enemies),

Chapter Summary

In Part 1, I examine three examples of "ecofiction," novels that encourage an ecocentric view of the world. Chapter 1 is devoted to Michel Tournier's *Gemini* (*Les Météores*, 1975), Tournier's monumental third novel after *Friday* (*Vendredi ou les limbes du Pacifique*, Grand Prix du roman de l'Académie française, 1967) and *The Ogre* (*Le Roi des Aulnes*, Prix Goncourt, 1970). Tournier never claimed to be an environmentalist, so it would be a stretch to align him with any sort of radical ecological discourse. Yet his works exude a philosophy constructed around a love and respect for nature. The first section of his *Célébrations* (2000), for example, is entitled "Naturalia." It includes the essay "The Tree and the Forest" ("L'arbre et la forêt," 13–18), a nostalgic remembrance of childhood days wandering through forests while vacationing in Germany. Another essay, "Defense and Illustration of Weeds" ("Défense et illustration des mauvaises herbes," 23–27), laments monoculture and the loss of biodiversity in France through the use of herbicides to kill unwanted wild plants like poppies, bachelor's buttons, thistles, and dandelions. His short story "Tom Thumb Runs Away" ("La fugue du Petit Poucet"), a parody of Charles Perrault's famous tale, decries the reign of the automobile in Paris, extolls the vegetarian lifestyle, and tells a tale of the awesome power of trees. On the last page, the hero dreams that he metamorphoses into a chestnut tree; Robinson in *Friday* and Paul in *Gemini* have similar visions. The closing pages of Tournier's intellectual autobiography, *The Wind Spirit* (*Le Vent Paraclet*, 1977), are a meditation on the absolute, "that flower of metaphysics" (247) whose opposite poles are incarnated in the island and the garden.

Like all Tournier novels, *Gemini* is centered on a myth. Here he explores twinship, symbolized by the constellation representing the mythical twins Castor and Pollux, born from an egg laid by their mother Leda after she had been seduced by Zeus in the form of a swan. *Gemini* explores the myth and meaning of twinship, as identical twins Jean and Paul grow up in a strange fraternal world where they communicate in a "language of the wind" known only to them: "Aeolian" (52). Jean wants to break the stifling bond of twinship,

---

Serge Audier also distinguishes between progressive ecologists, interested in global issues, and conservative ecologists, attached to their nation or *terroir*.

and embarks on an epic journey, pursued by his brother. The voyage prompts Tournier to reflect on the ambiguous nature of *temps* (time and weather), reminiscent of Jules Verne's *Around the World in Eighty Days*. The book begins with the image of a young Michel Tournier watching the wind turn the pages of Aristotle's *Meteorology*, as he sits reading on a Brittany beach. Thus, meteorology will be one focus: the extraordinary tides of Brittany, wind and its various connotations, weather and its polysemic partner time. Here Tournier draws on the research of J. G. Frazer, who, in *The Golden Bough*, mentions many civilizations where twins are said to magically control the weather. A second subject of enquiry will be gardens of various designs, encountered by the twins as they travel through Tunisia, Iceland, and Japan. A third will be landfills, the dubious domain of the twins' flamboyant Uncle Alexandre, self-proclaimed "king and dandy of garbage men" (*Gemini* 69). These marginal spaces become central to the novel and will be studied in the light of contemporary material ecocriticism, such as Jane Bennett's *Vibrant Matter* and Baptiste Monsaingeon's *Homo detritus*.

Chapter 2, which examines Stéphane Audeguy's *The Theory of Clouds* (*La Théorie des nuages*, 2005; Prix Maurice-Genevoix, 2005; Prix littéraire Québec-France Marie-Claire-Blais, 2007), will continue in the vein of meteorology. In this extraordinary first novel about the men who shaped our understanding of clouds, Audeguy proposes a provocative interpretation of "human geography." Richard Abercrombie, traveling around the world in the 1890s to compile an atlas of clouds in texts and photographs, abandons science for a new obsession: female genitalia. His atlas, instead of containing scientific information, becomes a collection of photos of women's sex organs. Often the word "origin" is written beside the pictures, a reference, as Audeguy states in the interview in the appendix to this book, to Courbet's painting *L'Origine du monde* (*The Origin of the World*, 1866). Audeguy develops a micro-cult of sexuality with origins in the macrocosm of the sky and earth, recalling "the sexualized world" that Mircea Eliade, in *The Forge and the Crucible*, observes in many pre-modern societies.

Chantal Chawaf's *Mélusine des détritus* (2002) is the subject of Chapter 3. The young heroine, like her namesake, the medieval serpent woman from France's Poitou region, flourishes when near a stream or in a forest. She has the misfortune, however, to live next to a busy highway, and, constantly exposed to diesel fumes, she has contracted asthma. Jean, endlessly driving on the highway for his job, fancies himself as the knight errant who will save the "fairy" from the detritus of modern civilization, including a nuclear power plant that looms over Mélusine's city. Chawaf's novel is a bitter critique of nuclear power and modern industry, and the pain they have inflicted on people. It is also a lament for the loss of character in French regions, whose languages and histories are disappearing with the standardization brought on by globalization.

Part 2 (chapters 4 and 5) discusses "the animal question," as it is called in France, in two novels: Vercors's *You Shall Know Them* (*Les Animaux denaturés*, 1952) and Olivia Rosenthal's *Que font les rennes après Noël?* (What Do Reindeer Do after Christmas?, 2010), which has not been published in English. *You Shall Know Them* considers the boundaries between humans and animals decades before it became a major issue of ecocriticism. British anthropologists, in New Guinea looking for fossils of what was then called the "missing link" between humans and apes, are astonished to discover a living tribe of primates who seem to be exactly what they are searching for. Unscrupulous businessmen want to use the creatures as slave labor, and a great debate ensues: Are they animals or humans? What defines a human being? How can these hominids be saved from "the law of the strongest" which, in the guise of Nazism, had just swept across a horrified Europe? Published shortly after the Second World War at the height of the existentialist movement, the novel explored a key question that also concerned Vercors's friend Camus: What is the fate of human dignity, devastated by years of war and centuries of racism and imperialism? This chapter attempts to sort out the consequences of an encounter between humanistic existentialism and the ecocentric world view of philosophers like Michel Serres, Catherine Larrère, and Bruno Latour.

Que font les rennes après Noël? won the Prix du livre Inter in 2011. We follow the life of the narrator from a young girl to a woman of 44, in paragraphs written in the second person. Her story—of a misfit who loves animals and longs for emancipation for both herself and them—alternates with paragraphs narrated by animal professionals— a wolf trainer, a zookeeper, a research scientist, a stock farmer, and a butcher—describing their daily interactions with animals. The reader slowly begins to understand that the problems this marginal woman faces are not unlike the problems we inflict on animals and hopes that liberation will soon come to them both. My study of Rosenthal's novel will be based on, among other research, extensive interviews with Boris Cyrulnik, Élisabeth de Fontenay, and Peter Singer, published in *Les Animaux aussi ont des droits* (Animals Too Have Rights); and Charles Patterson's controversial essay *Eternal Treblinka*, which compares the modern abattoir to Nazi death camps.

Part 3 deals with environmental skeptics. Chapter 6 studies two novels by Jean-Christophe Rufin of the Académie française, *Globalia* (2004) and *Le Parfum d'Adam* (The Scent of Adam, 2007). Rufin is concerned with the dark side of deep ecology: ecological terrorism and the authoritarian potential some see in it, in part because of the historical link between environmentalism and the Third Reich. *Globalia* is a dystopian science fiction novel inspired by Alexis de Tocqueville's *Democracy in America* (1835–40), which expressed the fear that the United States might someday succumb to a "tyranny of the majority." Globalia features all the negative aspects—potential and real—of globalization and twenty-first-century America: unbridled advertising, addiction to television and its variations, indifference to reading, political apathy, cynical dealings with the countries of the South. It is the only remaining country on earth; the rest is disorganized and violent "non-zones." Thanks to medical advances, people are living much longer, and so a despotic gerontocracy rules Globalia, based on the principles of deep ecology. Drawing from Catherine and Raphaël Larrère's *Du bon usage de la nature*, I will study the non-zones as an example of the concept of "hybrid objects." I will also examine the political nature of the novel, as suggested by Rufin's early essay, *La Dictature libérale*.

Le Parfum d'Adam, a thriller about ecological terrorists bent on reducing the population of the world's poorest, continues Rufin's critique of deep ecology. Like Luc Ferry's *The New Ecological Order*, Rufin's novel targets the antihumanist aspect of the "Deep Ecology Platform." As in *Globalia*, an afterword links the novel—about a plot to poison the water supply of Rio de Janeiro's largest *favela*—to the real world. Rufin is especially inspired by American radical ecology, which he considers much more dangerous than its European counterpart. Rufin remarks that, as a doctor who spent more than 20 years working for humanitarian organizations, he frequently heard troubling talk questioning the value of his quest to help the poor: perhaps it would be better to let nature take its course and, as Malthus saw, reduce the overpopulated poor through famine and epidemics (*Parfum d'Adam*

756). Lest the reader consider his plot far-fetched, Rufin cites several deep ecologists, including William Aiken, who wrote in *Earthbound: Essays in Environmental Ethics* (1984) that it is our duty to eliminate 90 percent of the human race (*Parfum d'Adam* 757).

Chapter 7 explores a rarity in ecological writing: humor. Iegor Gran's irreverent and controversial satires question the validity of much that French ecologists hold sacred, such as the efficiency and altruism of NGOs, and the sincerity of environmental heroes like ecologist, photographer, and filmmaker Yann Arthus-Bertrand and Nicolas Hulot, a popular environmental activist and Minister of Ecology from 2017 to 2018. Gran's *O.N.G!* (NGO!, Grand Prix de l'humour noir, 2003) and *L'Écologie en bas de chez moi* (Ecology in My Basement, 2011) are cautionary tales for environmentalists who take themselves too seriously. The first novel recounts the antics of two NGOs forced to share a building. Their lofty ideals cannot prevent them from going to war over petty issues like parking places; the narration of the war recalls the bawdy black humor of Rabelais and Voltaire. The principal target of *L'Écologie en bas de chez moi* is Arthus-Bertrand. Gran pitilessly critiques his famous environmental documentary *Home* (2009), which Gran accuses of opportunism, piousness, and antihumanism. Certain formal elements of *Home*—the stirring music, the aerial views—bear comparison to Leni Riefenstahl's *Triumph of the Will*, which glorified the 1934 Nazi congress in Nuremberg. Gran, like Rufin, raises the uncomfortable association between ecology and the ideology of some groups of the extreme right.

Finally, I conclude with a discussion of the relevance of a humanist ecocriticism, one that conceives the human and the natural as parts of a continuum, rather than two sharply divided phenomena. It is a call to reject the humanism that has come to us from the Judeo-Christian and Cartesian traditions, what Lévi-Strauss, in an article on Rousseau, refers to as "a humanism, corrupted at birth by taking self-interest as its principle and its notion" (*Structural Anthropology* 41). Martin Gibert calls this type of humanism "exclusive," because it upholds the supremacy of humans; he declares that it is time to replace it with an "inclusive humanism" that extends the "circle of morality" (173) to animals. Similarly, Cary Wolfe, in *What Is Posthumanism?*, describes how his vision of "posthumanism" involves new boundaries between humans and animals, which since Descartes have been regarded as "diminished or crippled versions of that fantasy figure called the human" (45).

This posthumanist remains a humanist: "Just because we direct our attention to the study of nonhuman animals, and even if we do so with the aim of exposing how they have been misunderstood and exploited, that does not mean that we are not continuing to be humanist—and therefore, by definition, anthropocentric" (99).

In France, farmer-philosopher Pierre Rabhi and sociologists Edgar Morin and Michel Maffesoli, among others, have recently led the movement for a new humanism. Rabhi's *Manifeste pour la terre et l'humanisme* (Manifesto for the Earth and Humanism, 2008), is a plea for an "enlightened humanism" (87–88) to alleviate the "world food tragedy" (17). He is one of the pioneers of agroecology, an agricultural practice that takes into consideration "water management, reforestation, the fight against erosion, biodiversity, climate change, economic and social systems, the relationship between the human being and his environment" (74–75). Rabhi laments the loss of enchantment and beauty, a love for the world that he calls "the symphony of the earth" (59). In *Écologiser l'homme* (Ecologize Man, 2016), Morin describes the paradox of "European humanism" (78): one form led to the long and cruel domination of colonial rule, another to the emancipation of the colonies. It is this second humanism that we need "to dig up or reinvent" in order to "ecologize man" (22). In *Écosophie* (Ecosophy, 2017), Maffesoli declares that a postmodern "progressive philosophy" (13) is finally supplanting the Promethean "progressism" (12) that has dominated the modern age. Like Rabhi, he calls for a "reenchantment" of a world that has forgotten how to enjoy the present, a "disenchanted" (29) world fixated on progress towards an unknown future.

The Appendix consists of interviews I conducted with Stéphane Audeguy and Iegor Gran. Audeguy explains the genesis of his *Theory of Clouds*, expounds on his ideas on humanism and ecology, and reacts to Pope Francis's encyclical on the environment. Iegor Gran expresses his aversion to *Home*, recalls readers' and journalists' intense reactions to *O.N.G!* and *L'Écologie en bas de chez moi*, and, as an immigrant from the Soviet Union living in Paris, shares his unique perspective on environmentalism, in which he cannot help but see certain authoritarian tendencies.

Part 1

Three French Ecofictions

The daytime belongs to the birds and then they are the sole masters of the silvery hills. ... Woe to the slow or injured birds that linger on the rubbish dumps after the passing of the evening trains! Hordes of rats surround them, bite out their throats, and tear them to pieces. This is why, as you walk the hills, you come at every step upon shreds of fur or tufts of down, the leavings of a diurnal and nocturnal rhythm by which the hills are divided between the rule of fur and feather.

—Michel Tournier, *Gemini* 210

Marseille landfill at Entressen, Istres, France, 1997. Photograph by Frank Pourcel.

Chapter 1

Time, Weather, and Waste: Michel Tournier's *Gemini* (*Les Météores*)

> As the sea is to the shore so the wind is to the cloudy air; so, when the wind drops, this very straight and thin cloud is left, a sort of wave-mark in the air.
>
> —Aristotle, *Meteorology*, bk. 2, part 8, p. 39

> All the elements nurture us. The earth gives its harvests and its ores, the sea its fish, fire cooks our soup, and air fills our lungs. But these comforting functions are insignificant compared to the colossal forces that the elements can unleash. The thunderstorm or the tempest possess at once a cosmic majesty and an eternal innocence, conferring on them a sacred dimension.
>
> —Michel Tournier, "Douceurs et colères des éléments" 205

Gemini opens with a report of the weather on 25 September 1937 in the English Channel and along the Brittany coast. The narrator describes the surges of waves and the gusts of wind that flutter the pages of the book 12-year-old Michel Tournier sits reading on Saint-Jacut beach: Aristotle's *Meteorology*. Weather—especially the mighty tides of Brittany and the chaotic turmoil of the troposphere—will be one of the principal themes of *Gemini*. The troposphere—"sphere of changes"—is the lowest part of the earth's atmosphere, where all weather phenomena originate. The French title—*Les Météores*—clearly conveys the significance of weather to the novel. *Météores* does not refer to shooting stars or meteorites, rather it evokes an older meaning of the word: "any atmospheric or meteorological phenomenon" ("Meteor," *Oxford English Dictionary*).

We have seen that in his *Mirror of Ideas*, Tournier contrasts the historical and geographical novel. If Tournier's second novel, *The Ogre*, is his most historical, written "in letters of blood" (*Mirror of Ideas* 55) describing Nazism's seduction of children, *Gemini* is his most geographical, because natural occurrences like weather and tides, and spaces shaped by humans, such as gardens and landfills, "play as vital a role as men and women" (54). As we shall see, "time" will also be an important topic of *Gemini*, especially as it relates to "weather" (both denoted by *temps* in French). However, Tournier stresses that, while historical time is linear, "irreversible," and mostly "catastrophic" (54), geographical time, even if it is subject to "capricious and unpredictable" weather, is "fundamentally optimistic," because etched into the eternal return of the seasons.

Tides

"You are the writer of the low tide," declares the artist Patricio Lagos to Michel Tournier in "Patricio Lagos ou le passage de la Ligne" (160). In this essay in *Le Crépuscule des masques* (The Twilight of Masks) Tournier describes the tides of Normandy and Brittany that he knows so well: that "ephemeral landscape" where the sea, ever changing and "eternally young," washes the rocks of the land, stratified "like the wrinkles of a very old face" (165). In other works of Tournier, littoral waters symbolize conflict. In *The Midnight Love Feast* (*Le Médianoche amoureux*) two "taciturn lovers" walk through the low tide, metaphorically sinking into the sludge of their silence. In *Friday*, when the waves wash an unconscious Robinson Crusoe onto a desert island, he will begin a decades-long struggle between his old life as a "civilized" Englishman and his new life, which at first seems "savage," and then gradually evolves into ecological awareness and appreciation of nature. But it is in *Gemini* that the tides play their most essential role.

As a young boy, Paul's twin Jean is obsessed by *le temps* in both senses of the word: time and weather. His favorite toys are his cuckoo clock and his barometer. Paul has his own clock and barometer—the twins have everything in double—but Jean's are slightly in advance of Paul's. In other words, Jean's cuckoo will go off a few seconds ahead of Paul's; likewise, the figure on Jean's barometer (a boy with an umbrella) will more accurately predict the weather than Paul's (a girl with a parasol). These two toys of time and weather, slightly out of sync, give Jean the hope that perhaps he may one day escape his twin and the oppressive identicalness of their lives. For Paul, the clock and the barometer constitute an irritation, for he is the conservative twin, and desires to preserve at all costs what he considers the superior form of life that is twinship.

Yet it is the tides that separate the twins more than anything. Paul is attracted by their theoretical "mathematical simplicity and regularity" (*Gemini* 128), but horrified by the reality of their unpredictability, due to the many factors that govern them: "The tide is a clock run mad, suffering from a hundred parasitic influences—the rotation of the earth, the existence of submerged continents, the viscosity of the water and so on—that defy reason and overset it." It is a mathematical system "warped, dislocated and fractured" (128).

Jean is particularly obsessed by the low tide. Sometimes, on summer nights, he would wake up trembling, as if pulled by "the great, wet, salty expanse the ebb had just uncovered" (128). Followed by his reluctant brother, Jean would run miles through the muddy sand until he finally arrived at the first ripples of the incoming tide. His passion for the low tide is twofold. First, unlike Paul, he is energized by the "capricious and unforeseeable aspect of the tides," and their "elemental force" (129). More important, however, is the "silent *cry* of helpless desolation" (129) emanating from the countless marine creatures abandoned by their watery element, perhaps left to die:

> The things that the ebb lays bare weep for the flood tide. The mighty glaucous mass fleeing toward the horizon has left exposed this living flesh, complex and fragile, which fears assault, profanation, scouring and probing. ... It is one vast lamentation, the weeping of the suffering shore, dying beneath the direct light of the sun with its terrible threat of drying out, unable to bear its rays except when broken, cushioned and fragmented by the liquid, prismatic depths. (129)

Upon reaching the edge of the returning ocean, Jean rejoices in the knowledge that he has answered "the mute appeal of those thousands upon thousands of thirsty mouths" (129) that will soon be saved. Like a salty John the Baptist announcing the coming of the Savior, he declares: "I am the forerunner, the herald of the marvelous good news" (130).

Tournier evokes the intertidal zone in other works, suggesting that for him it is an important metaphor for marginals everywhere. Patricio Lagos, the sand sculptor and dancer of *Le Crépuscule des masques*, had previously appeared in the first story of *The Midnight Love Feast*, "The Taciturn Lovers." Yves Oudalle lives on the Normandy coast, near Mont Saint-Michel, where he catches shellfish in the low tide. In this area that he describes as "the reverse of the ocean" (*Midnight Love Feast* 15), life is dominated by time, "the rhythm of the tides," whose cadence is closely associated with weather and the seasons: "solstices, equinoxes, spring-tides, syzygies" (15). He speaks of the "joy of long hours spent roaming the beds of water plants, the mud flats, pools, rocks, lagoons, and quicksands" (15)—"the foreshore, that ambiguous, contentious, magical zone, alternately covered and uncovered by the rise and fall in the level of the sea" (15).

One September, Yves and his wife Nadège are walking at low tide after a powerful "equinoctial tide had given the bay a devastated, frantic, almost pathetic air ... Yes, there was mystery in the air, almost tragedy" (16). They come across an extraordinary sand sculpture of two lovers embracing. As the flood tide rises and tears away at the statue, Lagos—adding to the mysterious and tragic ambiance of the scene—dances to the destruction of his art. Obsessed by time, Lagos seeks to unite dance—an art of the present moment—and sculpture—"the art of eternity," in this art of "ephemeral sculpture" (18): "'My sand sculptures live,' he declared, 'and the proof of this is that they die. ... I celebrate the pathetic fragility of life'" (18). Clearly Lagos, like Jean, reflects Michel Tournier's concern for the tenuousness of all life, especially for those living on the margins, represented by the ecologically precarious space of the littoral.

In "Michel Tournier, un écrivain écologiste?," Arlette Bouloumié suggests that Tournier's Germanophilia contributed much to his love of nature. We have already mentioned the essay in *Célébrations*, "L'arbre et la forêt," in which Tournier reminisces about his boyhood visits to the Black Forest and the Thuringian Forest. But it was especially his penchant for German Romanticism—and writers like E. T. A. Hoffmann, Ludwig Tieck, and Achim von Arnim—that heightened his interest in the environment: "His German education, his knowledge of German Romanticism—evocative of a living, sacred cosmos, thus more mystical than French Romanticism—sensitized him to a respect for nature" (Bouloumié, "Michel Tournier, un écrivain écologiste?" 92).

I have remarked elsewhere (*Tournier élémentaire* 135) how Jean's attraction to the space revealed by the low tide reveals his romantic soul, as does his desire to visit exotic lands, and his individualist revolt against the prison of twinship. It is not surprising that such a person would be attracted to the low tide. In *The Lure of the Sea*, Alain Corbin suggests that European romantic literature was especially fascinated by this intertidal zone and, in a sense, "discovered" it, much as the romantics discovered the beauty of Alpine summits formerly considered terrifying—another "territory of the void":[1]

> This territory of the void ... was henceforth to exert a growing fascination, and to become in turn the scene of quests on foot, built on the model suggested by walking fishermen. ... On this uncertain surface, ... individuals strongly experienced the interlocking solar and lunar rhythms. The alternation of days and nights became coupled with and complicated by that of the ebb and flow. ... The obscene bottom of the sea [is] miraculously exposed and temporarily available for the scientist's observation and the artist's vision. (116)

The exposed obscenity of the ocean floor during low tides is a product of what Corbin calls in *Le Ciel et la mer* (The Sky and the Sea) the rich "imaginary of the depths" (42) in Western thought. The ocean conceals unimaginable monstrosities, as well as the sublime secret of the origins of life (43).

Like the landfills that I will examine shortly, the suffering creatures of the "no man's land" where sea meets land represent the marginals of *Gemini*: first, the physically and intellectually disabled children who live at "the hill of the innocents" (*Gemini* 41) in Jean and Paul's Breton village, Pierres Sonnantes; second, homosexuals, notably the twins' flamboyant Uncle Alexandre, owner of six municipal landfills; and third, the twins themselves, who, Paul admits, are monsters, in the etymological sense (monster is related to *montrer*, "to show"),

---

[1] The French title of Corbin's essay is *Le Territoire du vide*, or "territory of the void." It refers to the muddy space between the liquid sea and the solid shore at low tide.

since they are considered curiosities by non-twins, exploited as children in a television commercial for binoculars, for example. Paul compares himself and his twin brother to the "innocent" disabled of Pierres Sonnantes, "a tribe apart, obeying different laws from other people, and therefore feared, hated and despised" (120). Some of these marginals will perish on the shore. Nine of the "innocents," fatally attracted to the blinking lighthouses of the Breton coast, drown at sea one night when their rickety old boat crashes on the rocks. Alexandre, stalking two young boys on the docks of Casablanca, dies from 17 knife wounds, but only after he thrusts his sword-stick through their hearts.

In *Water and Dreams*, one of his essays on the material imagination of earth, water, fire, and air, Gaston Bachelard[2] defines his task as one of rectifying what he sees as a problem with aesthetic philosophy: the fact that *form* has always been given more attention than *matter* (2). He believes that matter precedes form, expressing his materialism in this way: "*[I]t is matter that governs form.* ... The *imaginary* does not find its deep, nutritive roots in *images*; first it needs a closer, more enveloping and material *presence*" (119, 121; emphasis original).

Bachelard devotes a chapter to "Water in Combination with Other Elements." He calls the "union of water and earth ... one of the fundamental schemes of materialism" (104), strangely neglected by philosophers. For Bachelard, amorphous substances like dough, paste, mud, and clay are "the basis of a truly intimate materialism in which shape is supplanted, effaced, dissolved. ... The problem of form is given a secondary role" (104). Jean's beloved intertidal zone is such an "intimate" matter. His barefoot run through the wet sand is a liberating, exhilarating, and ultimately erotic act: "My cries, my groans and broken words indicated nothing more than the all-powerful attraction that the great wailing emptiness of the shore abandoned by the tide exerted over me" (*Gemini* 130). The night of adventure ends back in bed, as the twins make love in their particular incestuous, homosexual, and "oviform" manner (*amours ovales*), culminating in "seminal communion" (131).

---

2   Tournier attended Bachelard's philosophy courses at the Sorbonne in 1942 and was profoundly affected by his books on the material imagination, centered on the four traditional elements. Tournier dedicated his *Mirror of Ideas* to Bachelard.

When Jean and Paul run through the low tide, and when the disabled children and Alexandre come to their watery deaths, it happens at night. For Bachelard, the material imagination, besides valorizing the marriage of water and earth, is also fascinated by the combination of water and night. He explains how, for many writers,[3] the phenomenon of night is materialized:

> [Reverie] about substances is so common and so invincible that the imagination commonly accepts dreams of an active night, a penetrating night, an insinuating night, or of a night that invades the substance of things. Then Night is no longer a draped goddess, no longer a veil that stretches over Land and Sea; Night is *made of night*. Night is a substance, is nocturnal matter. Night is understood by *material* imagination. (*Water and Dreams* 101; emphasis original)

For Gilbert Durand, cultural anthropologist and disciple of Bachelard, night, like all "nyctomorphic symbols" (88), almost always has a negative connotation, inspiring terror and anguish (88–93). In *Gemini*, night intensifies the awesome elementary power of the ocean, veiling the chaos of the littoral zone, where saltwater meets sand, in fearful mystery. The mighty tides of Brittany and Normandy regulate this privileged borderland for a geographical writer like Tournier, who sees in the intertidal zone an apt metaphor for those cast off from society. For the ecologist, it is an area of prime importance, due to the diverse plants and invertebrate sea creatures that populate this fragile area.[4] The tides also illustrate the fusion of "time" and "weather" in the French word *temps*. Tides are linked to time because they follow a daily and monthly cycle: they usually repeat about every six hours, and reach their apogee during the syzygies (the new and full moons, when the earth, moon, and sun are aligned). They are also meteorological phenomena affected by atmospheric pressure and winds, and thus connected to weather. Like the weather, the tides are cyclical, changing with the eternal succession of the seasons.

---

[3] Bachelard cites in particular Edgar Allan Poe's "The Descent into the Maelström" and George Sand's *Visions of Night in the Country*.
[4] France's worst ecological disaster occurred off the Brittany coast in December 1999, when the oil tanker *Erika* sank, devastating coastal wildlife.

Time and Weather

In *The Wind Spirit*, Tournier notes his debt to Jules Verne's *Around the World in Eighty Days* for "[t]he underlying subject of *Gemini*": "the lost coincidence of the two meanings of *temps* (time, weather) followed by the restoration of identity" (225). In Verne's novel, the wealthy Englishman Phileas Fogg wagers £20,000 with his club members that he and his French valet Passepartout can circumnavigate the world in 80 days. Fogg is a man of time, "a stickler for promptness and regularity" (*The Wind Spirit* 225), a "walking timepiece" who "knows all the world's almanacs and schedules by heart" (226). Their journey, "made *against wind and tide*" (226; emphasis original) will have to overcome many meteorological obstacles, and this is why the Frenchman is key to Fogg's victory:

> Passepartout with his blunders and tantrums embodies those obstacles, because for him, as a Frenchman, Time and Weather are one and the same, and he finds it normal that the hours counted out by the clock should be splattered with rain and illuminated by sunshine. While Fogg is identified with his chronometer, Passepartout is the man of the changing heavens, always in the grip of some unpredictable humor. ... Fogg wins only by accepting his servant's confusion of Time and Weather. It is Passepartout who informs Fogg that by traveling from west to east, that is, ahead of the sun, he has gained twenty-four hours and is therefore returning to London after eighty days and not eighty-one as measured on his chronometer. Hence he has won his bet. It takes Passepartout's empirical, concrete, solar perception of time to recognize this simple fact. (226–27)

What is the connection between Verne's and Tournier's novels about time and weather? One could consider Paul a modern Phileas Fogg. He "views the heavens in an astronomical sense; he is rational, mathematical, and takes things to be totally predictable" (227–28). And like Passepartout, Jean loves unpredictability—of the tides and of life—and strives to free himself of the bond of twinship. *Gemini* is a story "of the triumph of chronology over meteorology," but also "of the intrusion of dawns and clouds into the clockwork of the heavens" (228); in other words, the synthesis of time and weather. Paul travels the world in search of Jean, who finally has broken away. Paul sees his real task, however, as something much more ambitious:

> That is to acquire a hold over the troposphere itself, to command meteorology and make myself master of rain and shine, no less! Jean has fled, swept away on the currents of the atmosphere. I can fetch him home, yes. But ... in the process I may become myself the shepherd of winds and clouds. (323)[5]

Tournier defines Paul's voyage in search of his twin as a "journey of initiation" (*The Wind Spirit* 230), which culminates in his "ritual mutilations" (*Gemini* 444). While attempting to escape from East to West Berlin[6] via a poorly constructed tunnel, he loses both left limbs in a cave-in. Transposing Henri Bergson's conception of time as "alteration" (change) to space, Tournier concludes that Paul's journey is "translation" (movement) plus alteration, since his very body has been altered. At the end of the novel, Jean has disappeared, and Paul, fighting through the pain of his recent amputation, is immobilized in a chair in Pierres Sonnantes, observing the earth, the sea, and the sky. Through his severed left members, he now identifies with the forces of meteorology. He imagines his left hand and foot protruding from the bandages and reaching out to the world. He is astonished by his new "hyperawareness" as he stares through binoculars at the garden. His "godlike eyes penetrate the mass of growing plants," which he now sees "with an incomparable clarity and brilliance" (444). This final chapter is named "The Extended Soul." Paul as human "subject" has been redefined to include such "objects" of nature as the sky and the wind. As the sun sets over the Atlantic, Paul marvels: "The blazing

---

5   In *The Wind Spirit*, Tournier explains the mythological association between twins and the weather. Referring to J. G. Frazer's *The Golden Bough* (1890), he states that in some cultures, "twins do indeed control the clouds and the rain ..., for a twin birth indicates a mother of exceptional fertility, and rains make the earth fertile" (215). Frazer writes that "There is a widespread belief that twin children possess magical powers over nature, especially over rain and weather" (39). This is the case for certain tribes in central India, southeastern Africa, British Columbia, and Peru. In the latter country, Indians believed "that one of each pair of twins was a son of the lightning; and they called the lightning the lord and creator of rain, and prayed to him to send showers" (40).
6   The divided city of Berlin is a metaphor for the split twinship of Jean and Paul.

sky became my own wound. I gazed in fascination at those vast, flaming subsidences of which I was the tortured consciousness. My suffering body covered the whole sky and filled the horizon" (439). Paul describes his new state as *porosity*:

> I realize that I am in direct contact, plugged in to the birth of a barometric body, a pluviometric, anemometric, hygrometric body. A porous body through which all the winds of heaven may breathe.[7] No longer the useless organism rotting on a mattress but the living, breathing witness of the meteors. (441–42)[8]

The novel ends with Paul's report of the approaching weather. His left side

> is resting a long way off on two anticyclones, one situated off northeastern France, the other off the southwest of England … [T]he sun is bright and keen and is causing the snow to evaporate *without thawing*. A transparent, rainbow mist trembles above drifts of hard, unbroken snow. The snow is vaporizing without melting, without running, without softening.

---

7 In *Écosophie*, Michel Maffesoli employs similar vocabulary as a metaphor for understanding "the spirit of the times": "This 'anemoscopy,' to repeat a classic theme, this observation of the atmosphere and the winds that traverse it, is primordial if we want to understand the 'climatic' variations which, for all of human history, are the motor of existential dynamism" (27).

8 In *French Écocritique: Reading Contemporary French Theory and Fiction Ecologically*, Stephanie Posthumus detects the same "porosity" in Marie Darrieussecq's *Le Pays* (The Country, 2005). Posthumus describes how the protagonist Marie experiences an "exchange of matter," becoming an "ecological subjectivity" (54) by which the subject is no longer limited to humans but expanded to include the environment. Much like Paul at the end of *Gemini*, Marie seems to fuse with sea and sky as she observes her beloved Atlantic: "Your molecules mix with the sky and water, solitude spreads out. Words and things move apart, thinking no longer follows, signs become unmoored; and the self gapes open full of salt water" (54; Posthumus's translation of Darrieussecq, *Le Pays* 84). Marie frequently visits the House of the Dead, where she communicates with the ghosts of her grandmother and brother. Posthumus concludes that "[i]n the end, collective subjectivity emerges both from porous bodies becoming landscape and a *socius* in which the living and dead circulate" (57). In *Gemini*, is Jean, the missing twin, also dead? "No," writes Michel Tournier. "He has simply been absorbed by his twin thanks to this journey through qualitative space, this profound process of alteration and initiation, this conquest of the heavens with their weather by this man of time" (*The Wind Spirit* 230).

This is called sublimation. (452; emphasis original)

"Sublimation," the last word of this epic novel, is indeed "a process by which a substance undergoes a change of state from solid to gas (or vice versa) without passing through the liquid phase" ("Sublimation," *Oxford English Dictionary*), like the "vaporizing" snow that Paul describes. But more importantly, "sublimation" describes Paul's apotheosis. He has been initiated by his ritual mutilation—as well as by the metaphorical amputation he suffered when Jean disappeared—into the state of "dispaired twinship" (*Gemini* 447). Jean has become his left side, his "extended soul" reaching far into the troposphere. This is the "mystery" and "miracle" of dispaired twinship: ubiquity (447). It is also an alternative definition of "sublimation," synonymous with "perfection": "Something which has been transformed into a higher, nobler, or more refined state; the purest or most concentrated product of, the quintessence; the height or acme of" ("Sublimation," *Oxford English Dictionary*).

Gardens

As the twins travel across the world—Jean fleeing the stifling geminate cell, Paul in pursuit, seeking to preserve it—they encounter several types of gardens: the lush oasis of Djerba, an island off the coast of Tunisia; the greenhouses of Iceland; the Zen and miniature gardens of Japan. Jean meets Ralph and his mortally ill wife Deborah in Venice, and accompanies them back to Djerba, where he helps care for Deborah until she dies a short time later. They had constructed their earthly paradise 40 years earlier, creating a small oasis out of the desert, itself surrounded by the sea. It is the type of refuge that Bachelard would have associated with the "Jonah complex." Like Jonah in the belly of the whale, the garden emanates a sense "of gentle well-being, of well-being that is warm, that is *never under attack*. It is truly an absolute of interiority, an absolute of the happy unconscious" (*Earth and Reveries of Repose* 109; emphasis original). In contrast to the sterile desert bordering it, however, the garden—like Deborah—will succumb to time: "[U]nlike the unchanging and eternal desert that surrounds them, this house and garden keep, in their fashion, a record of time, preserving traces of everything that comes and goes, of all that they have experienced of growth, resorption, change, decay and rebirth" (*Gemini* 335). Their house, surrounded by plants and trees, is dark, and seems to have grown in time, an interior extension of the garden: "It is a terrestrial, telluric house, provided with the vegetable extensions it demands, the product of a long, visceral growth" (336).

Deborah dies in the midst of a fierce storm that destroys house and garden. Ralph buries her in the garden and, like Paul who becomes one with the meteors at the end of the novel, Deborah's self merges with the earth, as Ralph explains: "It was Deborah's garden. Now, it is Deborah. ... She is everywhere, in the trees and in the flowers. ... Her feet became roots, her hair leaves and her body a trunk. ... And when the garden was finished, Deborah disappeared into the earth" (344). Once again, Tournier suggests that the human subject is limitless, that we have an intimate bond with our environment.

From Tunisia, Paul continues his quest to find his twin, whom he discovers has left for Japan, with a short stop in Iceland. In Iceland, he visits the stinking hot sulfuric mud and steam springs at Namaskard. "This is the fury of the subterranean hell against the surface, against the sky. The subterranean world is pouring out its hatred, spewing in the face of heaven all its vilest, most scatological abuse" (365). Then he discovers the greenhouse town of Hveragerdhi, situated on an active geothermal zone not far from Reykjavik. He is amazed to find, in this anti-Djerba so close to the Arctic Circle, the same plants he had seen in Deborah's tropical garden, "simply by virtue of the fires within the earth" (367). He is struck by the artificiality of the two gardens, which are anything but natural in their location: Djerba is too dry for such luxuriant vegetation, Iceland is too frigid. Both gardens represent the triumph of the underground; pumps bring precious phreatic water to Deborah's garden as the thermal springs provide heat to the greenhouses:

> These two gardens are the expression of the blooming, precarious victory of the earth's depths over its surface. And how extraordinary it is that the inferno of rage and hatred I saw unleashed at Namaskard should here be tamed and industrious, laboring to bring forth flowers, as though the devil himself had suddenly put on a straw hat, picked up a watering can and taken to gardening. (367)

As Paul's plane from Reykjavik to Tokyo crosses the Arctic Circle and flies over Greenland, Tournier—through the narrative voice of

Paul—reflects on the future of the massive ice-covered island, as well as the future of humanity:

> [E]verything here is pure, uninhabited, uninhabitable, frozen, carved in ice. A country left in cold storage until the time comes for it to live and to bear life. A country held in reserve, preserved in ice for the future use of mankind. When the new man is born, then the protective covering of snow over this land will be withdrawn and it will be bestowed on him, brand-new and virginal, preserved for him from the beginning of time ... (371)

This curious passage suggests that Tournier had concerns about global warming at the time (the 1970s) when the concept was competing with theories of global cooling.[9] He muses about the thawing of the permanent ice cover of Greenland, which someday will become a "virginal" paradise for "the new man." Tournier appears to be adopting a posthumanist point of view, implying that humanity as we know it will one day disappear, and some type of "posthuman" life will regenerate from the thawed polar regions.

Finally, Paul reaches Japan and discovers the perfection of the Japanese garden. Alternating narration between Paul and Shonin, a master gardener, Tournier explores several aspects of the Japanese garden. First, Shonin explains the meaning of garden stones, which are kept whole, not broken by a sculptor: "Why torment the stone and make its soul despair? The artist is a beholder. The artist carves with his eyes ..." (372). Gardens are made for contemplation, and the eye of the stone collector is the secret, lost soul of the garden:

> You will see in tenth-century gardens stones selected at that period by collectors of genius. ... But the tool for collecting them has been lost forever: the collector's eye. ... The stones with which [the garden] is filled are the work of an eye which, while leaving behind the evidence of its genius, has carried away the secret of it forever. (373)

---

9   The *Washington Post* published an article on 11 January 1970 entitled "Colder Winters Herald Dawn of New Ice Age." It quoted climatologists who predicted that a cold snap that began in 1950 could be the start of an ice age lasting hundreds of years.

The garden, the house, and its inhabitants form one being, a "living organism" (374). Garden stones must be partially buried, rooted in the earth, because for the Japanese gardener, stones are alive: "A stone is neither dead nor mute. It hears the crash of the waves, the ripple of the lake, the roaring of the torrent and it laments if it is unhappy, and that lament rends the heart of a poet" (374). Every garden also has an *Oku* stone. It is invisible to the eye, buried. It "animates the whole composition ... while remaining unperceived, like the soul of the violin" (375).

The Zen garden, created from dry landscape materials, is the most poetic and the most "austere" (380). Its paradox lies in "the contrast between wet and dry" (380). Rocks represent mountains and waterfalls, while raked sand or gravel symbolizes rivers or the sea. One does not walk in such a garden: "only the eye is allowed to wander, ... only ideas meet and embrace" (380). The minimalism of the Zen garden is meant to inspire infinite meditation: "In its apparent bareness, the Zen garden contains potentially all the seasons of the year, all the countries of the world and all the states of the soul" (380–81).

Finally, Shonin describes the miniature garden, whose dwarf trees must appear old; their gnarled trunk and branches symbolize great age and wisdom. The mystery of the miniature garden "is contained in this precept: *Possession of the world begins with the concentration of the subject and ends with that of the object*" (388; emphasis original). "Concentration" may be understood as condensation or contraction: as the thinker concentrates on the garden, he becomes smaller and smaller, as his rapt attention brings his understanding of the world into intense focus. The smaller a garden is, "the greater part of the world it embraces. ... So the scholar in his humble home, the poet at his desk and the hermit in his cave can possess the whole universe at will. They have only to concentrate enough to disappear into the miniature garden" (391).

This valorization of the small recalls Gilbert Durand's concept of "gulliverisation," seen in tales like "Tom Thumb" and the alchemical doctrine of the homunculus. The power of the small is a "reversal of the solar values symbolised by virility and gigantism" (Durand 204).[10] Indeed, Bachelard devotes a chapter of *The Poetics of Space* to

---

10 Tournier has shown his appreciation of the power of the small and the non-virile in other texts. In the Introduction, I mentioned "Tom Thumb Runs Away." In this short story appearing in *The Fetishist*, the diminutive hero learns

"Miniature." Sounding like Shonin, he writes: "The cleverer I am at miniaturizing the world, the better I possess it. But in doing this, it must be understood that values become condensed and enriched in miniature" (150). Among other authors, Bachelard quotes Charles Perrault, whose clever "Tom Thumb," outwitting the ogre, proves that "the infinitesimal is master of energies, small commands large" (166). He also cites a text of Cyrano de Bergerac that describes an apple as an entire universe, whose sun is the seed at the center (151). Again, like the Zen gardener, Bachelard speaks of the "cosmicity" (162) of the miniature:

> Thus the minuscule, a narrow gate, opens up an entire world. The details of a thing can be the sign of a new world which, like all worlds, contains the attributes of greatness.
>
> Miniature is one of the refuges of greatness. (155)

The subject of the miniature garden leads us to "Sophia's Misfortunes," the final chapter of Tournier's *The Wind Spirit*. Here Tournier meditates on genius, wisdom (*sophia*), and the absolute. For the ancient Greek philosophers, "Sophia was the absolute best, the Sovereign Good" (*The Wind Spirit* 233–34). Tournier laments that the "great ancient wisdom is dead" (244), killed notably by Rousseau and Kant. Rousseau's *Emile* (1762) was a "hymn to the moral conscience, ... a full-scale attack on speculative reason" (*The Wind Spirit* 235). Kant's fatal blow was struck by his *Groundwork of the Metaphysics of Morals* (1785), according to which, "morality must supplant wisdom as a guide to living and acting properly" (*The Wind Spirit* 237). We can, however, rediscover wisdom in the quotidian. Echoing his thoughts on

---

the lessons of ecology from an effeminate anti-ogre, Monsieur Logre. Another short story in the same collection, "The Red Dwarf," tells the story of a bitter and murderous dwarf who finally finds peace through the tenderness of the children who enthusiastically applaud him after his circus act. Finally, in "The Prophet of Unisex," Theodore Zeldin quotes Tournier speaking about his aversion to gender stereotypes: "I detest the Opera, because it so often presents a caricature of femininity and virility. I despise virility" (Zeldin 43). Nietzsche, in aphorism 51 of *Human, All Too Human*, part 2, also celebrates "the ability to be small": "One has still to be as close to the flowers, the grass and the butterflies as is a child, who is not so very much bigger than they are. ... He who wants to partake of *all* good things must know how to be small at times" (323). I am grateful to David Farrell Krell for pointing out this passage to me.

the miniature gardens in *Gemini*, Tournier proposes "a miniaturization of the ancient wisdom" (244), "an atomization of the absolute" (246).

Tournier explains that, etymologically, the absolute "is that which has no rapport with, no relation to anything else" (246). The absolute escapes us, because our lives "weave a constant web of relations" (246); ours is a relative existence in which meaning depends on our ability to compare and contrast persons and things. To attain the absolute, we must do like the Japanese gardener: our gaze must linger over a rock or a tree "as though it were the only thing that existed in the world" (247).

Tournier ends his autobiography with a reflection on two places where the absolute "takes on its most exalted forms" (247). First, referring to his novel *Friday*, he finds the absolute in the desert island, since it is completely cut off from the rest of the world. Crusoe's island is timeless: "The sea air effaces the differences between months and drowns the seasons in uniformity" (248), allowing Crusoe to enjoy eternal youth. Tournier prefers a second dwelling of the absolute, the garden, and in this very personal passage he specifically describes his own walled garden around his presbytery house in the village of Choisel, where he lived from 1957 till his death in 2016. Unlike the timeless island, the garden and the man who lives there are subject to the cycle of seasons and the advance of time. In his small, peaceful garden, bordered by a church and the cemetery where he now lies, Tournier, like the Zen practitioner, experienced time "compressed into one mystical moment" (249): "I suddenly become aware that time has been compressed, that space has shrunk to those few square feet enclosed by a stone wall, and that a single living thing—my garden—flourishes in the exorbitant immobility of the absolute" (249). Like Deborah in *Gemini*, Michel Tournier had a garden; now he is the garden.

Uncle Alexandre's Landfills

The most scandalously entertaining character in all of Tournier's *œuvre* is surely Jean and Paul's Uncle Alexandre, the self-described "swashbuckling" "dandy garbage man" (*Gemini* 69, 74). In 1934, upon the accidental death of his oldest brother, Gustave, Alexandre inherits the family business, TURDCO (The Urban Refuse Disposal

Company), consisting of six municipal landfills—Rennes, Deauville, Paris, Marseille, Roanne, and Casablanca—dedicated to the "task of repurgation" of waste (28). TURDCO is an inspired translation of SEDOMU (Société d'enlèvement des ordures ménagères urbaines). "Repurgation" refers to the "recovery" or "recycling" of waste, but the word has an obvious moral connotation. Bouloumié notes the connection to "purge" or "purgatory" ("*Les Météores*, Notice" 1626), and the dictionary defines it as "moral or spiritual cleansing; purification by the removal of corruption, sin, guilt, or similar evil" ("Purgation," *Oxford English Dictionary*). In *Homo detritus*, Baptiste Monsaingeon, recalling the anthropologist Mary Douglas's analysis of pollution and taboo, stresses the negative moral connotation of rubbish (*ordure*). *Ordure* is related to the Latin *horridus*, thus waste is seen as a threat to "the social or cultural order" (Monsaingeon 28): the filth of garbage suggests the stain of sin.

As for Tournier's SEDOMU, Alexandre is homosexual, and the French acronym—suggesting "sodomy"[11]—links garbage and homosexuality, while the scatological English translation links garbage to human waste. The connotation is clear: Homosexuals, like garbage and excrement, are unwelcome. The former live on the fringes of society, while the latter are abandoned to collection areas outside of cities. In her admirable dissertation on "the aesthetics of waste," Melissa Dunlany emphasizes the explicit connection between trash and human outcasts: "It is no coincidence that Alexandre's invented abbreviation for household waste, *ordures ménagères*, is *oms*, a homonym of *homme*, man" (42). Pary Pezechkian-Weinberg goes a step further, asserting that *oms* recalls not only *hommes*, but *homos* (66; cited in Dunlany 42 n. 10). In the following sections, I will analyze the beautiful and horrifying chapters devoted to the three landfills that contribute most to Tournier's complex metaphor of garbage: Roanne (on the River Loire, between Lyon and Vichy), Marseille, and Paris.

---

11 This connection is made, for example, by Arlette Bouloumié, *Les Météores*, "Notice" 1624, and by Susan Petit, *Michel Tournier's Metaphysical Fictions* 51.

Roanne

Alexandre is immediately "attracted by the negative, ... *inverted* aspect of this industry" (*Gemini* 28; emphasis original), the perfect profession for the homosexual hunter he prides himself to be. Like a cat, he is a predator (71), and with a lightning glance he can detect his new sexual quarries—Eustache and Daniel, "those flowers of the muck" (85)—among the Roanne refuse workers. More than his eyes, his nose possesses *"intelligence"* (72; emphasis original), and this olfactory talent allows him to appreciate the subtle aromas of his landfills: "The smell of refuse ... is an infinitely complex cipher which my nose is never done with decoding. ... How could anyone be bored amid a display of such richness, or so uncouth as to reject it out of hand as a bad smell?" (72). Alexandre identifies with the dump, and rejects any technique, such as recycling or incineration, that aims to reduce the volume of refuse. When Roanne city council members express a desire to recycle the wool that local textile factories contribute to the dump, Alexandre characterizes them as bourgeois, greedy, and anal retentive:

> Middle-class cheeseparing! Always terrified to throw anything away, like a miser hating to let go of anything. ... It's the dream of a completely constipated city. Whereas what I dream of is an entirely disposable world where a whole city could be thrown on the scrap heap. (68)

Alexandre is impressed by the "wealth and wisdom" (68) of Roanne's garbage. The combination of the gray wool with an inexplicable quantity of discarded books—usually prime targets of ragpickers,[12] who recuperate and sell them to paper manufacturers—

---

12 Compagnon ("Le moment du chiffon") and Monsaingeon (43–63) recount how ragpickers (*chiffonniers* or *biffins*) were essential players in the trash industry until after World War I. They were also called rag and bone men, after the two most important items they recuperated from trash. Rags were invaluable to the paper industry, which produced paper from recycled textiles until the mid-nineteenth century, when a process to make paper from wood pulp was invented. Recuperated bones had many uses. They were the raw material for buttons, gelatin, and phosphorus for matches. Monsaingeon describes the marginality of ragpickers, one of the most despised professions, considered "the refuse of the bourgeoisie" (44–45). His description reminds a reader of *Gemini* of Alexandre and his workers. Ragpickers were proud and "ferociously

leads Alexandre to call it "cerebral rubbish" (73) or "gray matter" (72), because its "fibrous substance ... has a certain affinity with the intricate synaptic substance of the human brain" (73). Would it not be a shame to recycle or burn this treasure? The dump is no "infernal place" (68). On the contrary, it is "a world parallel to the other, a mirror reflecting what makes the very essence of society, and every dump has its value, which may vary but is always positive" (68).

The paradox of Alexandre's concept of the landfill is that it is—as we saw above—a "negative," "inverted" (28) space which nevertheless, as a mirror of society, has a positive value. This is pure Tournier, whose novels abound with what he calls benign or malignant inversion,[13] "a mysterious operation which, without causing any apparent change in the nature of a person or thing, alters its *value*, putting less where there was more and more where there was less" (*The Wind Spirit* 102). Most people, whom Alexandre would disparage with terms like middle-class, heterosexual, or respectable, would place a negative sign on landfills. But Alexandre, "emperor of dust" (*Gemini* 29), "king and dandy of garbage men" (69), declares the positivity, superiority even, of "monstrous" people—the disabled, twins, homosexuals—and hellish spaces—landfills—confined to the fringes of society.

---

independent" from the "good citizens" of France (44). Their profession was rendered obsolete by the invention of the garbage can (*poubelle*) by the *préfet* Poubelle in 1883, and later by technical progress in the removal of waste from cities, along with increasing knowledge of hygiene. Ragpicking was formally banned in France in 1946 (63). Soon after began France's "Trente Glorieuses," the post-World War II economic boom that saw the beginning of a "throw-away" consumer society and the rapid development of construction (highways, ports, railroads, etc.), an industry responsible for 72 percent (247 million tons) of the waste generated in France (Lindgaard 39). Recuperation of waste, which had existed for centuries, was now seen as too expensive. Urban sewage would no longer be used to fertilize nearby farms; rags, bones, and metals would be permanently discarded. Waste treatment would now be defined by the "abandonment principle" (Monsaingeon 55, 66–67), until the emergence of a "green economy" (Lindgaard 41–42) in the later decades of the twentieth century.

13 An example of benign inversion is the transformation of Robinson Crusoe in *Friday*. Under the influence of Friday, Crusoe ceases to exploit the resources of the island, adopting instead a symbiotic relationship with nature. Abel Tiffauges, protagonist of *The Ogre*, recognizes that Auschwitz is a malignant inversion of the Nazi military boarding school where he works to recruit young boys.

The idea of landfills as the mirror of civilization, or "the other side of production" (Monsaingeon 28), is an oft-repeated trope in *Homo detritus*. The ubiquity of waste and pollution on the land, in the sea, and in the air prompts Monsaingeon to rename the Anthropocene Age the Poubellocene Age (15; see also Lindgaard 38), which one could translate as the Garbagocene Age, or, to borrow Dunlany's term, the "Garb-Age" (10). In an ominous posthumanist vision of the world, Monsaingeon designates the progeny of *Homo sapiens* as *Homo detritus*, the very inversion of *Homo economicus*: a "negative mirror of human rationality erected as the structural principle of the market economy" (18). *Homo detritus* is the "ideal discarder," the natural successor of the "ideal consumer" (18).

Since the early twentieth century, incineration has been an alternative to storing garbage in landfills. In theory, burning trash could be used to produce energy, but because of the enormous volume of water in dumps, incineration was not always profitable (61). Alexandre visits the incinerator at Issy-les-Moulineaux in the Paris suburbs, to see if such an installation would work in Roanne. The Roanne refuse workers take a fierce stand against the project, because of potential job losses. Alexandre is against the idea, too, but predictably, his reasons are more poetic: "[T]he fires of the incineration plants are akin to the fires of the Inquisition. To our eyes, beyond all doubt it is our bodies and our independent souls they are conspiring to cast into the flames" (*Gemini* 87), and he dreads the visit to the hellish plant as Dante must have dreaded following Virgil into the Inferno. And then his thoughts turn from burning garbage to events in Germany, where Hitler has begun rounding up homosexuals, Jews, and other minorities. He recalls a conversation with one of his workers:

> "Incineration! Incineration!" he kept repeating. "All very fine for the Maccabees! I've always been one for incinerating Maccabees. No profit in a Maccabee, so shove him on the fire, quick! It's clean, it's thorough, and what's more it gives him a little taste of where he's going to, eh! … But burning rubbish! That's wicked, that is!" (86)[14]

---

14 The Maccabees were a family of Jewish rebel warriors. Hanukkah commemorates the Maccabean revolt against the Seleucid Empire (167–160 BCE). I have made one important change to the published English translation. The translator

Alexandre clearly sympathizes with minority humans like himself who, metaphorically, are one with the landfills, body and soul. The anti-Semitic worker also values the dump and the garbage within, but his valorization of the marginal plainly does not extend to all of humanity.

The threat of an incinerator eventually leads to a strike by the Roanne refuse workers, resulting in an accumulation of garbage in the city. Alexandre marvels at the "splendors" of the tall garbage "sculptures" overrun with rats. They are "multicolored shrines" celebrating a new feast of the eerie rubbish world. It is the inversion of Corpus Christi: instead of the metaphorical body of Christ being displayed in a monstrance, it is the celebration of "Corpus Ganesh" (151), the elephant-headed Hindu deity that fascinates Alexandre because it is usually accompanied by a rat. Alexandre contemplates the beauty of trash that has not been "battered, humiliated and robbed of its worth by barbarous treatment" (151) like incinerating or crushing:

> For the first time, thanks to the strike, it has been given to me to see and to praise rubbish in its primordial freshness and innocence, spreading its flounces unrestrainedly.
>
> There is something far beyond mere aesthetic satisfaction in the winged happiness that carries me about the town. There is a sense of conquest, the satisfaction of ownership. For the centrifugal motion which drives urban refuse outward to the periphery of the town, to the waste ground and public dumps, along with stray dogs and an entire fringe society, that motion has been stopped by the strike and has started to go into reverse. The garbage has taken over. (151–52)

For a few heady days, at least, Alexandre's "fringe society" has taken power. But he knows that he is not witnessing a revolution; it is merely a respite from oppression.

In the chapter "Aesthetic of the dandy garbage man" (74–76), Alexandre reveals his ideas on beauty. Sounding much like the

---

failed to convey the extreme anti-Semitic tone of the character, because she did not translate Tournier's *macchabée* literally, using the neutral term "body" instead. Such a translation renders much less powerful the correspondence Alexandre identifies between garbage incineration plants and Nazi concentration camps.

decadent Des Esseintes in J.-K. Huysmans's 1884 novel *À rebours* (*Against Nature*),[15] Alexandre explains why he values copies of art or furniture more than originals:

> The idea is more than the thing and the idea of the idea more than the idea. Wherefore the imitation is more than the thing imitated, because it is the thing plus the effort of imitation, which incorporates the possibility of reproducing itself, and so of adding quantity to quality. (74)

Since copies often end up in the rubbish, Alexandre is in an ideal position to pursue his collection: "After all, what is rubbish but the great storehouse [*conservatoire*] of things multiplied to infinity by mass production?" (75).[16] His fondness for imitation extends to food. He

---

15 Des Esseintes prefers artificial to real flowers; dissatisfied with the drab natural color of a tortoise shell, he encrusts it with countless precious stones, and the animal perishes from the added weight; instead of going to a seaside resort, he adds salt to his bath water to simulate the sea, etc. Artificiality and imitation define his aesthetics: "Artifice," remarks the narrator, "seemed to Des Esseintes to be the distinctive stamp of man's genius. 'Nature has had her day,' as he put it, 'she's finally worn out the mindful patience of the man of refinement through the sickening uniformity of her landscapes and her skies. ... Moreover, there's not a single one of her inventions, reputed to be so subtle and so grandiose, that human ingenuity cannot create'" (Huysmans 54–55).

16 Has Alexandre found a copy of Walter Benjamin's recently published "The Work of Art in the Age of Mechanical Reproduction" among the books abandoned in the Roanne dump? Alexandre's own "essay" on aesthetics seems to refute Benjamin's concept that an original work of art possesses an "aura" or "authenticity" ("The Work of Art" 220–21) that a copy cannot possibly have. For Benjamin, the uniqueness of the art of antiquity is associated with magic or religious rituals, but the aura "withers in the age of mechanical reproduction" (221). Alexandre, however, is an apologist for "the process of production-consumption-disposal" (*Gemini* 75). For him, reproductions have far greater value than originals because of their sheer numbers, and even acquire something akin to Benjamin's aura, a copy "being the original encapsulated, possessed, integrated, and even multiplied—in short, considered and spiritualized" (74). Benjamin and Alexandre would at least agree in their bitter opposition to fascism and its "politics which Fascism is rendering aesthetic" ("The Work of Art" 242). Tournier examined the seductive appeal of Nazi aesthetics in *The Ogre*. When accused of romanticizing Nazism, he replied in a *Newsweek* interview: "You think Hitler didn't have his attractions? I simply point out how Nazi propaganda was focused on children, to woo them into Fascism with all the attractions of the Wagnerian side of Nazism. When people

declares his "weakness for disguised food": vegetables made to look like meat, and above all, fish, "that imitation meat" (70).

Later, Alexandre will propose that a landfill is not only the conservatory of beauty, but also the dwelling place of the absolute. When the mysterious aristocrat Fabienne de Ribeauvillé speaks to him of "the gentleness of the refuse dumps" (166),[17] he wonders how such a woman could share his love of garbage:

> Has she also understood that what is there is a civilization pulverized and reduced to its first elements, whose functional relations with mankind have now been broken? The repository of the everyday life of the moment, made up of objects which, because they are useless, are thereby elevated to a kind of absoluteness? ... A society defines itself by what it throws away—which instantly becomes an absolute—domestic refuse and homosexuals in particular. (170)

Alexandre believes that the landfill is an "archeology of the present" (170), a civilization literally broken down to its basics. He would agree with the great French anthropologist Marcel Mauss, who reportedly said that "[t]he most common objects are the ones that teach us the most about a civilization. ... Digging through a pile of rubbish, one can reconstitute the entire life of a society" (*Homo detritus* 25). Objects in the dump have been abandoned by humans and cast off to the fringes of the city because they are useless—pure form, containers without content. Earlier in this chapter I quoted the end of *The Wind Spirit*, where Tournier defines the absolute as "that which has no rapport with, no relation to anything else" (246), like Robinson Crusoe's desert island. Landfills—islands of filth and rubbish cut off from the livable world—would seem to fit his definition. In *Friday*, Crusoe realizes that anyone who ever knew him believes he is dead; he is utterly cut off from the rest of the world, existing *absolutely* between heaven and hell,

---

tell me I estheticize Nazism, I quote Léon Blum, who said, 'Communism is a technique, Socialism a morality and Fascism an esthetic'" (qtd. in J. Krell, "Michel Tournier's 'Degenerate' Art" 154).

17 Fabienne's remark recalls Victor Hugo's praise of urban sewers in *Les Misérables*: "Each thing bears its true form, or at least, its definitive form. The mass of filth has this in its favor, that it is not a liar. ... The sincerity of foulness pleases us, and rests the soul" (1127).

in a sort of "Limbo of the Pacific" (123). Alexandre, too, wonders if he is truly alive, when he later takes up residence in the ghostly, isolated world of the Saint-Escobille landfill:

> Saint-Escobille is actually nothing but the white shadow of Paris, its negative image ... . [O]ught it not rather to be called *limbo*? It seems to me that vague, colorless, diaphanous word, with its mingled suggestions of the life before and the hereafter, suits this faceless, voiceless plain rather well. Am I still alive? (*Gemini* 236)

Landfills possess an absolute quality because they are places of separation and death, where the undesirable parts from the desirable. Gérard Bertolini explains that the French word for "garbage" (i.e., organic waste) is *déchet*, from the Latin *cadere*, to fall, via *choir*, and is related to "decadence," "cadaver," and "to die." The first syllable of *déchet* indicates separation. Bertolini states that "[g]arbage [*déchet*] is in fact placed under the sign of alterity" (50). Garbage is "not me" (50): it is strange, other, and dangerous.

Marseille

When Alexandre approaches the Miramas landfill near Marseille, he is struck by the strange foliage of the trees. Instead of leaves, "soiled paper fluttering in the wind" (*Gemini* 208) graces their branches. This visual pollution is caused by the persistent mistral wind that sends paper from the dump flying into the trees, whose "unclean foliage sprouts with unusual luxuriance" (208). By night, "black waves" of rats carry on their "infernal sabbath" (209–10); by day, the seagulls rule, and a "whirlwind of beaks and wings" (212) harasses the workers on their bulldozers, working the "white hills" (208) of the enormous dump.

Operating between 1912 and 2010, the Miramas landfill (also known as Entressen, after another nearby village) was at one time the largest landfill in Europe, a 60-meter mountain of garbage. Monsaingeon cites Miramas as a prime example of "the principle of abandonment" (67). Before it was built, household waste from the Marseille region was used to fertilize nearby agricultural fields, a common practice throughout France (Monsaingeon 39–43). Agricultural exploitation of waste stopped in the twentieth century; all refuse was destined to be abandoned in dumps and thus, as Monsaingeon puts it, garbage was invented. The Miramas site was notorious for its pollution: contemporary articles (see Broqua n. pag.; Clarke n. pag.)[18] describe the enormous and destructive gull population; photographs show trees suffocated by paper and—since the 1960s—plastic bags. Miramas is an "ecological scandal" (Broqua n. pag.), principally because of decades of pollution of the water table. Nevertheless, the site is slowly recovering. The gulls have left, trees have grown back and are no longer garnished with paper and plastic. A biogas facility now burns away the methane emitted by decomposing material, in the process providing enough electricity to service 16,000 homes. But it will take at least another 30 years to clean up the water table (Clarke n. pag.).

Tournier named the chapter devoted to Miramas "Fur and Feather" because of the ghastly battles at dusk and dawn between the rats and the gulls. In the most horrific scene, Alexandre's young lover Daniel is eaten alive by hordes of rats crazed by the mistral, as he searches for Alexandre's quarters. Alexandre is living in a converted railway car in the midst of the dump, "one more step toward [his] absorption in the refuse" (*Gemini* 209). Repulsive images of rats and gulls intensify Tournier's probe into "this negative side of life" (209). For the "bourgeois" whom Alexandre despises, it is a purgatory in need of purgation, a home to disease-spreading pests, decomposing and polluting filth, and the basest of human beings. Alexandre, again questioning if he is alive or dead, wishes that the Paris–Lyon–Marseille train that roars past the dump each day would stop just once at his "pale, silvery half-world":

> Windows will be lowered, heads poked out, startled and frightened by the strange, bleak terrain. Then I shall make a speech to those visitors from another planet. The dandy garbage man will inform them that they are newly dead. That they have been wiped from the face of the earth and passed over to its underside. (209)

Indeed, neither the dead nor the living count for much at Miramas. When Alexandre reports finding a body (Daniel's) in the "white hills" (220) of the dump, the *gendarmes*

---

18 See also "1912–2012: La décharge d'Entressen ou d'Arles?," which cites a description of the landfill in *Gemini*.

had other things to think about! In the white hills? That's a place that the police steer clear of. Outlaw country. The body probably belonged to a ragpicker, a secondhand dealer, a garbage collector or some tramp. The settlement of a score between Arabs, Piedmontese, or Corsicans. I understood that we were outside society. (220)

But it is September 1939, Germany has invaded Poland, and France has ordered a general mobilization. "Well, let them carve each other up, these respectable, heterosexual citizens," declares Alexandre. "We, the outcasts, will stand by and watch them" (220).

Alexandre's descriptions of Roanne's garbage are essentially static. He admires the majestic garbage "sculptures" that grace the city during the strike. He reflects on the archeological relics—absolute in their uselessness—that fill the dump. He ponders the timeless infinity of the limbo in which he lives. Miramas, on the contrary, is a living, moving mountain: bulldozers carve out hills, the mistral blows all manner of trash through the air, gulls fly and dive, rats gallop through the trash, and it is all-out war between nocturnal fur and diurnal feather (210). The perpetual movement of Miramas brings to mind Jane Bennett's essay *Vibrant Matter: A Political Ecology of Things*. In the spirit of "material ecocriticism," Bennett questions the divorce of subjects (humans) from objects (everything else) and suggests that a "vital materiality" dwells in all things. Her reference to trash on the first page could have been written with the disastrous Miramas landfill in mind. She encourages us to not "ignore the vitality *of* matter and the lively powers *of* material formations, such as the way ... our trash is not 'away' in landfills but generating lively streams of chemicals and volatile winds of methane as we speak" (vii; emphasis original). Bennett, a political scientist, believes that knowing the power of things has a political effect: "How, for example, would patterns of consumption change if we faced not litter, rubbish, trash, or 'the recycling,' but an accumulating pile of lively and potentially dangerous matter?" (viii). Like Tournier, Bennett admires Spinoza,[19] specifically for "his idea of conative bodies that strive to enhance their power of activity by forming alliances with other bodies," and "his faith that everything is made of the same substance"

---

19 Tournier writes in *The Wind Spirit* that, for him, Spinoza's *Ethics* is the most important book after the Gospels.

(x). Thus all matter, not just human matter, is vibrant, and possesses "thing-power": "the curious ability of inanimate things to animate, to act, to produce effects dramatic and subtle" (6). Again, Bennett alludes to the power of trash, quoting Robert Sullivan's *Meadowlands* (1998), a "Thoreauian travelogue of the New Jersey garbage hills outside Manhattan" (5):

> The ... garbage hills are alive ... there are billions of microscopic organisms thriving underground in dark, oxygen-free communities. ... I found a little leachate seep, a black ooze trickling down the slope of the hill, an espresso of refuse. In a few hours, this stream would find its way down into the groundwater of the Meadowlands; it would mingle with toxic streams. ... But in this moment, here at its birth, ... this little seep was pure pollution, a pristine stew of oil and grease, of cyanide and arsenic, of cadmium, chromium, copper, lead, nickel, silver, mercury, and zinc. ... A few yards away, where the stream collected into a benzene-scented pool, a mallard swam alone. (Bennett 6)[20]

Gemini similarly confers "thing-power" on all matter. What passes for a "character" in the novel goes beyond Jean, Paul, Alexandre, and other humans. We have seen, for example, how the low tide is an ensemble of characters—vegetable and animal—suffering while exposed on the muddy sand. And the Miramas landfill is teeming with "life": human, nonhuman, organic and inorganic. The "force of things" (Bennett 1–19) in *Gemini* is in part due to personification. The creatures of the low tide and the things in the garbage dumps are a powerful metaphor for the plight of the various outcasts of society. But the power of the tides and the landfills goes beyond mere personification. We have seen how the tides, in their unpredictability, seem to have a mind of their own (*Gemini* 128), and how Jean is attracted by their "elemental force" (129). As the moon's and sun's gravitational pull attracts the earth's waters, so Jean is drawn by a "pull on him of the great, wet, salty expanse the ebb had just uncovered" (128). The landfills are ambivalent spaces. As personification they represent the marginals with whom Tournier obviously sympathizes, but they are

---

20 Bennett quotes Sullivan, *Meadowlands*. Doubleday, 1998, pp. 96–97.

also powerful and uncanny "malignant inversions" of the world of *Homo economicus*, stark and shadowy versions of the absolute.

Paris

Alexandre's next stop is the landfill that serves Paris: Saint-Escobille in Île-de-France, 70 kilometers southwest of Paris.[21] He will stay there through the "phony war" (September 1939–May 1940), and leave a month or so after 14 June 1940, the beginning of the German occupation of Paris. Once again, we appreciate the "vital materiality" of things and places in the novel. Alexandre imagines Paris as a pump. First, it sucks the life out of "this dead land, desert and sterilized" (*Gemini* 235), then the garbage train pierces the vacuum, pumping "thirty-five wagonloads of refuse come from the capital to the center of the dump every morning" (235).

In 1939 the garbage arriving from Paris was normal. Faded chrysanthemums from cemeteries arrived after All Saints' Day, and, a few days after Christmas, the "train was overflowing with beribboned Christmas trees and empty champagne bottles" (236). But early in June 1940 things change. The Paris exodus begins: thousands of Parisians fleeing towards the south any way they can, by car, bicycle, or on foot. Alexandre is horrified by the contents of the first train to arrive after the exodus and the subsequent German occupation. The train driver opens the side panel of a car, "and an avalanche of limp bodies bounced and tumbled at our feet. Dogs! Hundreds of thousands of dead dogs!" (246).[22] The driver explains that the fleeing Parisians abandoned their dogs, and the Germans rounded up the roaming packs: "Guns, pistols, bayonets, sticks, lassos, a real massacre!" (247). Thus dogs become yet another marginal group pursued and executed by Hitler. Alexandre calls the Saint-Escobille train a "ghost train" (236), because it backs

---

21 Saint-Escobille operated from 1898 to 1968; garbage was delivered by train from Paris. In 2017, after 15 years of protests led by l'Association pour la défense de la santé et de l'environnement (ADSE), a project to build another giant landfill there was defeated (Dutheil n. pag.).
22 In *The Wind Spirit* (220), Tournier explains that the delivery of dead dogs is based on real events, related to him by Louise Falque, who worked at the Saint-Escobille landfill in June 1940.

into the dump in the early morning with no headlight to show the way. He imagines the driver sporting a skull for a head. The imagined horror of the ghost train turns real in this scene, and a reader cannot help but associate the ghost train to the Holocaust trains that were already transporting victims to the death camps.

Alexandre's dog Sam could have been one of the dead dogs delivered that day, for Alexandre had lost him on a memorable bicycle trip to Paris in late June. Like Des Esseintes in *Against Nature* (also translated as *Against the Grain*), Alexandre is "fond of going against the grain" (240), and he decides to cycle north to see empty Paris, passing the "chaos" of the southern exodus. He approves the mess of abandoned vehicles and furniture at the side of the road: "it was the refuse collector's triumph, a paradise of salvage, the dandy garbage man's apotheosis" (241). His joy is short-lived, because in Paris he loses Sam, drawn away by the scent of stray dogs. He spends the night alone near the Palais de Chaillot, across the Seine from the Eiffel Tower, and is awakened by the sound of German officers preparing for an important photograph:

> I knew him at once, the Great Heterosexual, Chancellor Adolf Heterosexual, the brown devil who has put to death in his horror camps as many of my brethren as fell into his hands. This meeting had to take place, and nowhere else but in the shadow of the Eiffel penis. The prince of refuse come from the ends of his rubbishy empire and the vulture of Berchtesgaden descended from his airy charnel house were bound to look one another in the eyes on Sunday, June 23, 1940, while the sunshine of the year's longest day burst in a fanfare of light. (244)

When Alexandre returns to Saint-Escobille without Sam, his solitude is total. He is as forgotten as the tons of garbage that surround him. In an intertextual nod to Tournier's first novel, Alexandre compares his isolation to Crusoe's limbo of the Pacific: "How welcoming was Robinson Crusoe's island, how it swarmed with friendly presences compared to my desert of refuse!" (241). He and his workers set about the task of burying the dead dogs, from which "there rose a silent barking, one unanimous howl that drilled through my brain" (247). As they cover the dogs with lime, Alexandre meditates one last time on the aesthetics of the landfill. Although a dump may be very deep, it is essentially superficial, because every layer is similar, like an onion's "superimposed skins" (248). It is mostly containers emptied of their content, forms without substance: "The substance of things ... has all gone, used up, swallowed, absorbed into the city. The refuse—the anti-city—piles up the skins. After the substance has melted away, the form itself becomes substance" (248). Thus the material of the landfill is a "pseudo-substance, which is nothing but an accumulation of forms" (248). The superficiality of the landfill serves two functions, "possession" and "celebration." First, its area (*superficie*) delineates the borders of the material, "thus ensuring *possession* of the thing or substance" (248). Second, the labels and tags of the various objects are *celebrations*: they declaim the virtues of the product and tell the consumer how to use it. But "since the thing, the substance is no longer there, this possessing encloses emptiness, this declamation bursts upon the void, so becoming absolute and absurd" (248). Alexandre is indeed in his element, inhabiting an absolute non-world—like limbo or hell—but in the end pure form, useless and absurd. He will survive the war, but in time he loses interest in garbage and in life (266) and will die an absurd—perhaps suicidal—death, "boy hunting" (270) on the dark, dangerous docks of Casablanca.

Chapter 2

Cloud Erotica: Stéphane Audeguy's *The Theory of Clouds* (*La Théorie des nuages*)

History shows again and again how nature points out the folly of men.

—Blue Oyster Cult, "Godzilla"

[N]ever has experience been contradicted more thoroughly than strategic experience by tactical warfare, economic experience by inflation, bodily experience by mechanical warfare, moral experience by those in power. A generation that had gone to school on a horse-drawn streetcar now stood under the open sky in a countryside in which nothing remained unchanged but the clouds, and beneath these clouds, in a field of force of destructive torrents and explosions, was the tiny, fragile human body.

—Walter Benjamin, "The Storyteller" 84

Man lives *erotically*. The geographer who modestly and patiently studies the relationship between humans and the Earth would thus be a disciple of Eros, an *erotologist*, an expert in *erotology*.

—Luc Bureau, *Terra erotica* 9

In the opening paragraph of his novel *The Theory of Clouds*, Stéphane Audeguy introduces one of his major themes, the complex relationship between the two meanings of *temps*, "time" and "weather": "All children become sad in the late afternoon, for they begin to comprehend the passage of time. The light starts to change. Soon they will have to head home, and to behave, and to pretend" (3). Unfortunately, in this and other passages, the English translation obscures the time/weather ambiguity, much more evident in the original French: "Vers les cinq heures du soir, tous les enfants sont tristes: ils commencent à comprendre ce qu'est le temps. Le jour décline un peu. Il va falloir rentrer pourtant, être sage, et mentir" (*Théorie des nuages* 13).[1] The time is five in the evening, a melancholic moment when day is turning to night. Time is not a clock on the wall; it is intimately related to the position of the sun in the sky. And the sun is a key actor not only in the cycle of time, but also in the round of the seasons with their varying weather patterns.

Also on the first page, we meet Akira Kumo, a retired couturier living on the rue Lamarck in Montmartre. He has just hired a librarian named Virginie Latour to classify his considerable collection of materials related to clouds.[2] Kumo loves to talk about clouds, and it is through his storytelling that Virginie learns about the men who shaped our knowledge of clouds: Luke Howard (the only historical character in the novel), a pharmacist from London, whose cloud classification in the "Essay on the Modification of Clouds" (1804) was much admired by Goethe; Carmichael, a painter of clouds, driven to suicide by their dangerous beauty and infinitely unfathomable structures; Richard Abercrombie, a Scottish meteorologist whose journey around the world began with the goal of assembling a complete photographic cloud atlas, and ended with the compilation of the mysterious and notorious Abercrombie Protocol. The chronology-meteorology question, like its relative history-geography, was a key factor in the lives of these cloud pioneers.

In order to understand these concepts in Audeguy's novel, it will be useful to consult a philosophical essay by an author who has been

---

[1] Normally I will quote the published English translation (*Theory of Clouds*), but translation issues will occasionally make it necessary to quote from the original French text (*Théorie des nuages*).

[2] The proper names are well chosen. Kumo means "cloud" in Japanese, and Jean-Baptiste Lamarck, the great naturalist, also had an interest in clouds: he proposed a five-type classification in 1802, just before Luke Howard's more famous four-type classification (cirrus, cumulus, stratus, nimbus) (*Theory of Clouds* 9).

a major influence: Michel Tournier. "Chronology and Meteorology" and "History and Geography" are two of the 58 pairs of words whose similarities and contrasts Tournier playfully examines in *The Mirror of Ideas*. The first element of these pairs is clearly related to time, the second to space, an opposition that Tournier examines in a third essay, "Time and Space."[3] We noted in the last chapter how Tournier's thoughts on "the lost coincidence" (*The Wind Spirit* 225) between time and weather were inspired by Jules Verne's *Around the World in Eighty Days*. Tournier writes that Verne's novel best represents the "collision of meteorology and chronology" (*Mirror of Ideas* 82) in the concept of *temps*. Phileas Fogg is a precise man of chronology, obsessed by clocks and schedules, whereas his French valet Passepartout personifies the unpredictability of meteorology, "because he is the man of improvisation and resourcefulness in ... 'foggy' situations" (82). The chronology-meteorology homonymy of *temps* is justified, according to Tournier, by the seasons, "characterized by meteorological portraits," but occupying "a very precise place on the calendar" (82). The chronological precision of the seasons, however, is belied by the fickleness of the weather.

History and geography are not homonyms, but opposites, and Tournier wonders why in France these "incompatible" (53) subjects—"somber" history and "optimistic" geography (54)—are traditionally taught by the same teacher. Yet if history is fundamentally time and geography space, Tournier remarks that geography has its temporality as well, again embodied by the seasons:

> Historical time is an irreversible succession of unpredictable and almost always catastrophic events, the most common of which is war, the absolute evil. Geographical time, by contrast, is inscribed in the regular cycle of the seasons. Certainly, meteorology plays here its capricious and unpredictable games. But even rains, storms, fog, and clear weather obey more or less the order of the four seasons that array them in their traditional colors: spring, pink; summer, green; autumn, gold; winter, white. (54)

---

3 Tournier, a student of German philosophy, bases his analysis of time and space on Kant's *Critique of Pure Reason* (1781). In Part 1, "Transcendental Aesthetic" (his term for the "science of all the principles of sensibility *a priori*" [22]), Kant differentiates between time and space as follows: "Time is the formal condition, *a priori*, of all phenomena whatsoever. Space, as the pure form of all external intuition, is a condition, *a priori*, of external phenomena only" (31).

The first instance of the interaction between time (or history) and meteorology (or geography) is during Kumo's narration of Luke Howard's journey to the European continent in 1815. A pacifist and Quaker, Howard volunteers to aid the victims of the bloody Napoleonic Wars. When Howard arrives at Waterloo shortly after Napoleon's defeat, the narrator describes the contrast between the consequences of history—corpses decomposing on the ground—and the innocence of the sky, abode of the atmospheric phenomena that used to be called meteors: "The rains, at long last, ceased. The stench of rotting carcasses and gangrenous wounds rose slowly skyward [*vers le ciel radieux*]" (*Theory of Clouds* 84). Napoleon's army had been hindered by the rain and mud: marching was difficult, weapons were damp, and the French attack on the Prussians had to be delayed. This certainly contributed to Napoleon's defeat, which Audeguy calls "meteorology's revenge" (84), for three years earlier Napoleon had mocked a scientist who had attempted to convince him of the importance of clouds—and weather predictions—to warfare. Napoleon's arrogance and "imperial stupidity" ("impériale bêtise," *Théorie des nuages* 105) was such that he never understood the potential might of the weather even after his experience in 1812, when for the Russians winter proved to be "a powerful and indefatigable ally, one that would attack day and night, and by night even more fiercely than by day" (*Theory of Clouds* 84–85).

The next character to encounter time and weather is the painter Carmichael. Kumo tells Virginie that clouds present a danger for artists who lose themselves in their dizzying abyss. The edges of one appear "like another cloud, and those edges yet another, and so on. Every part of a cloud, in other words, reiterates the whole. Therefore each cloud might be called infinite, because its very surface is composed of other clouds, and those clouds of still other clouds, and so forth" (44). Carmichael's insane obsession with clouds and his inability to depict their infinite changes leads him to a fallacious—and fatal—insight regarding *le temps*. He declares that time and weather are essentially the same; moreover, that they are both spatial. Carmichael abolishes temporality, leading him to conclude that death does not exist:

> He knew with absolute certainty that chronological and climatic time were one and the same thing. The contractions of the

adiabatic clouds[4] were the expression of this periodicity, of the cyclic nature of time, in the same way the seasons are. Cycles, endless cycles. Everything moved and nothing changed. This thought made Carmichael euphoric: What we call "time" isn't chronological but spatial; what we call "death" is merely a transition between different kinds of nature. (95–96)

Believing that the particles that make up his wife and himself will endure, he poisons her before taking his own life, naively certain that "embracing death opened up new possibilities for life" (96).

The Theory of Clouds extends the meaning of clouds beyond the conventional definition. The eruption of Krakatoa in August 1883 was "the most powerful explosion [*bombe naturelle*] the world had known in several thousand years" (78), "the largest cloud ever recorded" (79). Although the eruption and ensuing tsunamis killed tens of thousands of people, Audeguy adds that, unlike the unnatural bomb dropped over Hiroshima, the "titanic forces" (79) of the volcano were without murderous intent, merely the natural build-up of enormous pressure. After the initial eruption, the cloud, traveling around the earth for several years, actually changed the climate in many places, lowering temperatures and disrupting the normal cycle of the seasons:

> The volcano continued to prove lethal through the air. The heated cloud made up of stone pulverized by the explosion didn't dissipate so easily; indeed, it lasted for years. Because of its size it could not be dispersed by the winds, and was itself a storm of dust, water, and wind. First it arched up, reaching a height of ten miles, and for a time seemed to remain immobile: then, a few hours later, like a slow-moving predator, it began to stretch out across the atmosphere, its mass crushing millions of tons of cold air, which, pushing the cloud, sent it spinning slowly into the Northern Hemisphere, altering climates as it went. (80–81)

Krakatoa is undoubtedly a representation of nature's force, but for Audeguy this massive cloud also symbolizes nature's ultimate helplessness in what Michel Serres calls the "objective war" (*Natural*

---

4 The translator helpfully explains that "'adiabatic' refer[s] to the point at which no heat can be gained or lost between a cloud and the surrounding atmosphere" (*Theory of Clouds* 95).

Contract 10–11) that humans have been waging against it. Nature will never destroy humans, Audeguy writes; only humans will accomplish that feat: "Krakatoa had taken thousands of victims but it did not have the power to destroy humanity. Humanity could only be obliterated through self-destruction. For nature, this marked the beginning of the end" (*Theory of Clouds* 82).

One of the central ideas of *The Theory of Clouds* is humankind's insatiable appetite for destruction, be it, in the vocabulary of Serres, "subjective" annihilation of other humans or "objective" destruction of nonhuman entities. This recalls Tournier's essay on "Time and Space," in which he declares "humanity's race towards self-destruction through bloody tribulations" (*Mirror of Ideas* 101) to be the very essence of historical time. Audeguy has seized upon two tragic events as twin defining moments of the twentieth century: the Third Reich's attempt to exterminate European Jews, and the atomic bombings of Hiroshima and Nagasaki by the United States. These two concurrent catastrophic man-made clouds are inseparable in the author's mind: "It was while dreaming of the cloud formed by the unspeakable explosion of Hiroshima and the indescribable smoke from the chimneys of Auschwitz that I wrote my first book: *The Theory of Clouds*" ("De la nature de quelques choses" 243).

The bombing of Hiroshima is the focal point of Audeguy's commentary on the folly of humanity's war on itself and on nature. Akira Kumo has a memory problem. Born in Hiroshima in 1946—he thinks—but living in Paris since 1967, he recalls little of his previous life in Japan, except perhaps the preference for Caucasian prostitutes that he developed as a young graphic art student during the American occupation. In 1997, he begins to collect every work he can find on clouds and meteorology, and his collection is soon recognized as one of the most remarkable in the world. Yet he does not understand the reason for his sudden passion, and this incomprehension haunts him:

> There was … one question to which he had no answer, and it involved his obsession with clouds. His profession had taught him that sometimes it was best not to overanalyze things, that leaving them in shadow was the right course. Yet he couldn't help feeling that an answer lay in wait for him somewhere, crouched like a beast hidden in the dark jungle of memory. He shivered at the thought that one day it might leap out at him and in one swift and terrible motion devour him whole. (*Theory of Clouds* 43)

Stéphane Audeguy's The Theory of Clouds (La Théorie des nuages)

And this is what happens one day in 1996, when he is struck by the truth of his birth: it was in 1933, not 1946. He was nearly 12 when the bomb fell on his city. The trauma of the explosion—that spared him because he was swimming under water but incinerated his little sister on the shore—had erased 12 years from his memory. "From that moment onward, the tissue of his life started unraveling—not all at once but inexorably" (70). Twice he will attempt suicide; the second time he will succeed.

The lethal cloud of Hiroshima has been haunting his unconscious since that day in August 1945 when the bomb obliterated his memory along with the city. He finally understands his fascination with clouds when he recalls the moment he realized that his vaporized sister has become a part of the atmosphere: "[I]t meant that her body had vanished into the air and that her spirit would wander the earth like a ghost until the end of time" (225). Kumo will be reunited with his sister when, on the final page of the novel, Virginie scatters his ashes into a fierce storm:

> Some were probably shot straight up into the upper layers of the atmosphere and would not settle back down for quite some time. With a little luck, those ashes might ride upon one of the high-altitude currents that flow constantly above us at speeds greater than two hundred and fifty miles per hour, and which are the true authors of the weather down below. She imagines that some of these ashes might mingle with the remaining particles of Krakatoa's volcano, or even the vitrified traces, still radioactive, of a little girl vaporized on the banks of the Ota River. (266)

Kumo reveals his personal trauma during his conversations with Virginie, and in letters he writes to her while she is in England researching the Abercrombie Protocol. These narratives are an opportunity for Audeguy to present his own thoughts on the Hiroshima and Nagasaki bombings, such as why two bombs were dropped, and how the targets were chosen (127–30). In a letter to Virginie, Kumo explains that two attacks were necessary because the Americans had two types of atomic bomb and wanted to test both. The five cities on the target list had to be cities that had so far been spared war damage, so that the effects of the bomb could be more cleanly measured. Kyoto, originally on the list, was removed because of its cultural importance. The four remaining cities—Hiroshima, Kokura, Nagasaki, and Niigata—were targeted based on logistics, including cloud cover. Hiroshima's misfortune was that, unlike the others, it had cloudless weather on August 6, 1945. Hence, like Napoleon's costly defeats at Moscow and Waterloo, Japan's destruction was closely linked to weather. As the bomb fell towards the people of Hiroshima, history obliterated geography, time annihilated space:

> Here was a unique moment in a century of iron and fire, in the silence of a cloudless sky that seemed to have absorbed time and space, with the exception of this tiny brilliant dot heading toward them. Then the moment vaporized. The bomb had gone off at precisely the designated height. (130)

Audeguy briefly brings together the cloud of Hiroshima and the ashes of the Holocaust when Kumo—in another letter—describes the apocalyptic scene that he witnessed in the moments following the explosion. The mushroom cloud, born in blinding light, soon turns dark as night, and black rain—nuclear fallout—begins to pour down:

> The holy book the Americans worshipped foretold the end of the world, a tale of blood and fire in which the wicked were punished. Over the city was hanging a single gigantic cloud straight out of that story, come to earth. It was as if the flattened city, reduced to nothing, was floating above itself, as if this cloud had absorbed all the ash the city had exhaled—the dust of roads and buildings, and bodies as well. At the other end of the earth, in northeast Europe, Jews and gypsies and political prisoners and others had also disappeared into ash, and had been for years, but the world had looked elsewhere. (226)

The evocation of the apocalypse recalls the opening of the sixth seal in Revelation 6.12: "[L]o, there was a great earthquake; and the sun became black as sackcloth of hair, and the moon became as blood." The comparison of the black sun to sackcloth of hair links the cloud of Hiroshima to the ashes of the Nazi concentration camps, where tons of shaved human hair were used to make cloth, blankets, and socks for the German war machine.

Thinking back to that morning in 1945, Kumo realizes that the terrible power of the atomic bomb and the ensuing black rain ushered in a new era, when humankind's war on nature would signal a suicidal war on humanity itself: "Looking at the ink-like droplets, Akira tried not to think about his sister. Two hours before these drops, she had been a young girl and now her body fell as rain, and this had become a world in which such a thing—and many other things besides—was conceivable" (227). Kumo's recounting of the Hiroshima bombing is the culmination of one of the novel's critical points: The West has appropriated science and technology in the interest of war, simultaneously ensuring power over weaker countries and domination over nature.

For Audeguy, nuclear power, be it for war or power generation, symbolizes excessive human pride, or hubris, which one might translate in French as *la démesure humaine*. This is the subtitle of the philosopher François Flahault's *Le Crépuscule de Prométhée* (The Twilight of Prometheus), an essay on the dangers of progress. Flahault begins his study by commenting on the Chernobyl nuclear disaster, and the ironic symbolism of the bronze statue of Prometheus erected in nearby Pripyat, a nuclear city founded in 1970 principally to house employees of the plant, then evacuated and abandoned shortly after the catastrophic accident in April 1986. The statue depicts a triumphant Prometheus, the benefactor—and some say creator—of mankind, stealing fire from the gods in order to give it to humans, who had fallen out of favor with Zeus. As Prometheus gave humanity quasi-divine power with his gift of fire, the Soviets used nuclear technology to bring the gift of electricity to the people, as Lenin had promised:

> "Communism," Lenin had declared, "is Soviet power plus the electrification of the entire country." The electric light bulb was, in some ways, the new Eucharist. Sixty years after the October Revolution, Soviet propaganda could brag about having mastered the atom, inexhaustible source of the energy of progress. (Flahault 11)

Prometheus has long symbolized the unlimited potential of humankind, whose advancement, thanks to creative use of technology, knows no bounds. A passage from Aeschylus's *Prometheus Bound* reveals that humans' uncontrollable desire to obtain mastery over nature was actually a second "gift" of Prometheus. When the Chorus asks Prometheus—now strapped to the rock—what he has done to offend Zeus, he replies that, besides giving them the technology of fire, he had "caused mortals to cease foreseeing doom" (250). At that time, it is said, humans knew in advance the day of their death. Henceforth, they would be ignorant of this fact; instead, Prometheus "placed in them blind hopes" (253). Thus Prometheus, despite his name which means "forethought" (84–87), does not enlighten humankind; he instead blesses them—or condemns them—with the kind of blind optimism that causes them to fight on against their mortality by harnessing technology to become ever grander, ever hopeful that they will one day conquer nature.[5]

Flahault believes that in the Western philosophical tradition it is Descartes who best formulates the "Promethean ideal" (14) that humankind should dominate nature, and even challenge God. In *Discourse on the Method*, Descartes famously declares that "knowing the force and the action of fire, water, air, the stars, heavens and all other bodies that environ us" will "render ourselves the masters and possessors of nature" (Part 6; qtd. in Flahault 15). In a later work, *The Passions of the Soul*, Descartes extols the power of free will, which "in a certain measure renders us like God in making us masters of ourselves" (Article 152, *Philosophical Works* 401; qtd. in Flahault 15).

Prometheus's crime was doubly chastised by Zeus: Prometheus was chained to a rock in the Caucasus, where an eagle would eat his liver every day; and his human friends were punished when Zeus sent them Pandora, the first woman, who released evil into the world when curiosity compelled her to open the beautiful *pithos* given her by the gods. Flahault describes the Chernobyl disaster as a modern example of the consequences of Promethean hubris. After the explosion, the Prometheus statue was moved from Pripyat, now a ghost city, to the entrance of the devastated power plant, where, Flahault writes, instead of celebrating humankind's mastery of the atom, it now "gives homage to the army of liquidators"[6] (13), many of whom died in the "titanic struggle" (12) to deal with the consequences of the tragedy.

Flahault's description of Chernobyl's reactor number four is reminiscent of Audeguy's account of the eruption of Krakatoa and the ensuing cloud that changed the climate around the world. Flahault writes: "Like an erupting volcano, it spews out into the sky a flame 170 meters high. Almost 50 tons of nuclear fuel evaporates. The famous radioactive 'Chernobyl cloud' first burned the neighboring pine forest, then spread

---

5 For a discussion of this passage, see "Introduction to *Prometheus Bound*," by David Grene and Richard Lattimore.
6 "Liquidators" is the name given to the thousands of workers recruited to clean up the accident.

over Western Europe and Scandinavia, even reaching North America" (12). One might say that, like the "bombe naturelle" (Audeguy, *Théorie des nuages* 98) that was Krakatoa, the Chernobyl explosion was "without murderous intent" ("sans intention maligne," 100). Yet Chernobyl, like Hiroshima, was clearly an act of hubris, the arrogance that fails to recognize the limits of human technological inventiveness.

The Paris Exposition universelle in 1889 embodies for Audeguy the optimistic faith in human progress that would eventually lead to the tragedies of nuclear power misused. Organized for the one hundredth anniversary of the French Revolution, the exposition sought to restore Paris's tarnished reputation as a world capital. It was a marvel of modernity, centered around the Eiffel Tower, evoking the "Progress of Civilization" (*Theory of Clouds* 133) and the power of engineering, industry, and science. Beneath the tower was the ornate Fountain of Progress, which Audeguy describes in terms that hint at the veiled peril of unbridled progress:

> The fountain was a masterpiece of industrial art that continuously recycled its foamy water, thanks to a motor ingeniously hidden under the pool. People admired the technical prowess of the thing and gazed at it silently while their guides explained what it signified—and warned that the water wasn't drinkable. (133–34)

The fictional meteorologist William S. Williamsson, nemesis of Audeguy's protagonist Richard Abercrombie, personifies the spirit of the Exposition. Like a cross between Descartes, a Baptist preacher, and a modern technological utopian, he predicts humankind's mastery over nature and the advent of a golden age. In the future there will be no deserts, since

> we will have learned to move clouds and to control the rains … . And that wouldn't be all, because they who control the clouds also control agriculture. … [T]he earth will be a vast garden in which we will live in the Golden Age about which the mythologies and religions have informed us; man will be good; our grandchildren will see the desolate plains of Canaan blossom again. The science of our descendants will fulfill the prophecies of our ancestors. (151–52)

But like the atomic bomb, which begins as a bright point of light but ends as a sinister cloud from which deadly black rain falls, the optimistic reign of Prometheus has reached dim twilight, technological progress having served the cause of violence and conquest:

> Prometheus now appears less radiant, darkened by twilight clouds. First because last century saw industrial power used in the service of total war—a "storm of steel"[7] raining down on both the living and the decomposing dead—then a series of totalitarian regimes, all of which claimed to create the new man. "The mechanisms," writes Jean-Pierre Dupuy, "that explain the extraordinary dynamism of modern society, and hence its inextinguishable thirst for energy, are the same as those that explain its tendency to self-destruction."[8] Second because as the sun inevitably meets the horizon, Promethean dynamism is colliding with the limits of the planet. (Flahault 16–17)

The Promethean ideal clearly considers humans the masters of nature. The realization of the horrific consequences of such an attitude is what causes a profound metamorphosis in Richard Abercrombie, who gradually had been losing interest in scientific investigation as he left Europe far behind. Now in Indonesia taking photographs for his cloud atlas, he heads upriver with two hunters into the jungle of Borneo. He is struck by the deafening noise of the rain forest, and realizes that, contrary to the animals in English forests, located so close to towns, these animals are completely indifferent to humans, unaware that the human being is the "supreme predator" ("prédateur supreme," *Théorie des nuages* 219), killing for recreation, not survival. Left alone to rest in a clearing for a short time, Abercrombie is elated to come across a large orangutan with her baby. They stare at each other, and "in the eyes of a beast that had never before come across those of a man, there was absolutely nothing the slightest bit savage" (*Theory of Clouds* 189). Sadly, the animals pay for their lack of fear, as one of the hunters shoots the mother from several hundred feet away, then walks up and calmly snaps the neck of the baby.[9]

---

7   This is the title of Ernst Jünger's memoir about World War I, published as *In Stahlgewittern* in 1920.
8   Flahaut quotes Jean-Pierre Dupuy, *Retour de Tchernobyl. Journal d'un homme en colère* (Return from Chernobyl: Diary of an Angry Man). Seuil, 2006, p. 99.
9   In a personal interview, Stéphane Audeguy revealed that his character Richard Abercrombie is loosely based on Ralph Abercromby (1842–97), a

In an article entitled "De la nature de quelques choses,"[10] Audeguy examines our ambiguous relationship with nature. Agreeing with the Vercors of *You Shall Know Them*,[11] he declares that although we are part of nature, we are nonetheless denatured animals, and this "denaturation" is what allowed Hiroshima and Auschwitz to occur (245). Our bond to nature is predatory, like that of the hunter to the orangutan.[12] Audeguy prefers the word *arraisonner/arraisonnement*, a nautical term that means to forcibly board and seize a ship: "We have seized [*arraisonné*] nature, like a ship: we board and search it, we believe we own it. ... Boarding and seizing [*arraisonnement*] is the very direction of our civilization; it determines its progress, but it also conceals a morbid, mad fantasy that threatens humanity itself" (244).[13] Our desire to commandeer nature is thus the same Promethean hubris that Flahault exposes in the Chernobyl disaster: we treat nature as a stockpile of energy to be used by human technology, which is ultimately uncontrollable and leads to humanity's self-destruction.

After that day in the jungle, Richard Abercrombie will never again

---

well-traveled Scottish meteorologist and author of *Seas And Skies In Many Latitudes: Or, Wanderings In Search Of Weather* (1888). Audeguy has a copy of a lithograph featuring Ralph Abercromby proudly standing behind an orangutan he has just shot. The fictional Abercrombie, who detests hunting, is profoundly changed by his travels and becomes closer to nature; his historical namesake, however, remained an avid hunter.

10   "On the nature of some things," a tribute to Lucretius's *On the Nature of Things*.
11   See below, Chapter 4.
12   In an interview Audeguy cites the novels of Jules Verne as excellent illustrations of our predatory instinct, "of the Western fantasy of enclosing, of circling the globe. Verne expresses something of the capitalistic, scientific, and commercial grip on the world that is still true: predation" (Guichard 21).
13   *Arraisonner* has been used by French translators of Heidegger to convey the term *Ge-stell*, usually translated in English as "enframing." The term captures the threatening essence of technology—reducing nature to a "standing reserve"—that Heidegger describes in "The Question Concerning Technology" (1953). David Farrell Krell explains the hostile nature of *Ge-stell* in his introduction to Heidegger's essay: "[T]he question concerning the essence of technology confronts the supreme danger, which is that this one way of revealing beings may overwhelm man and beings and all other possible ways of revealing. Such danger is impacted in the essence of technology, which is an ordering of, or setting-upon, both nature and man, a defiant challenging of beings that aims at total and exclusive mastery" ("Introduction to The Question Concerning Technology" 285).

photograph a cloud. The shame he feels at the killing of the orangutan will alter him forever:

> Much later, when Abercrombie no longer felt competent to judge his contemporaries, or to read his journal, or to debate issues of the day; when he was no longer the man of science he was thought to be; and when he would wonder what had happened to him, seeking in his past the source of his transformation, he would invariably be drawn back to this very moment in the clearing. (*Theory of Clouds* 189)

The Abercrombie Protocol will no longer be about clouds, it will be about women, as the once puritanical Scotsman's obsession changes from meteorology to sexology. Over a century later, Akira Kumo comes into possession of the Protocol, which no one outside the Abercrombie family has ever seen, and is surprised to see that only the first few pages contain pictures of clouds:

> Most disturbing of all were those photographs of women's sexual organs—numbering in the hundreds—on the book's facing pages.
> The images could not be explained away as having ethnographic or anthropological value. The women posing in them were wearing no clothes; no folk art, jewels, or tattoos were visible. The photographs weren't ... as crude as typical pornography. The images were simple, unadorned. Great care had been taken to highlight every detail ... . The recto page was covered with drawings, the same design, repeated over and over. Kumo could see they were of shells, animal heads, women's vaginas; a few clouds as well. Each entry was dated. (165)

The Theory of Clouds metamorphoses at this point into a theory of bodies, as Gallimard's famous scarlet cover band proclaimed,[14] and a novel about clouds of all sorts—natural and unnatural—turns into a kind of environmental erotica. If Abercrombie's photographs are solely of women—at first full-length, then limited to torsos—his drawings alternate between vaginas and nonhuman objects: seashells, animal heads, and clouds. For Audeguy finds sexual analogies between the

---

14 Below the title—*La Théorie des nuages*—appeared the provocative bright red band: "... et des corps" (and bodies).

macrocosm of the world and the microcosm of the human body, in the tradition of ancient and medieval thinkers, such as the alchemists of the Near and Far East studied by Mircea Eliade in *The Forge and the Crucible*. Eliade devotes a chapter to "the world sexualized," "a general conception of cosmic reality seen as Life and consequently endowed with sex; sexuality being a particular sign of all living reality" (36). Eliade recalls the gynecological symbolism of the sacred Earth Mother in traditional societies, where mineral substances were thought to "'grow' in the belly of the earth after the manner of embryos. Metallurgy thus takes on the character of obstetrics. Miner and metalworker ... collaborate in the work of Nature and assist it to give birth more rapidly. In a word, man, with his various techniques, gradually takes the place of Time: his labours replace the work of Time" (8).

In "Nature as Female," Carolyn Merchant explains that from Antiquity through the Renaissance, the prevailing world view saw nature as a living organism with a double personality: normally a kind, "nurturing mother," the earth would at times become "wild and uncontrollable," unleashing violent storms, floods, droughts, etc. (10). This organic view encouraged respect and restraint from humans. Merchant echoes Eliade when she recounts the sacred vocation of miners who entered the earth's vagina, and the "awesome responsibility" of metallurgists who engaged in "the human hastening of the birth of the living metal in the artificial womb of the furnace" (11).

The Scientific Revolution, seeking to impose mechanics and rationality on the world, seized upon the notion of nature's destructive side, "nature as disorder," and determined to master and dominate the earth. Nature was no longer viewed as a living being and was thus ripe for exploitation: "the new images of mastery and domination functioned as cultural sanctions for the denudation of nature. Society needed these new images as it continued the processes of commercialization and industrialization, which depended on activities directly altering the earth" (11).

This mechanistic world view did not of course completely destroy ecological consciousness. Merchant cites Spenser (*Faerie Queen*, 1595), Donne, and Milton (*Paradise Lost*, 1667) among several sixteenth- and seventeenth-century authors who condemned mining as a rape of the earth. Spenser, for instance, considered mining to be a sin of avarice, and comparable to lust: "Digging into the matrices and pockets of earth for metals was like mining the female flesh for pleasure. ... Both mining and sex represent for Spenser the return to animality and earthly slime" (Merchant 29).

Ecofeminists have for some years been fighting against this ancient association of women and nature. Annette Kolodny, for example, in "Unearthing Herstory," describes how a 1969 Berkeley protest called the "Battle for People's Park" revealed a deeply ingrained American fantasy, "a daily reality of harmony between man and nature based on an experience of the land as essentially feminine—that is, not simply the land as mother, but the land as woman, the total female principle of gratification" (171). The conquest of the American wilderness was in large part a violation of this "land-as-woman" (176). Kolodny calls for a "new symbolic mode" to govern our relationship to landscape, because "we can no longer afford to keep turning 'America the Beautiful' into *America the Raped*" (178).

In "The Ecology of Feminism and the Feminism of Ecology," Ynestra King writes of the shared voicelessness of women and nature (as Élisabeth de Fontenay would later describe the silence of the beasts). Without feminism, ecology is incomplete: "The special message of ecofeminism is that when women suffer through both social domination and the domination of nature, most of life on this planet suffers and is threatened as well" (King 25).

A first hint of correspondences between the macrocosm and microcosm is found early in Audeguy's novel. He devotes several pages to Goethe, whose interest in meteorology led him to admire Luke Howard's research on clouds. Goethe researched morphology as well, and Audeguy envisions the similitude Goethe may have observed between clouds and the human brain: "He even imagined that the brain of man was like a cloud, and thus that clouds represented the heavenly seats of thought, connecting the human and the divine" (*Theory of Clouds* 17). Many of Abercrombie's sketches in the Protocol will reveal the same connection, spiraling cloud-like lines shrinking into forms resembling tiny brains (*Theory of Clouds* 206).

But female sexuality is obviously what most interests the author and his character. Audeguy explicitly states that the photos in the Protocol have no cultural value (*Theory of Clouds* 165): no clothing or markings hint at the women's ethnicity; nor is the pubic hair "airbrushed" as it might have been had Abercrombie wanted to conform to his own cultural tradition (see Brooks 17; Gaillard 428–29). Abercrombie increasingly excludes the women's faces from his photos, "focusing

Stéphane Audeguy's The Theory of Clouds *(La Théorie des nuages)* 69

only on the subject's midriff, which had the effect of dehumanizing the sexual organ, creating landscapes of pure flesh, lunar, as it were, or volcanic" (*Theory of Clouds* 205–06). Virginie, annotating and cataloguing the Protocol, is struck by the diversity of the scores of vaginas pictured, as Abercrombie must have been, for "Rather than refer to *the* female sexual organ in the singular, Abercrombie henceforth used the plural" (206).[15] In close-up photography, the sexual organs lose their humanity, and take on the relief of rocky, mineral landscapes. Gynecology merges with geology to form a geography of the body. Scribbled next to the photos are more and more enigmatic words like "similitude," "origin," "parallelism" (206); and, finally, the last word of the Protocol: "infinite" (245).

"Similitude" and "parallelism" are linked to two other obsessive ideas of Abercrombie: "isomorphism" and "analogy." He even dreams that a "chair of analogy" will be created for him at the University of Cambridge. He is clearly fascinated by the correspondences he has discovered between nature and humans, giving "human nature" a radical new meaning. The word "origin" that he repeatedly writes is undoubtedly an authorial reference to Gustave Courbet's (in)famous oil painting *L'Origine du monde* (*The Origin of the World*, 1866), whose photographic quality inspires Peter Brooks to call it "a decisive gesture toward hyper-realism in the representation of the nude" (142), and Françoise Gaillard to comment on its "photographic realism" (429), shockingly different from the portrayal of female nudes accepted by the Academy at the time, which showed only a hairless "little mound,

---

15 The italics in this quotation are Audeguy's. His insistence on the plural (*des sexes*, not *un sexe*) translates as an articulation of female subjectivity. His character Abercrombie is hardly an ecofeminist; indeed, Virginie notes that he never quite got over the idea that all the genitalia in his photos were unique and diverse. But Audeguy's italics underscore the dignity of these women who—like Descartes's nature—are mastered and possessed by men. This plural is a plea to save women from male violence, as is Derrida's use of "animals" (*animaux*, or *animots*) to refer to that other silent minority: "I would like to have the plural *animals* heard in the singular. There is no Animal in the general singular, separated from man by a single, indivisible limit ... among nonhumans, and separate from nonhumans, there is an immense multiplicity of other living things that cannot in any way be homogenized, except by means of violence and willful ignorance, within the category of what is called the animal or animality in general. From the outset there are animals and, let's say, *l'animot*" (Derrida, *The Animal that Therefore I Am* 48).

shiny as lard or alabaster, revealing the well-named mons Venus but not the labia" (428). In his 2012 essay *Opera mundi*, Audeguy suggests that *L'Origine du monde* should not be considered pornographic, because (as in most of Abercrombie's photographs) the woman's face is not pictured. What makes an image pornographic, he states, is the concurrence between the permitted view of the face and the prohibited, transgressive view of the sexual organs (37). Like Abercrombie's pictures, Courbet's painting is faceless, thus dehumanized.[16] It is a landscape that Audeguy describes as "an extraordinary valley, whose folds, infinitely delicate, seem like supple and living lava flows" (38). Courbet himself must have been sensitive to the correspondence between *L'Origine du monde* and a particular landscape, for it is tempting to see a marked similarity between this painting of a vulva and the many paintings he made of the source of the Loue, a small river that flows out of a cave near his hometown of Ornans in Franche-Comté. Audeguy comments: "It is difficult to not associate the wide opening of the karstic resurgence,[17] this narrow valley, with the valley of *L'Origine du monde*" (38).[18] Courbet scholars have all noted the resemblance between his canvases of the human "origin" and the geological "source" (see Nochlin 82). Moreover, their similarity corroborates Eliade's recounting of gynecological myths of the Earth Mother in the archaic "world sexualized," such as the Zuni myth of the origin of the human race, whereby the first humans climbed upward through four "cavern wombs," until they finally emerged on the surface of the earth (*The Forge and the*

---

16 Françoise Gaillard's reading of *L'Origine du monde* is quite similar. "Nothing louche or libidinous in this realist representation of the genitals devoid of both eroticism and obscenity." Courbet's framing of the painting only allows us to see "pure genitality ... deprived of its most desirable feature: the woman" (429–30).
17 "Karstic" refers to the limestone composition of the cave from which the spring emerges.
18 In these two quotations Audeguy draws attention to the fluid nature of the female sexual organs with terms like "lava flow" and "karstic resurgence." His descriptions of Virginie's "oceanic orgasms" (*Théorie des nuages* 146) also connect the human body to the forces of nature, as he explains in an interview:
> In this scene of solitary pleasure, what was important for me is that we have a woman who rains. ... There is a kind of mystique around the orgasms of these "gushing" women [*femmes fontaines*]. But as for me, I associate this type of orgasm with rain and thus with clouds. Also, I found it interesting because masturbation infers autonomy. This scene gives her a universe. (Guichard 27)

Crucible 40). The source of the Loue is a karstic spring that mysteriously emerges from a rocky grotto in the Jura Mountains, having flowed for some distance underground. For Courbet, the stony birth of the river is a metaphor for the birth of human life, just as it was in many mythologies. Eliade cites numerous myths of "stone parentage," or *petra genitrix*, "the notion that stone is the source of life and fertility, that it lives and procreates human creatures just as it has itself been engendered by the earth" (43). Finally, Linda Nochlin wonders if Courbet's two paintings may be clues to the origin of art itself:

> In an article entitled "The Origins of Art," Desmond Collins and John Onians attempted to "trace back" historically the origin of art to the engraving of crude but recognizable vulvas on the walls of caves in Southern France during the Aurignacian Period, about 33,000 to 28,000 B.C. According to this scenario, masculine desire literally led lusting but frustrated Aurignacian males to represent in stone the desired, absent object—the female sex organ—and thereby to create the very first artwork. In the light of this assumption, all other artworks ought to be considered simulacra of this originating male act, and representation must itself be considered a mere simulacrum of that desired original. (81–82)

So perhaps the troubling photographs of Abercrombie's Protocol are not so out of place, not such a departure from the original scientific task at hand. For, as seen in the preceding examples, the erotic bond between humans and landscapes is as ancient as humankind itself. In *Opera mundi*, Audeguy refers to two modern French writers whose work illustrates this connection. In Sade's *Justine*, for instance, the narrator proclaims the "strange desire" (39) to be Mount Etna, and the character Almani becomes in effect a human volcano through the sex act. Baudelaire's "La Géante" is at the same time a woman and a mountainous landscape (34); in the last two lines of the sonnet the poet, exhausted after a day of climbing, wants nothing more than "To sleep nonchalantly in the shadow of her breasts, / Like a peaceful hamlet at the foot of a mountain." Analogy, or isomorphism—the term he prefers—becomes Abercrombie's new science (*Theory of Clouds* 246). Although it leads meteorology nowhere, it does serve to actualize the archaic belief of a necessary bond between macrocosm and microcosm: a link between nature and humans. Abercrombie stumbles upon the link in his own way, seeing it between clouds and "the altar of his private religion between the thighs of women," which Virginie admits is "no more or less crazy a cult than any other" (259). The key to understanding Abercrombie's odd science is the last term that he scrawls in his notebook: "infinite." This concluding word is his best description of the limitless irregularities in both natural and human geography. One could never truly measure, he believes, "the sinuosity, the anfractuosities" (245) of a mountain side, a vaginal wall, a cloud, or the coast of Cornwall, of which he says, "[t]he tiniest irregularity itself consists of even tinier irregularities, and so on, such that we would have to conclude that the coastline was infinite" (245). We would lose ourselves in the infinity of nature, as Carmichael, the painter of clouds, lost his mind when he attempted to illustrate the infinite *mise en abyme* he perceived in clouds. As Audeguy succinctly puts it in *Opera mundi*, the analogy between the human body and nature comes down to our inability to fully comprehend the complexities of either: a "confrontation between the limitlessness of desire and the unthinkable infinity of nature" (39).

Nature's very condition is desire, contends Luc Bureau, a Canadian geographer, in *Terra erotica*: our relationship with nature is erotic. Nothing has changed since Plato's *Symposium*, when the doctor Eryximachus declared that Love's empire extends over all of nature, human and nonhuman alike (Bureau 54). For Bureau, Eros is the greatest of the gods; he even makes an appearance in the harsh Old Testament, most notably in the *Canticle of Canticles*, a love poem infused with nature metaphors. Here "the work of Eros rests on the principle of the indissoluble unity of the world. Saintliness and pleasure, nature and man, good and evil, strength and gentleness coexist without hostility" (Bureau 63). One is reminded of the beautiful passages in Michel Tournier's *Friday*, in which Robinson Crusoe's sexuality turns towards the "vegetable way" ("voie végétale," 115), and he begins a love affair with the soft earth of a valley. His erotic relationship with the island is accompanied by readings from the *Canticles*:

> Thy lips are like a thread of scarlet, and thy speech is comely: thy temples are like a piece of a pomegranate within thy locks. ... Thy two breasts are like two young roes that are twins, which feed among the lilies. (127)

Stéphane Audeguy's The Theory of Clouds (La Théorie des nuages) 73

Robinson's sexuality, like Abercrombie's, is an inextricable bond between the human and the nonhuman, the microcosm and the macrocosm.

Bureau laments the fact that for many of us, nature and Eros have nothing in common. When Eros abandons nature, the world is nothing but faded matter: "Without the voluptuous titillation of Eros, nature is but a silent aggregate of matter, a bare body, like the debris of a dead star. Without Eros, the places of the Earth are but pieces of space reduced to nothing but their physical or geometrical attributes" (71). Desire, he writes, is an attribute not only of humans but also of the earth:

> Without desire, man is nothing more than a statue of salt. Without desire, the Earth is but a speck of dust in the Universe, a dead star, at most, a deformed geometric shape. It is under the auspices of Eros that a pact is made between man's desire and the Earth's desire. (73)

Bureau calls himself an erotologist ("*érotologue*," 9). "I've made my choice," he writes: "Among all the gods known or unknown, chaste or unchaste, benevolent or malevolent, there is only one I would like to teach me of worldly adventures: Eros, he who ensures the union of the primordial elements and who arouses love's desire" (59). Tournier's Robinson Crusoe likewise sheds his puritanical past to become an erotologist when his "elemental" (*Friday* 211) sexuality changes elements: his love affair with the earth is verticalized, redirected towards the heavens: sky, sun, constellations. He no longer experiences the "harsh stab of desire" of genital sex, but instead a solar or cosmic sexuality: "My sky-love [*amours ouraniennes*] floods me with a vital energy ... . If this is to be translated into human language, I must consider myself feminine and the bride of the sky" (212). His days are identical; he lives in an eternal present. "[M]y days," he writes in his Log-book, "[have] rearranged themselves [*se sont redressées*]. No longer do they jostle on each other's heels. Each stands separate and upright, proudly affirming its own worth" (204). This passage inspires Gilles Deleuze to write, in his *Postface* to the novel, that Robinson's existence has become a "generalized erection" (317).

Like Robinson, like Luc Bureau, Audeguy's protagonist Abercrombie is truly an erotologist. Robinson's mind is filled with erotic images from classical mythology: "Venus, the Swan, Leda, the Twins ... I grope in search of myself in this forest of allegory" (Tournier, *Friday* 214). Similarly, Abercrombie's analogies lead him to conclude that "everything in the universe reverts to the same forms. The world consists of recurring combinations of these forms" (Audeguy, *Theory of Clouds* 207). Vaginas and clouds, his two personal obsessions, rule Abercrombie's universe. They are not only analogous but infinitely complex, as the final word of the Protocol suggests.

Where did Stéphane Audeguy find inspiration for this troubling and truly original novel? I have already mentioned his debt to Tournier's *Friday* and *Gemini*. I sense that Tournier would have seen in Audeguy a kindred spirit, if he had read the article in *Le Monde des livres* in which Audeguy states that "I never write about nature, but I hope to write with nature" (Beuve-Méry n. pag.). Like Tournier's two novels, *The Theory of Clouds* treats nature as a subject, rather than a lowly object lorded over by humans. Audeguy thus accomplishes an important task that ecocritics have assigned to the contemporary writer. Nathalie Blanc, for instance, citing Lawrence Buell's *Writing for an Endangered World*, insists on the writer's capacity to evoke nature "as an independent actor and not simply as a frame around human experience" (Blanc 19), giving nature the status of subject, not object (24). Moreover, she maintains that fiction must not settle for imitating nonhuman nature, but aim for "a renewal, even a revolution, in the way we comprehend nonhuman nature" (22). In this undertaking, Audeguy has admirably succeeded. Readers of *The Theory of Clouds* will never again look at clouds without being reminded of volcanic eruptions and nuclear annihilation, not to mention the lacy veil of Eros.

Stéphane Audeguy is not a "nature writer" in the American tradition initiated by Thoreau and Emerson. He says, "In my novels there are no descriptions of pure nature. There are on the other hand characters that are not human" (Beuve-Méry n. pag.), like clouds and their simulacra: volcanoes, the explosions over Hiroshima and Nagasaki, the ashes of Auschwitz. *The Theory of Clouds* bears some resemblance to Rousseau's *Reveries of the Solitary Walker*, in that it "draws attention to the intense feelings linked to the perception of nature" (Beuve-Méry n. pag.). But one must go back to Roman antiquity to find Audeguy's most compelling influence. In "De la nature de quelques choses" (On the Nature of Some Things), Audeguy suggests that "Nothing has changed since Lucretius. Everything is possible" (248). The Latin poet's *On the Nature of Things* is an epic poem about all things big and small,

Stéphane Audeguy's The Theory of Clouds (La Théorie des nuages)

material and immaterial: the principle of atomism that structures the universe, nature, and its phenomena; the creation of the world and the development of civilization; human psychology, biology, sexology, and mortality.[19] Scientific and philosophical, it nevertheless opens with a prayer to Venus, goddess of love, "power of life," who can "hush the winds and scatter the clouds" (5). Lucretius, celebrating the dispersal of wind and clouds in the wake of Venus's arrival, prefigures the transition in Abercrombie's life from clouds to sex. The Roman poet prays that Venus vanquish her bellicose lover Mars "by the never-healing wound of love" (34), so that "tranquil peace" will finally replace "barbarous war" (32) among mortals. *The Theory of Clouds* carries a similar message. Who would not prefer the work of Abercrombie—which converts cirrus, cumulus, stratus, and nimbus clouds to a "cult" of sexuality—to the folly of warring nations, whose technology has invented the "very particular kind" of cloud that rose above Hiroshima, "a tall cloud, anchored to the ground by an enormously long stalk: a cloud on a pedestal, like a grotesque mushroom" (*Theory of Clouds* 226)?

---

[19] See Martin Ferguson Smith's informative introduction to *On the Nature of Things*.

Chapter 3

A Fairy in the Age of Prometheus: Chantal Chawaf's *Mélusine des détritus*

> So many times, in the course of this war and before that in the preceding one, I waited to hear that scream ring out, the scream buried for nine centuries under the ruins of the Chateau of Lusignan!
>
> —Breton, *Arcanum 17* 60

> In a world where nature is dominated, polluted, pocketed, ecotouristed, warming, melting, bleaching, dissipating, and fleeing toward the poles—detritus is both its curse and its alternative.
>
> —Patricia Yaeger, "The Death of Nature and the Apotheosis of Trash; or, Rubbish Ecology" 338

Rooted in the serpent-woman stories common to many mythologies, the myth of Mélusine was born in the late fourteenth century in western France. First composed in prose by Jean d'Arras (1393) for the Duc de Berry, then in verse by Coudrette (1401) for the Sire of Parthenay, the myth served to confer a semi-divine origin upon the noble house of Lusignan, a prominent family in the Poitou region since the tenth century. The Lusignan lineage included crusaders who became kings of Cyprus, Jerusalem, and Armenia.

The myth of Mélusine shares the tripartite structure common to fairy stories (Harf-Lancner 113): a meeting between the hero and heroine, a pact, and a transgression. The hero, Raimond, has just accidently killed his uncle during a boar hunt. Disconsolate, he wanders through the forest alone and chances upon the beautiful Mélusine sitting near a spring, for water is this fairy's element. Eventually, Mélusine agrees to marry him on one condition: that he promise never to see her on Saturday. Unbeknownst to Raimond, on this day she assumes her fairy form—a serpent from the waist down—while in her bath. Raimond honors the pact, but after many years of happy marriage blessed by ten male children,[1] Raimond's jealous brother spies on Mélusine in her bath and reveals her secret to Raimond. Raimond denounces his wife, Mélusine disappears, and the Lusignan family falls into decline. The departure of Mélusine is one of the iconic images of the myth. She jumps from the Lusignan castle tower and flies around the castle three times, each time emitting a heart-rending cry, and then disappears. These "cries of the fairy," evoked by Gérard de Nerval in his celebrated poem "El Desdichado," and by André Breton in *Arcanum 17*, lie at the heart of Chantal Chawaf's Mélusine story.

Mélusine fascinates by her ambivalence. It is easy to forget that this fairy of the forest, streams, and rivers is also part human: her father was a mortal. Mélusine imprisons her father Elianas in a magic mountain in Northumberland as punishment for having betrayed her mother, Pressine. He had watched her bathing their daughters, thus breaking the pact that had been the condition of their wedding. Because Elianas had not willfully violated his oath, Pressine curses Mélusine for this act of revenge. Mélusine will become a serpent from the waist down every Saturday in her bath. She may only marry on the condition that her husband never see her on Saturday. If he honors the pact, she will live a human life, have children, found a powerful dynasty, and die a natural death. If the pact is broken, she will be cursed to renounce her humanity and live eternally as a fairy.

---

1   Mélusine's sons are truly remarkable. All except two have a curious physical deformity. Some go on to be heroes and kings. Urien, who will become king of Cyprus, has one red and one green eye. Antoine, despite a lion's paw growing out of his cheek, will nevertheless become Duke of Luxembourg. Others are monstrous murderers. Geoffroy Big-Tooth, whose huge tooth resembles a boar's tusk, is cruel and hot-tempered, and burns down a monastery, killing his own brother. Son number eight, nicknamed Horrible, huge and cruel, has three eyes, and murders two of his wet nurses by biting their breasts off. The sons evoke Mélusine's own ambivalence: for some, she is divine, for others, diabolical (see J. Krell, "Between Demon and Divinity").

Pressine explains that Mélusine's dilemma is the fatal attraction to human nature inherited from her father: "Your mortal descent from your father's side, without doubt, drew you and your sisters towards his human nature" (Jean d'Arras 71). Yet Mélusine plays her human role well: soon she finds a husband and becomes a sort of businesswoman. All the while preserving her special relationship to the earth and water, Mélusine, like a fabulous construction company CEO, reveals an extraordinary talent for clearing forests and building castles and churches. In a few days, with the help of "a great number of landscape workers and woodcutters" (143) who mysteriously appear, she cuts down all the trees and raises up the walls and towers of the great fortress of Lusignan, a "strange and prodigious" (145) feat that leaves her entourage stupefied. This "wondrous" fairy,[2] by her choice to become human, distances herself from nature to bring culture and architecture to this forest-covered region. Moreover, through her ten sons, as her mother predicted, she founds, "a noble and powerful lineage who will accomplish great feats" (71). Her devotion to the human race, her building and child-bearing exploits make her a sort of female Prometheus; she is a mythic figure who expresses an optimistic vision in which humanity, thanks to hard work and innovation, will forever progress and become more perfect.

In *Mélusine des détritus* (2002), Chantal Chawaf[3] proposes a new interpretation of the myth, in which the reader cannot help but question the wisdom of Mélusine's desire to become human. For this novelist, the 11 centuries of Western civilization gone by since the founding of the house of Lusignan mark a dystopian regression, rather than progress. I will first study her bitter repudiation of industrial society, before examining the problematic of maternity, an essential theme of Mélusine which, for Chawaf, is closely related to voice and words. This preoccupation with language is manifested by the strange cry of the protagonist—a modern Mélusine—and also by our disembodied, "backward language"—the flesh made word—that she analyzes in her

---

2 The name Mélusine means "wondrous" or "wonder," according to Jean d'Arras (145). However, Laurence Harf-Lancner believes that "this explanation of Mélusine's name remains enigmatic" (Coudrette 62 n. 18).
3 Chantal Chawaf is the author of over 30 novels and essays. Chawaf is her husband's name, and *Mélusine des détritus* is the only book she has published under the name given her by her adoptive parents: Marie de la Montluel.

essay *Le Corps et le verbe: la langue en sens inverse* (The Body and the Word: Backward Language, 1992).

Chawaf's young protagonist is named Mélusine. Like her namesake, she lives not far from Poitiers, in a fictitious village situated in the south of the historical region of Berry. Mulac is a sad little place and retains nothing of its past glory. Now it is not much more than an intersection of two major highways. At first, the reader cannot tell if this new Mélusine is a human or a fairy. She is enchanting, but suffers from asthma and depression: her lungs have been poisoned by the diesel emissions from the trucks that rattle the house she shares with her aunt, and her anguish is intensified by the neighboring nuclear power plant that—rumor has it—threatens to wipe out the population. She will flee this "gray town" (7) with Jean, a businessman and modern knight errant who loves to cruise the highways on his mechanical steed, a fast little Citroën. Unfortunately, Jean, like his "ancestor" Raimond, will fail in this impossible task to make happy—or human—a displaced fairy, whose agonizing cry haunts the novel.

From the first page of *Mélusine des détritus*, Chawaf situates her heroine and her village in a twenty-first century that has forgotten its history. People have "levelled the tumulus where the Gallic chief was buried and built a low-rent apartment building on the site," and they steal stones from the feudal castle to build garages. The Romanesque cloister has become a parking lot (9), and "the eleventh- and thirteenth-century sculptures will soon be just powder and sand" (22–23). Progress is killing the past and offers nothing positive to Mulac's residents. Instead of looking forward to a better future, people have the impression of being forgotten. They will never reap the benefits of modernization, reserved for the ruling class:

> In this suffering town, we are all convinced that we are finished as human beings, condemned to be replaced by an improved human race; we feel backward, our nerves, veins, arteries, and capillaries products of generations of inbreeding. We think that the future will have nothing more to do with us. (9)

The past is dying and the mournful present, in which "bodies have no escape, and desire no outlet" (18), is sterile; moreover, the future seems to belong not to men, but to a strange race of supermen. Like the wasteland of Arthurian novels, the town is "suffering." This rhetorical device, named "pathetic fallacy" by the art critic John Ruskin, underscores Chawaf's holistic point of view: nature and humans are one and suffer equally from the ecological crisis that provides the backdrop for the novel. And it is above all Mélusine's anguished cry that expresses the symbiosis between humans and nature, as in the following passage, typical of Chawaf's engaged lyricism. Jean is stunned by Mélusine's cry:

> "Are you sick? Are you sick?"
> Were you sick? Oh! The whole planet was sick in you, sick of its nuclear power plants, sick of its nuclear fuel reprocessing plants, sick of its weapons, its nuclear, chemical, biological weapons, sick of its uncertainty, sick of its choices, sick of everything you felt as imminent, unbalanced, obvious, sick of the cooling towers looming over us. (213–14)

When Jean sees the "fairy" for the first time—"a girl illuminated by an invisible halo" (32)—Mélusine has an asthma attack. But her symptoms are much more complicated. Watching her scream out the window, Jean describes her attack as a cry for help and an accusation against the trucks that are poisoning the air she breathes:

> She screams to the trees, she begs the nests to shelter her, to protect her from the trucks. She casts her lament upon the wind, she screams out the window to mourn the earth doomed to perdition. ... Her screams were like those of a woman being raped, or tortured with a knife; the screams of her frustrated youth, the screams of her life and its broken, mad heartbeat, gasping in the indifference of a dead city. (32)

Mélusine's symptoms are as much psychological as physical: her outbursts express her "pain," "anguish," and "anger" at being in an asthmatic "prison." Thus, the doctors are skeptical, and take her asthma for hysteria (53). Jean suffers from his inability to love this strange woman, whose "family" includes trees, insects, and especially the river near her house, her only relief from the pollution. Mélusine is "not of his species" (40). During another asthma attack—when "she tries to empty her mucous membranes inflamed by the diesel fuel, to cough up the bottom of her throat and chest filled with gasoline fumes" (40)—Mélusine grumbles about the current condition of the human race:

Isn't humanity beautiful? Isn't it beautiful to want to cough up all your organs because you are so polluted and you have so many allergies! Pitiful heap of guts! Money owns the world, not you! ... Humanity is screwed! The planet no longer belongs to humans! They want to perfect us, they want robots. Go away, life! Into the garbage! Down with nature! Up with the end of the world! (41–42)

Vehicle emissions are not Chawaf's only target. As the dark nightmare of Hiroshima haunts Stéphane Audeguy's story of clouds, so the menace of the atom permeates Mélusine's world. Chawaf is not so much concerned with nuclear arms as with the risks of civil nuclear power: Those huge clouds of vapor (beautifully named *panaches* in French) pouring out of the cooling towers conjure up the possibility of accidental leaks, terrorism, and radioactive waste. When Chawaf was writing her novel, about 82 percent of French electricity was being generated by nuclear power plants, and she conveys the ubiquity of nuclear energy by placing reactors wherever Mélusine lives. There is one in Mulac,[4] her native town, and near the end of the novel, when Mélusine runs away to live in the heart of nature, isolated on the Normandy coast, there is a nuclear power plant a stone's throw from her little fisherman's cottage.

A storekeeper explains that she fears nuclear power above all because its effects are poorly understood:

You can't say for sure: "it's good, it's bad ..." ... I've lived my life, but what about my daughter? I want her to be able to have children ... And with the power plant, we don't know ... They tell us that everything has been done to prevent any foreseeable problems, but that, in the end, they're not really sure about anything ... (98–99, 101)

Chawaf is most critical not of the reactors themselves, but of the radioactive waste, treated at la Hague in Normandy, and transported by train to the nuclear waste repository at Gorleben, a small town in northern Germany: "The gloves, the boots, the protective suits, the

---

4 In *L'Érotique des mots* (186), Chawaf reveals that the Mulac plant is based on the Civaux nuclear plant, not far from Poitiers, on the River Vienne. I thank Nannette Mosely for this reference.

tools, scrap iron: everything that might have been contaminated by radionuclides will end up in the bowels of the earth, hoping that the earth will accept them ... Because the people of the earth will not" (198). Chawaf's anthropomorphism is again clear here. She is sorry that the earth cannot—like the anti-nuclear protesters—refuse to accept the waste.

Chawaf's anti-nuclear discourse recalls the "nuclear criticism" movement that began when *Diacritics* published its summer 1984 issue, *Nuclear Criticism*, featuring a transcription of a lecture by Jacques Derrida: "No Apocalypse, Not Now (Full Speed Ahead, Seven Missiles, Seven Missives)." The Reagan administration and the "evil empire" are in the midst of a cold war, kept cold by nuclear deterrence, and human society, says Derrida, "hangs by the thread of nuclear rhetoric" (24). Humans who study the humanities, rhetoric, language—like those listening to Derrida's talk at Cornell—are therefore not incompetent to discuss the nuclear crisis, despite its scientific complexities understood by few. Derrida likens the nuclear threat to literature, because it is essentially imaginary. Yes, the United States used nuclear bombs against Japan in 1945, but that was to end a conventional war, not to begin a nuclear war:

> Some might call it a fable, then, a pure invention: in the sense in which it is said that a myth, an image, a fiction, a utopia, a rhetorical figure, a fantasy, a phantasm, are inventions. It may also be called a speculation, even a fabulous specularization. The breaking of the mirror would be, finally, through an act of language, the very occurrence of nuclear war. (23)

There is, of course, a realistic component to the nuclear crisis, "the massive 'reality' of nuclear weaponry," and "[o]ne has to distinguish between this 'reality' of the nuclear age and the fiction of war" (23).

Similarly, the bleak predictions of *Mélusine des détritus* are closely allied with language and narrative. The power company tries to allay the fears of the townspeople, but people do not buy its discourse: "they are not really sure about anything" (Chawaf, *Mélusine* 101). In "Knowledge of the Future: Future Fables," Richard Klein recalls Derrida's distinction between the two French words for "future," *futur* (predictable events, like the sun rising tomorrow morning) and *avenir* (unknown events, like a terrorist attack or a total nuclear war): "To borrow another of Derrida's metaphors, the *futur* is what we can see ahead on the horizon—horizontally; whereas the *avenir* falls vertically on our heads, out of the blue" (175). Mélusine suffers from the reality of pollution, but her "hysteria" (Chawaf, *Mélusine* 53) stems from the unknown *avenir* in which human beings will be reduced to unthinking robots. Culture, literature, and language will cease to exist or be drastically reduced. This fear of the unknown future is illustrated by Mélusine's incoherent, guttural screams during her asthma attacks. For Derrida, the new danger of nuclear annihilation is "the destruction of the archive," "the remainderless and a-symbolic destruction of literature" ("No Apocalypse" 27, 28). All memory will be wiped out, as if all the libraries in the world had been set ablaze: "Literature, in Derrida, is exemplary of the fragility of the nuclear age, where memory itself, the archaizing functions of social memory, which allows the dead to be mourned, may be destroyed" (Klein 177).

Chawaf finished her novel shortly after the terrorist attacks of 11 September 2001. It is clear that the threat of terrorism through nuclear proliferation is one of her central concerns about the future of Mélusine's world. Like nuclear war, 9/11 has become a fable, a horror story about an uncertain but deadly *avenir* that threatens to obliterate the future and the human work of mourning:

> The terror of terrorism, the terror of the trauma, what makes the event inappropriable in the present, is that the terrible events it signifies have not yet happened, and can't be predicted (the worst is never certain), but can be imagined, in a fable. It is the future dimension of the event [the attacks of September 11] that happened in the past, four years ago, that gives it the power, says Derrida, to continue to haunt us—to prevent us from mourning the loss, doing the work of mourning, in order to incorporate the memory of those people and things we lost. "What is at stake," he says, "is nothing less than the existence of the world, of the worldwide itself." (Klein 178)[5]

The young heroine of *Mélusine des détritus* faces the dilemma that Derrida describes: her very existence is in peril, a victim of the uncontrolled nuclear and industrial expansion of our Promethean society. Like her fairy ancestor, this Mélusine "of the post-industrial

---

5 Klein quotes Derrida, *Philosophy in a Time of Terror*. Edited by Giovanna Borradori, University of Chicago Press, 2003, p. 99.

era" (Chawaf, *Mélusine* 65) is a marginalized being, caught between technological progress and nature. Like Ondine, in Jean Giraudoux's eponymous play, her nature "is nature itself" (1.7), and she cannot survive in the polluted atmosphere that asphyxiates her. "'What happens to a girl of nature,' wonders Jean, 'when one takes her nature away?'" (Chawaf, *Mélusine* 40).

We are reminded of Luce Irigaray's 1986 talk to women of the Italian Communist Party, gathered to discuss "Life after Chernobyl," just a few months after the catastrophe. Irigaray's "A Chance for Life" ties women's sexual temporality to the rhythm of the universe, echoing Mircea Eliade's statement in *The Forge and the Crucible*, quoted above in Chapter 2, that many ancient thinkers held "a general conception of cosmic reality seen as Life and consequently endowed with sex" (36). Irigaray speaks of women's "double temporality":

> This female temporality is hormonally complex and in turn has consequences for the organization and general equilibrium of the body. But every stage in this development has its own temporality, which is possibly cyclic and linked to cosmic rhythms. If women have felt so terribly threatened by the accident at Chernobyl, that is because of the irreducible relation of their bodies to the universe. (200)

Controversial as this statement may be,[6] it resembles the message that Chawaf is sending to her readers. As Chawaf believes that the patriarchy, through the Bible, has usurped language, so Irigaray believes that science is essentially masculine. And when this science goes horribly wrong, as it did at Chernobyl, perhaps women suffer inordinately.

---

6 In *Fashionable Nonsense: Postmodern Intellectuals' Abuse of Science*, two physicists ridicule postmodern thought, and many of the leading proponents of "French Theory." The authors are Jean Bricmont and Alan Sokal, perpetrator of the famous "Sokal Hoax," in which he succeeded in publishing a deliberately nonsensical article in the journal *Social Text*. They react to Irigaray's statement on Chernobyl as follows:
> Here Irigaray falls straight into mysticism. Cosmic rhythms, relation to the universe—what on earth is she talking about? To reduce women to their sexuality, menstrual cycles, and rhythms (cosmic or not) is to attack everything the feminist movement has fought for during the last three decades. Simone de Beauvoir must be turning in her grave. (Sokal and Bricmont 123)

And perhaps this is why Chawaf chose a woman named Mélusine, the French female myth *par excellence*, to represent human fear and suffering in this age of unbridled nuclear technology and pollution.

To recover lost nature, one can try to go back in time. When Jean decides to take Mélusine to Scandinavia to enjoy the pure air of the country of "The Little Mermaid,"[7] he is taking a Proustian journey in search of lost time. At least that is his impossible dream. He admits the folly of his idea by speaking in the conditional mood:

> We would drift into a world of legend and enchantment. We would be the nomads of time, escaped prisoners of the present, we would go back to the Neolithic, then to the Ice Age; we would go towards the dazzling, absolute light, the north of the north, the land where songs are sung in a mysterious tongue. We would go to the beginning of life, where nothing more would harm the serpentine body of my amphibian Mélusine, where nothing more would impede her journey to the waters of the beginning. (62–63)

In the original French, Jean does not say *nous* (we), but rather *on* (one), a relatively weak pronoun, less definite than *nous*, which would have suggested a stronger and more durable relationship between the fairy and the man. *On* does, however, translate Jean's dogged optimism that he and Mélusine, in spite of their differences and the fragility of their union, nevertheless are one. Jean himself remarks that the human condition, characterized by suffering, is not so different from the fairy condition: "Even if you are a fairy and I am a simple human, our Calvary is the same, a destiny without rest, a sin that cannot be forgiven, the sin of not knowing how to live" (71–72). The fairy-human couple are star-crossed, bound by an "irrational" (71) love that unites them "beyond insanity" (72). Jean begins to understand that "the spirit of Mélusine" (Markale 251–68) resembles Camus's absurd, where to be human means to desire the impossible, as Jean Markale explains:

> We are all the children of Mélusine. Our double nature, animal and human, our desperate attempts to leave the earth, escape

---

7 "The Little Mermaid" was published by Danish writer Hans Christian Andersen in 1837.

gravity and sprout wings to fly off into the sky, our inability to recognize ourselves as we are; all that makes us, in one way or another, like Mélusine's sons, the good and the bad, the normal and the abnormal. (254)

For Chawaf, the double nature of Mélusine is an appropriate symbol of the separation between body and language handed down through the Christian tradition. In *Le Corps et le verbe*, published ten years before *Mélusine des détritus*, she claims that we have lost the "carnal source" (7) of our language. While "in Genesis the body precedes the word, because the body exists before it knows that it exists" (18), in the Gospel According to Saint John, we read that "in the beginning was the Word, and the Word was with God, and the Word was God. ... And the Word was made flesh, and dwelt among us, and we beheld his glory" (John 1.1, 14). During the 12 centuries separating Genesis and the Gospels, a fundamental reversal took place:

> Thus, encouraged by the medieval Church, will be born—from the word that was made flesh, the word that takes the place of the flesh—a disincarnated language that will cut off everything— body, woman, organic mother, Eve, and everything sexualized and alive in the human being, including man himself—from the word. Language, taking itself for God, castrates its carnal humanity. And the body remains nothing more than a beast. (Chawaf, *Le Corps et le verbe* 20)

Chawaf's "disincarnated language" is a distinctly feminist perspective on the "great divide" ("le grand partage," Larrère and Larrère, *Du bon usage* 93) between scientific and pre-scientific, matter and spirit, humanism and naturalism: a heritage of Plato and Christianity by way of Descartes, Marx, and other modernist philosophers.[8] An effect of the divide is what two contemporary French intellectuals, Michel Maffesoli and Pierre Rabhi, refer to as the disenchantment of the world, borrowing Max Weber's expression ("Die Entzaüberung der Welt") to describe the debilitating effects of rationalization, technology, and capitalism. Chawaf's disoriented, depressed, and disenchanted fairy is an apt representative of this phenomenon.

---

8 For a detailed discussion of the great divide, see Larrère's *Du bon usage de la nature*, part one, chapter two: "Nature et humanism" (57–103).

Maffesoli is a sociologist who studied under Gilbert Durand. Like Durand, and Jung before him, Maffesoli believes that myths and legends structure the human psyche and inform our relationship to the world. In *Écosophie*, he calls for a "progressive philosophy" of a "return to the Real" (13). "Progressive" philosophy is the opposite of the "progressist," or Promethean myth of progress, which Maffesoli sees as the root of "the devastation of the natural and social world" (9). And the "Real" to which he wants to return is the reality of our origins, our roots, often manifested in our myths and dreams. For Maffesoli, the twenty-first century is still struggling with the death of Promethean modernism and the birth of a Dionysian postmodernism, which is a return to nature and the earth, or, more precisely, a fusion of the social and the natural.

Ecosophy is the antidote for disenchantment. It recovers myth, celebrates the earth, and re-enchants the world, precisely what Jean fails to do on his journey with Mélusine to the land of "The Little Mermaid." Bound to his fast car and endless highways, Jean is blind to the "world of legend and enchantment" (Chawaf, *Mélusine* 62) that is the privilege of the fairy. We have noted Mélusine's terror of the future: she does not feel like she belongs to this world and is obsessed by the alienation that she—and all human beings—will experience in an unknown dehumanized future *à venir*, darkened by the threat of nuclear power. Maffesoli stresses that in a disenchanted world, people live in fear of the future. Re-enchantment is characterized by "the enjoyment of the present. The famous *carpe diem*!" (Maffesoli, *Écosophie* 29). Poor Mélusine is too sick to enjoy the present in her polluted town.

In *Mélusine des détritus* and *Le Corps et le verbe*, Chawaf contends that language—especially the language of women—has been separated from the body thanks to the writings of the church fathers. *Écosophie* too laments the loss of the "feminine principle" (42). Maffesoli reminds us that in the West the gender of reason has always been masculine: *logos spermatikos* in Greek, *ratio seminalis* in Latin. Referring to Durand's *The Anthropological Structures of the Imaginary*, he remarks on the phallic quality of many of the images of cutting or separation characteristic of the imagination's "diurnal regime": "the cutting sword (symbol of discerning Reason), the plowshare digging the furrow (symbol of productivism), and the erect phallus (symbol of the pre-eminence of masculine agency)" (44). By contrast, Mélusine resides in the opposing "nocturnal regime" with other maternal symbols: closer to the earth, synthetic rather than dividing.

An important symbol of this shift is the agricultural landscape, in which nature and culture come together. Pierre Rabhi, an Algerian-born farmer, activist, and philosopher, who moved to the Ardèche region of southern France, is a proponent of organic farming, agroecology, and biodynamics.[9] In *Manifeste pour la terre et l'humanisme* (Manifesto for the Earth and Humanism), he critiques Western agriculture as an environmental catastrophe, because of practices such as the use of chemical fertilizers, which lead to a loss of microelements in the soil (27); persistent pesticides, which pollute soil and water (31); and treating cows, pigs, sheep, and chickens like "protein factories" instead of animals (28). Rabhi finds "magnificent ... poetic and symbolic resonance" in the word "food" ("nourriture"), which has unfortunately been superseded by "grub" or "chow" ("bouffe"): "overabundant, adulterated, manipulated, and polluted" (32).

Like Maffesoli, Rabhi believes that the environment is in a state of crisis, one which can only be overcome if—and, unfortunately, the "if" is huge—we turn our backs on modernism and embrace a "re-enchanted" postmodernism. His lyrical humanist and agricultural manifesto conveys a respect and awe for the mysteries of the earth: "A simple gardener ..., if observant, can perceive the creative force that programs the tiniest seed" (46). In a chapter called "Symphony of the Earth," Rabhi echoes Maffesoli's call for re-enchantment, harmony with nature, and nature as the "totality of the real":

> Before the world changes, must it not be re-enchanted? Mustn't we love and contemplate the world in order to find the energy to take care of it? It is this deep love of what I call the "symphony of the earth" which, more than the alarming reports of current and future disasters, inspires me to work at finding solutions. For an ecology that does not integrate this notion of a universal

---

[9] Rabhi describes agroecology as "a technique inspired by the laws of nature. It contends that farming must not limit itself to a technique; it must consider the milieu in which it is working and with which it constitutes a true ecology" (74). *The Oxford English Dictionary* defines biodynamic farming as "a method of organic agriculture based on the philosophy of Rudolf Steiner (1861–1925), in which the farm is viewed as a single self-sustaining entity, and which incorporates certain astrological and spiritual principles."

harmony of nature runs the risk of getting stuck in a world reduced to elementary phenomena, the domain of specialized scientific observation, to the detriment of the fundamental principle—let's cautiously call it "spiritual"—that represents the immense intelligence governing the totality of the real. (59)

The medieval story of Mélusine resonated like an enchanted symphony of the earth and waters. In contrast, Chawaf's jarring modern version brings to light what Maffesoli calls the "ontological cut" ("coupure ontologique," 44) between subject and object—body/spirit, body/language, animal/human, man/woman. However, one can nevertheless consider Chawaf's character to be an attempt to unite these halves or, to use Chawaf's image, "to heal the wound of separation" (*Le Corps et le verbe* 13). Mélusine responds to the author's call for "an ecology of writing and language" (67), a concept that she explains as follows: "Ecologists, like writers, are defending life in a threatened environment. Global life of the universe for ecology, individual life of language for the writer. ... Ecological and literary language share the desire to socialize nature where this socialization is lacking" (67).

Mélusine's cry is a scream from the depths of the earth, for she represents "the soul of the wounded and suffering world" (Saigal 191). For a feminist like Chawaf, it is the cry of all women, marginalized since "the Christian metaphor of the holy language only speaks of the Father and the Son," and because "Eve, the word of woman, is no longer there to dialog with Adam, the word of man, and so create the human word" (*Le Corps et le verbe* 21). A renewal of the female word is essential if we wish to rediscover our earth, ravaged by pollution, illness, and war. André Breton, exiled on Quebec's Gaspé Peninsula in 1944, during the darkest hour of the Second World War, made the same appeal to Mélusine and to all women, whom he considered—in the grand tradition of Western thought!—closer to nature than men:

> Melusina half-reclaimed by panic-stricken life, Melusina with lower joints of broken stones or aquatic plants or the down of a nest, she's the one I invoke, she's the only one I can see who could redeem this savage epoch. She's all of woman and yet woman as she exists today, woman deprived of her human base, prisoner of her mobile roots, if you will, but also through them

in providential communication with nature's elemental forces. (*Arcanum 17* 63)

How might we "redeem this savage epoch," characterized for Breton by the Nazi atrocities, and for Chawaf by "the barbarism" (*Le Corps et le verbe* 71) inflicted on human beings and our planet by men in power? Both Breton and Chawaf turn towards art. Breton suggests a "feminine" art, "against man and for woman," that might "bring man down from a position of power which, it has been sufficiently demonstrated, he has misused" (*Arcanum 17* 62). Chawaf's hope is that literature may bring "the living word back to its origin, through a fusional language in which the word and the flesh come together in the reality of our body" (*Le Corps et le verbe* 11).

It is precisely Mélusine's cry that strives—repeating Chawaf's plea—to "heal the wound of separation" (13) between language and the body. This split is as much personal as it is philosophical for Chawaf, given the tragic circumstances of her own birth.[10] Through her cry, Mélusine communicates the pain of her body that is one with the pain of the earth. To Jean it seems that this preverbal language he hears in her pained scream is announcing the end of humanity as we know it:

> This dialect of mewing and moaning, these sounds of a small wild animal, these hoarse emanations from an inflamed throat that signaled the waning of our native tongue, magnified in ancient and noble times by fairy tales and legends, were a premonition. Thousands of the earth's spoken languages were disappearing little by little. What would be left of language in a hundred years? An abstract? Just one language? Nothing at all? (Chawaf, *Mélusine* 204)

Mélusine's cry is visceral, an "inarticulate, unbearable … vomiting" (210) by which she expresses the "premonition that the earth was no longer for her" (211). Mélusine's cry is thus an appeal to the earth, but also a plea for the mother: "You were like an infant crying for your mother. Little by little, your cry, a convulsive fusion with the

---

10 Chantal Chawaf was pulled from the womb of her dying mother, mortally wounded during a bombing in the Paris suburbs in November 1943. Her father and an aunt also died when a bomb exploded near the car as they drove to the maternity clinic (Zupančič, "Déchirure" 220).

modern world, sickened you; the world became your nausea" (212–13). This new Mélusine, who lives with her aunt, has lost her mother, as the mythical Mélusine essentially lost hers through the curse, and as Chantal Chawaf lost hers during her traumatic birth.

Thus the cries of the two Mélusines are analogous. In the medieval legend, it is the "strange and mournful cry" (Jean d'Arras 609) of a fairy-woman condemned by a maternal curse to an eternal life she does not desire. In the novel of a twenty-first century spinning towards destruction, it is the quest for a female and maternal voice that will save us from a terrifying *avenir*, leading us instead back to our origins, "to coolness, fertility, the source, the gift of life, the gift of living life" (Chawaf, *Le Corps et le verbe* 12).

Part 2

The Animal Question

Even though you'd still like to receive the presents they bring, you wish they would leave Santa's sleigh for good, cut their yoke, and run off to the distant tundras of the East.

—Olivia Rosenthal, *Que font les rennes après Noël?*

Grazing reindeer in snowstorm. iStock.com/SeppFriedhuber.

Chapter 4

Ethical Humanism and the Animal Question: Vercors's *You Shall Know Them* (*Les Animaux dénaturés*)

> [O]n their own and without trying, animals have never ceased to make the border-boundary between humans and beasts an unsettled one.
>
> —Jean-Christophe Bailly, *The Animal Side* 5

In his introduction to ecocriticism, Greg Garrard writes that the broadest definition of ecocriticism "is the study of the relationship of the human and the non-human, ... entailing critical analysis of the term 'human' itself" (*Ecocriticism* 5). Nature writing and pastoral are no longer the foundations of ecocriticism, whose "key task" has become the "reconsideration of the idea of 'the human'" (15). Ecocritics long ago discarded Descartes's claim that animals are mere mechanical creatures possessing movement and a life force (*anima*), but lacking a thinking, reasoning, feeling *cogito* (*animus*).[1] As J. Baird Callicott explained in

---

1   Descartes's views on animals are succinctly summarized in a letter to the English philosopher Henry More, dated 5 February 1649. He explains that "there are two different principles causing our motions: one is purely mechanical and corporeal ..., and can be called the *corporeal soul*; the other is the *incorporeal mind*, the soul which I have defined as a thinking substance" (Descartes, *Philosophical Letters* 243; emphasis added). Descartes maintains that all animal motions originate in the corporeal soul; the incorporeal mind is exclusively human, and "we cannot at all prove the presence of a thinking soul in animals" (243). Descartes goes on to assert that animals are marvelous "natural automata." "Art copies nature," he writes, and thus animal automata—while clearly inferior to humans—are "more splendid than" the artificial copies produced by humans (244). At the end of his letter, Descartes states his principle reason for believing

1994, "The emerging postmodern model of nature is more organismic than mechanistic" ("Role of Technology" 67). The flourishing field of animal studies[2] confirms what pet owners have always known: that animals are not machine-like objects, but sentient, emotive subjects, and as such share "troubled boundaries" (Garrard 148) with human beings. One of the most intriguing French literary treatments of the human-animal continuum is undoubtedly *You Shall Know Them* (*Les Animaux dénaturés*), a little-known novel by Vercors (Jean Bruller), published in Paris several years after the end of World War II, at the height of the existentialist movement. While grappling with the question of what separates humans and animals, Vercors shows how "the question of the animal" (Calarco, *Zoographies* 4–6) is intimately bound up with notions of power, racism, imperialism, and capitalism.

You Shall Know Them recounts the adventures of Douglas Templemore, a journalist who joins a team of British scientists on a journey to New Guinea in search of the "missing link," a fossil then thought to be the transitional creature in the evolution from early hominids to *Homo sapiens*. The team is astonished to discover, instead of fossils, a living colony of primates. They conclude that these creatures are the intermediary species between apes and humans, and call them *Paranthropus erectus*,[3] or "tropis," a contraction of *anthropos* (human) and *pithecus* (monkey). The tropis possess some characteristics typically perceived as human: they live in caves, not trees; they have fire; they

---

that animals cannot think. Humans can communicate through words and signs by speaking, and, although some animals have voices and can make sounds, "it has never yet been observed that any brute animal reached the stage of using real speech, that is to say, of indicating by word or sign something pertaining to pure thought and not to natural impulse" (245). This then is the most consequential difference "between men and dumb animals" (245).

2 Some helpful essays on animal studies in France are included in the bibliography. For studies by or about French scholars, see referenced works by J.-C. Bailly, J. Birnbaum, M. Calarco, M. Calarco and P. Atterton, J. Derrida, É. de Fontenay, T. Garcia, D. Krell, K. Matignon, and D. Rosane. J. B. Callicott, C. Huggan, and H. Tiffin provide insight into, respectively, tensions between animal studies and environmental ethics, and the relationship between animal studies and postcolonial criticism.

3 The genus *Paranthropus* ("beside human") actually existed, first appearing between two and three million years ago, well before *Homo sapiens*, which has only existed for about two hundred thousand years. There does not seem to have been a species named *P. erectus*.

make and use tools; they bury their dead; they laugh. Physically, however, they resemble apes more than humans; and, significantly, they do not name one another: "any idea of differentiation, of individuality, was completely alien to them" (Vercors, *You Shall Know Them* 76). As scientists attempt "to settle definitely that famous question: are the tropis human?" (78), Vancruysen, an Australian businessman, plans to use these highly trainable "animals" that are adults by the age of ten for cheap labor in his wool mills. They will live in camps; the females will be forced to breed quickly, while most males will be castrated to improve their temperament. In a desperate attempt to save the tropis from slavery by proving that they are human, Templemore and the scientists artificially inseminate several female tropis. Templemore kills one of the offspring—after taking care to have his "child" baptized—and turns himself in to the police as a murderer. The second half of the novel follows the events of two trials that seek to determine 1) what is the definition of human and do the tropis fit that definition? and 2) did Templemore commit a crime, and if so, was it murder? Bernard Cocula calls *You Shall Know Them* an "anthropological fable." As in all fables, animals play an important role, but Vercors especially contemplates the border between animals and humans,[4] and the "question of questions, what is man?" (Cocula 149).

Like Camus and Sartre, Vercors is fundamentally a humanist, and he considers animals from the viewpoint of what Callicott calls "ethical humanism" ("Animal Liberation" 315–16). Callicott identifies three philosophical perspectives regarding the rights of nonhuman beings. First, "ethical humanism" (or "moral humanism") claims that only humans are worthy of "moral standing," for many possible reasons: "Only human beings are rational, or capable of having interests, or possess *self*-awareness, or have linguistic abilities, or can represent the future, it is variously argued" (316). Second, the "humane moralism" (316–18) of Peter Singer and others espousing Jeremy Bentham's utilitarian philosophy considers "sentience" the only attribute necessary for a being—even one "deprived of reason, speech, forethought or ... *self*-awareness" (317)—to warrant full moral standing. Third, "environmental ethics," based on Aldo Leopold's "land ethic" (311), takes a holistic rather than an atomistic view of nature like the first two

---

4   This aspect of *You Shall Know Them* is better conveyed by the title used in a 1976 New English Library translation: *Borderline*.

perspectives (319, 337). For Leopold, "the good of the biotic *community* is the ultimate measure of the moral value, the rightness or wrongness, of actions" (320). This point of view tolerates the sacrifice of individual creatures if it is in the interest of the collectivity. For Callicott, environmental ethics, which considers not only animals, but plants and geographical areas such as mountains, oceans, and wetlands (337), is far more inclusive than the first two perspectives. He concludes that

> [t]he debate over animal liberation … should be conceived as triangular, not polar, with land ethics or environmental ethics, the third and, in my judgement, the most creative, interesting, and practicable alternative. Indeed, from this third point of view moral humanism and humane moralism appear to have much more in common with one another than either have with environmental or land ethics. (337)

Callicott's essay is a good summary of the tension that has long existed between ecocriticism and animal studies, the first priding itself on its holistic world view, envisioning horizontal, symbiotic relationships among species, the second on its fight against speciesism and its protection of the interests of all animals. In a more recent article, "Animal Liberation and Environmental Ethics," Callicott slightly tempers his criticism of Singer and the animal liberation movement, conceding that "Animal welfare ethicists and environmental ethicists have overlapping concerns. From a practical point of view, it would be far wiser to make common cause against a common enemy—the destructive forces at work ravaging the nonhuman world—than to continue squabbling among ourselves" (147).

Despite his unabashed humanism, Vercors has much in common with today's environmental ethics, which, in the words of Callicott, "locates ultimate value in the 'biotic community' and assigns differential moral value to the constitutive individuals relatively to that standard" ("Animal Liberation" 337). The protagonist of *You Shall Know Them* will make the difficult choice—repugnant for some characters in the novel (notably Templemore's wife), and doubtless for many readers as well—to sacrifice his offspring for the good of the community of tropis; as a result of Templemore's sensational trial, the newly discovered species is deemed human and saved from slavery.

The Vercors is a majestic Alpine mountain range that dominates the horizon southwest of Grenoble. It is here that Jean Bruller served in the French army during the "drôle de guerre" that culminated in the French defeat in May 1940. Bruller quickly became active in the clandestine struggle against the German occupiers; like many French resistants, he chose a favorite geographical name as an alias, and thus it was under the name of Vercors that he carried out his resistance activities and eventually published his literary works. He is best known for a short narrative, *The Silence of the Sea* (*Le Silence de la mer*), the first publication of the underground, aptly named Les Editions de Minuit, co-founded by Vercors and Pierre de Lescure. Printed and distributed secretly early in 1942 in occupied Paris, the book recounts the passive resistance of a man and his niece, forced to house a German officer in 1941. The officer is a cultivated musician enamored of French culture and, despite the war, he is optimistic that Germany and France will soon put aside their differences and combine their greatest attributes— German music, French literature—for the greater good of Europe. His hosts' only response to his polite conversation is a defiant silence, which endures for six months.

For most readers, *The Silence of the Sea* epitomized, more than any other work of fiction, intellectual resistance against the occupation forces.[5] Yet Vercors was criticized by some for his pacifist humanism, his belief "in a possible marriage between the two former adversaries within a happy Europe," and his sympathetic portrayal of this "best possible German" who, as evidenced by the sensitive tone of the first-person narrator (the uncle), almost wins the friendship and affection of his two taciturn French hosts (Stokes 11). At this early point in the war, Vercors was still hopeful that Germany's humanistic traditions would triumph over the barbarity of the Third Reich.

His tolerance of Germany was short-lived, however, as towards the end of the war the horrors of the concentration camps and other Nazi atrocities, such as the massacre of Oradour-sur-Glane,[6] became known. Indeed, the shock of the camps led Vercors to forge what would be

---

5   Richard Neupert explains how "the clandestine book became a clandestine film" (64), when Jean-Pierre Melville wrote and directed a film version of *Le Silence de la mer*. A successful low-budget film, it was shot in 1947 without the permission of Vercors and without the authorization of the Centre national de la cinématographie (64). Finally released in 1949, "*Le Silence de la mer* was hailed by many as the greatest film about the German occupation of France" (67).
6   On 10 June 1944, 642 persons—including 452 women and children—were gunned down or burned alive by the 4th SS Panzer Regiment in the small

the focus of his *œuvre*: to elaborate a humanistic philosophy that could account for the animality of humans, and question the boundary between the human and nonhuman.

You Shall Know Them is Vercors's most complete fictional expression of that philosophy, which echoes Hannah Arendt's acute observations on the death camps and the truths they reveal about human nature in *The Origins of Totalitarianism* (published in 1951, a year before *You Shall Know Them*). Nazism, writes Arendt, "attempted to change man into a beast" (179). This change was affected through a three-part "murder" of concentration camp inmates. First, the "moral person" is destroyed; that is, he no longer perceives normal notions of right and wrong: "The alternative is no longer between good and evil, but between murder and murder. Who could solve the moral dilemma of the Greek mother, who was allowed by the Nazis to choose which of her three children should be killed?" (452).[7] Second, the "juridical person" must disappear. Once a person is interred, he ceases to exist in any legal manner. He is not even dead, since dead people at least merit a death certificate. And he is not a criminal, since criminals, having been convicted by a legal process, retain their juridical identity. Lastly, "total domination"[8] is achieved when the prisoner's "unique identity," or "individuality" (453), is killed. Individuals cease to exist. They become a mass of creatures to be exterminated, like faceless cattle crammed into a train headed to the abattoir:

> Total domination, which strives to organize the infinite plurality and differentiation of human beings as if all of humanity were just one individual, is possible only if each and every person can be reduced to a never-changing identity of reactions, so that each of these bundles of reactions can be exchanged at random for any other. The problem is to fabricate something that does not exist, namely, a kind of human species resembling other animal species whose only "freedom" would consist in "preserving the species." (438)

---

village of Oradour-sur-Glane (Haute-Vienne, Limousin). The motive for the massacre was allegedly the kidnapping of an SS officer by French resistants.
7   Albert Camus reported this incident in *Twice a Year* (21).
8   "Total domination" (437–59) is the title of the last section of Arendt's twelfth chapter, "Totalitarianism in Power."

Total domination was the goal of the concentration camps, at first run by the SA (Sturmabteilung), known for its sadism and perversion. Yet as horrifying as the SA's "blind bestiality" (453) was, Arendt stresses that they were "acts of *individual* bestiality" (454 n. 159; emphasis added). However, when the SS (Schutzstaffel)[9] effectively replaced the SA and took over the administration of the camps, brutality became just another element of the organizational structure: "The old spontaneous bestiality[10] gave way to an absolutely cold and systematic destruction of human bodies, calculated to destroy human dignity" (454). Mechanized killing techniques alleviated the guilt that a guard might feel upon killing a single prisoner. Mass murder anesthetized the SS. They did not murder humans, they murdered the human:

> The killing of man's individuality, of the uniqueness shaped in equal parts by nature, will, and destiny, which has become so self-evident a premise for all human relations that even identical twins inspire a certain uneasiness, creates a horror that vastly overshadows the outrage of the juridical-political person and the despair of the moral person. It is this horror that gives rise to the nihilistic generalizations which maintain plausibly enough that essentially all men alike are beasts. Actually the experience

---

9 SA: Storm Troopers, a Nazi paramilitary group founded in 1921, but superseded by the SS in 1934. SS: Protection Squadron, founded in 1922, commanded by Heinrich Himmler, 1929–45. The SS managed the concentration camps from 1934.

10 Arendt's vocabulary highlights the problematic connotations of the various forms of "beast" (*bête* in French). In our anthropocentric tradition, of which Arendt is of course a part, "bestiality" is synonymous with brute violence. Foucault showed how in earlier centuries even the more neutral "animality" connoted wildness and madness (Palmer 75). Philosophers such as Jacques Derrida and Élisabeth de Fontenay have rehabilitated the word "beast." In *The Animal That Therefore I Am*, Derrida reveals the irony of the words "bestiality" and *bêtise* (stupidity), nouns that can only apply to humans, not beasts: "One cannot speak ... of the *bêtise* or bestiality of an animal. It would be an anthropomorphic projection of something that remains the preserve of man" (41). At the beginning of *Le Silence des bêtes*, Fontenay writes that she will prefer *bête* over *animal* (25), and in *Without Offending Humans*, she says she "will never consent to define [humans] as human animals" (xiii). She gives back to animals the right to be called *bêtes* without negativity and insists on separating them from those who have done violence to them, those who have considered their inability to speak—their silence—a fault (*Le Silence des bêtes* 22).

of the concentration camps does show that human beings can be transformed into specimens of the human animal, and that man's "nature" is only "human" insofar as it opens up to man the possibility of becoming something highly unnatural, that is, a man. (454–55)

The Law of the Strongest

The French title of *You Shall Know Them*, *Les Animaux dénaturés*, suggests that Vercors would have agreed with Arendt's proclamation that human nature is anything but natural. Published seven years after the liberation of the concentration camps and the end of the war, the novel proposes to define the human animal, and to situate human nature within the whole of nature. A problem of human society that particularly interests Vercors is how the "law of the strongest"—whose insidious presence he sees in racism and capitalism—still menaces humanity.[11]

---

11 Rousseau, in his *Discourse on the Origins of Inequality* (*Second Discourse*), evokes the law of the strongest as one of the corrupting factors of civilization. "[N]atural or Physical" in the state of nature, the law of the strongest degenerates into "moral or Political inequality" (Rousseau, *Second Discourse* 18) with the advent of families and property that causes jealousy and quarrels (46), eventually leading to societies founded upon violence and conquest (55), and corrupt governments (59). The ogre of despotism, "raising its hideous head and devouring all it had seen to be good and healthy in all parts of the State" (64), consumes its people. Subjects, "engulfed by the Monster" of tyranny, become slaves (64–65):
> Here everything is brought back to the sole Law of the stronger, and consequently to a new state of Nature different from the one with which we began, in that the one was the State of Nature in its purity, and this last is the fruit of an excess of corruption. Besides, there is so little difference between these two states, and the Contract of Government is so completely dissolved by Despotism, that the Despot is Master only as long as he is the strongest. (65)

A century later John Stuart Mill, in his 1869 essay *The Subjection of Women*, uses the term to describe the condition of women in England, which is tantamount to slavery, "the legal subordination of one sex to the other" (1). In England, "the law of the strongest seems to be entirely abandoned as the regulating principle of the world's affairs: nobody professes it, and, as regards most of the relations between human beings, nobody is permitted to practise it." It is quite shocking, therefore, that in this country "the inequality of rights between men and women has no other source than the law of the strongest" (10).

For the protagonist of *You Shall Know Them*, the law of the strongest is illustrated first of all by the "relentless machine of capitalism" (Cocula 151), personified by the business "shark" (Vercors, *You Shall Know Them* 78) Vancruysen, who plans to exploit the tropis for slave labor, and secondly by the racism embodied by the Australian anthropologist Julius Drexler and his supporters. The discovery of the tropis prompts Drexler, who has ties to big business, to publish an article—heartily approved by, among others, the South African press[12]—challenging our conception of the human. Templemore summarizes the article in a letter to his fiancée Frances:

> The appearance of the tropis, [Drexler] concludes, proves that the oversimple notion of the oneness of the human species is inept. There is no human species, there is only a vast family of hominids, in a descending color scale, with the White Man—the true Man—at the top of the ladder, and at the bottom the tropi and the chimpanzee. We must abandon our old sentimental notions, and at last establish scientifically the hierarchy of the intermediate groups "improperly called human." (102)

Templemore, the *porte-parole* for Vercors, decries this "grimacing ghost of racial discrimination," where any "ethnical minority" can "be stripped of [its] human status and the rights that go with it." And where will the boundary be set between the human and the nonhuman? "Where it pleases the strongest!" (102).

Vercors is thus acutely aware of the heritage of the law of the strongest, which, as Rousseau and Mill established, has long corrupted human nature. Once again Arendt's *The Origins of Totalitarianism* can provide useful philosophical insight into Vercors's novel. Completed barely four years after the defeat of Nazi Germany, Arendt's first major book is a monumental analysis of how centuries of anti-Semitism and imperialism finally culminated in Nazi and Bolshevik totalitarianism. Like Vercors, Arendt charges the materialistic bourgeois or business class with operating under the law of the strongest, or what she often names the might-right doctrine:

---

12 Apartheid became the law of the land in 1948, just a few years before the publication of *You Shall Know Them*. In the novel, the *Durban Express* runs the headline "Are the Negroes human?" in response to Drexler's comments on the tropis (103).

> Imperialism must be considered the first stage in the political rule of the bourgeoisie … . [Its] privateness and primary concern with money-making had developed a set of behavior patterns which are expressed in all those proverbs—"nothing succeeds like success," "might is right," "right is expediency," etc.—that necessarily spring from the experience of a society of competitors. (*Totalitarianism* 138)

Imperialism was in part the inevitable result of the "superfluous wealth" (136, 149–51) created by overaccumulation of capital, which had to be exported to non-capitalistic areas of the world. Arendt cites the Marxist economist Rosa Luxemburg (1871–1919), who wrote in *The Accumulation of Capital* (first published in 1913) that the production system of capitalism "from the beginning had been calculated for the whole earth" (Arendt 148). Luxemburg defines imperialism as "the political expression of the accumulation of capital in its competition for the possession of the remainders of the noncapitalistic world" (Arendt 148 n. 45).

Arendt stresses the obvious link between imperialism and racism: the imperialistic politics of modern Europe have always had racism as their most "powerful ideology" (158). For Arendt the nation at the origin of racism is not Germany, but France, despite its proud tradition of enlightenment and revolution, and its publication of the *Declaration of the Rights of Man and of the Citizen* in 1789: "Yet it is this nation-creating century and humanity-loving country to which we must trace the germs of what later proved to become the nation-destroying and humanity-annihilating power of racism" (162). She locates the origins of modern European racism in the "class-thinking" (162) of the French historian Comte de Boulainvilliers (1658–1722) who, towards the end of the reign of Louis XIV, was a staunch defender of the nobility. In contrast to Rousseau, who in the *Social Contract* would endorse the "right of first occupancy" in property law,[13] Boulainvilliers

---

13   In Book I, ch. 9 ("On Real Estate") of *The Social Contract*, Rousseau writes: The right of the first occupant, although more real than the right of the strongest, becomes a true right only after the establishment of the right of property. Every man naturally has a right to everything he needs; but the positive act that makes him the proprietor of some good excludes him from all the rest. Once his portion is designated, he should limit himself to it, and no longer has any right to the community's goods. That is why the

was influenced by "might-right" or "right of conquest" doctrines. He theorized that the Gallo-Romans, who long occupied what is now French territory during the Roman Empire, were not in fact the ancestors of the French nobility. Since they were conquered by the Franks (a Germanic tribe) during the fifth century, right of conquest deems that the Franks be considered the true ancestors of the French noble class (Second Estate). The descendants of the Gallo-Romans are also French, concedes Boulainvilliers, but they belong to the inferior class of commoners (Third Estate). Boulainvilliers, writes Arendt, "based his doctrine solely on the eternal right of conquest and found no difficulty in asserting that 'Friesland [on the North Sea; now part of the Netherlands] ... has been the true cradle of the French nation'" (162).[14]

It is difficult to overemphasize the significance of the racist tradition embodied by writers like Boulainvilliers and Gobineau to Vercors's novel. Georges Cesbron points out how Vercors always championed the causes of the "weak" against the eternal power-wielding "tigers" (10). As the debris of the Second World War settles, it is clear that the law of the strongest has won out over Rousseau's gentle notions of compassionate humans living in a natural state. The "faculty of self-perfection" (Rousseau, *Second Discourse* 26) that elevated "Savage man" above animals now reads like irony, or merely another myth of a lost golden age. Rousseau perceived the desire to own property as

> right of the first occupant, so weak in the state of nature, is respectable to every civil man. In this right, one respects not so much what belongs to others as what does not belong to oneself. (142)

14 Boulainvilliers's beliefs were later shared by the better-known and more overtly racist Comte de Gobineau (1816–82), author of *The Inequality of Human Races* (*L'Essai sur l'inégalité des races humaines*, 1855). The "last heir of Boulainvilliers" (Arendt, *Totalitarianism* 171), Gobineau also believed that the French lower classes were of Gallo-Roman origin, whereas his endangered upper class—the Second Estate—descended from the Germanic Franks. He linked the decline of the aristocracy after the 1789 and 1848 revolutions to what he perceived as the general decay of humanity, which could be attributed to a sole cause: the miscegenation between the superior white Aryan race and the "pestilent congregation of ugliness" (107) that characterizes the two inferior races, black and yellow. He espoused polygenesis, the belief that each race has its distinct ancestor. Sixteen years after Gobineau's essay, Charles Darwin essentially disproved the theory of polygenesis in *The Descent of Man* (1871), and thus discredited Gobineau's refusal to accept monogenesis, according to which all human beings are thought to have one common ancestor.

the beginning of the evil that leads to inequality: it flourished under capitalism, imperialism with its attendant racism, and finally the evil reached its apogee under Hitlerism. Vercors would most certainly have agreed with Hannah Arendt's bleak prediction that, even after the horrors of the Holocaust, racism would not end with the Third Reich:

> Racism may indeed carry out the doom of the Western world and, for that matter, of the whole of human civilization ... . For no matter what learned scientists may say, race is, politically speaking, not the beginning of humanity but its end, not the origin of peoples but their decay, not the natural birth of man but his unnatural death. (*Totalitarianism* 157)

What Is a Human?

Vercors's concerns with racism go hand in hand with his struggle to define the human. Sir Arthur Draper, the judge presiding over Templemore's case, observes a London policeman directing traffic one evening, and muses that it is one thing to define types of persons based on their nationality, religion, or occupation, but understanding what makes a human human is quite another: "It's so much easier to define an Englishman, a judge, a Quaker, a Labor member, or a policeman, than to define a man pure and simple. ... The tropis are the living proof of this" (Vercors, *You Shall Know Them* 157). English law has no definition of the human, and so before a jury can decide if Templemore is or is not guilty of murder, a parliamentary committee must decide upon the "indisputable sign" (136)—be it a soul or something else—that differentiates the human animal from other animals.

Through the words of a government minister, Vercors underlines the crucial nature of the decision that is about to be made, which could one day pass from British law into international law: "All the rights and duties of man, of social groups, of societies and nations, towards one another, in all latitudes, of all creeds, would for the first time be founded on the very nature of Man, on the irrefutable elements that distinguish him from the Beast" (204). We see that Vercors's thoughts are never far from the atrocities of the recent war, for the attempt to find a universally accepted definition of the human inevitably brings to his mind the inhuman crimes judged at the

Nuremberg Trials, where "Human Rights" all too briefly triumphed over "Human Might":

> For do we not often see that what is a crime for one group of people is not one for their neighbors or their foes?—who may even extol it as a duty or an honor, as we could see in the case of the Nazis? And was it not useless to create in Nuremberg a new law which was not, in its very foundation, acknowledged equally by all? For today we find that, in the name of German traditions, the friends of the condemned drag that law from its lofty eminence as a safeguard of Human Rights down to the disgraceful level of a safeguard of Human Might—and we cannot crush them with the proof of their abject mistake. That is why today we see the Nuremberg laws,[15] in spite of all the hopes that went to their making, gradually dissolving into shadows, and in those shadows new crimes prepared. (205)

The fictional minister's lament is corroborated by history. Some five decades later, the Robert H. Jackson Center published an essay entitled "The Influence of the Nuremberg Trial on International Criminal Law,"[16] which states that "The Nuremberg trials established that all of humanity would be guarded by an international legal shield." Attaining this noble goal, unfortunately, was hampered by "the

---

15 Vercors's character cannot be referring to what are normally called the Nuremberg Laws (in French, *les lois* [plural] *de Nuremberg*). In the original French, he says "le Droit [singular] de Nuremberg." The Nuremberg Laws, enacted by the Nazi Party in 1935, legalized persecution of the Jews. An article in *Prologue*, a publication of the United States's National Archives (where the Nuremberg Laws have been kept since 2010), summarizes the laws as follows: "They stripped German Jews of their German citizenship, barred marriage and 'extramarital sexual intercourse' between Jews and other Germans, and barred Jews from flying the German flag, which would now be the swastika" (Bradsher n. pag.). The Nuremberg *Laws* obviously never occupied the "lofty eminence" that the minister describes in his flowery speech. He is clearly alluding, not to the Laws, but to the Nuremberg *Principles* of 1950, an attempt by the United Nations to codify crimes against peace, war crimes, and crimes against humanity—as determined during the Nuremberg Trials of captured Nazis. Difficult to enforce, the principles did not succeed, as the minister affirms, in safeguarding "Human Rights" from "Human Might."
16 Robert H. Jackson (1892–1954) was a Supreme Court Justice and Chief of Counsel for the United States at the Nuremberg Trials, in charge of prosecuting Nazi leaders.

inadequacy of the law and the willingness to do something to enforce such new principles" and,

> [w]hile the law limped lamely along, international crimes flourished. The horrors of the twentieth century are many. Acts of mass violence have taken place in so many countries and on so many occasions it is hard to comprehend. According to some estimates, nearly 170 million civilians have been subjected to genocide, war crimes and Crimes Against Humanity during the past century. (n. pag.)

After much debate, the committee finally concludes that there is in fact a "sign" that distinguishes humans from animals; unlike the Nuremberg Principles, this sign will be universally accepted. A bill is passed, and section 1 reads: "Man is distinguished from the Beast by his spirit of religion" (Vercors, *You Shall Know Them* 230). Section 2 explains that "spirit of religion" is to be understood in a broad sense: faith in a god, science, art,[17] philosophy, fetishism, totems, taboos, magic, witchcraft, ritualistic cannibalism, etc.[18] Although at first the tropis do not appear to possess a spirit of religion, eventually they are deemed to be human since some of them practice "a very primitive fire worship, a homage paid to its magic power of purification and exorcism" (237). The tropis are thus saved from the slave labor that Vancruysen envisioned for them in the Australian wool mills. As for Templemore, he is acquitted of the murder charge, since at the time he killed his offspring, the victim was not yet known to be human; moreover, its death was a necessary sacrifice in order to save the entire race.[19]

---

17 It may appear strange to include "art" as a manifestation of the spirit of religion. Yet Claude Lévi-Strauss, in a 1979 interview, comments that he is struck by our society's "veneration" of great artists. Our museums are "more or less the equivalent of temples in other societies," and to lose the works of Rembrandt or Michelangelo would be considered a "catastrophe." Unfortunately, he adds, when it comes to living plant and animal species, "infinitely more complex and infinitely more irreplaceable" than great works of art, we treat them "totally irresponsibly and offhandedly" (Lévi-Strauss, "L'idéologie marxiste" 14).
18 In the definition of "spirit of religion," the English translation inexplicably omits several important terms found in the original French edition: fetishism, totems, taboos, magic, and witchcraft.
19 As I discussed earlier in this chapter, this type of "sacrifice," while odious to

Existentialist Humanism and Human Dignity

The dénouement of the novel presents an existentialist manifesto of the human condition. Indeed, *You Shall Know Them* expounds on many of the ideas that characterized the burgeoning existentialist movement that came out of the Second World War. Like Camus and Sartre, Vercors the author was formed by the profound crisis from which Europe was just emerging. His literature is one of engagement, committed to the righting of the political and social wrongs he has witnessed. Sartre would doubtless disagree with Vercors's attempt to find a definition or essence of humanity, but Templemore's steadfast attempt to save the tropis proves his authenticity and his commitment to freedom; like Orestes in Sartre's *The Flies* (*Les Mouches*), he is condemned to act, to follow the difficult path of responsibility.

In the closing pages, the characters of *You Shall Know Them* come to grips with the real nature of the human condition. Echoing Rousseau, they agree that the tropis had "lived a wonderfully carefree life" (242), which will come to an end once they are educated like humans, and "become liars, thieves—vain, selfish, mean ..." (243). Frances, now Templemore's wife, remarks that happiness is not the lot of humans; yet she would not trade the pain of being human for the guiltless contentment of animals. Frances is surely expressing Vercors's affirmation that, in spite of the unspeakable evil that humans are capable of, the human spirit is incomparably beautiful: "This pain, this horror, that's the beauty of man. The animals must certainly be more happy, not feeling them. But I wouldn't for an empire change that pain and even that horror, and even our lies and selfishness and hate, for their unconsciousness, for their happiness" (244). In one of the most memorable passages of the novel, she suggests that the difference between animals and humans is that the former passively accept their state, while the latter actively earn their lofty position: "Humanity is not a state we suffer. It's a dignity we must strive to win. A dignity full of pain and sorrow. Won, no doubt, at the price of tears." Quoting Macbeth, who, after learning of his wife's suicide, mourns the terrible brevity and absurdity of life, Frances affirms that,

partisans of the animal liberation movement, would be tolerable in the context of the environmental ethics of Leopold and Callicott, which values the interests of the community over those of the individual.

on the contrary, life is worth living, worth fighting for: "The tropis will have to shed [tears], with a lot of blood, and sound and fury. But now I know, I know that all this isn't 'a tale told by an idiot, signifying nothing'" (244).

In this passage we clearly see Vercors's espousal of human exceptionalism. This aspect of his philosophy runs counter to the "antihumanist resentment" that Élisabeth de Fontenay (*Le Silence des bêtes* 44) detects in Lévi-Strauss. In effect, this excerpt from a chapter that Lévi-Strauss consecrates to Rousseau reads like a refutation of Vercors's humanism:

> In this world, more cruel to man than it perhaps ever was, all the means of extermination, massacre, and torture are raging. ... It is now, I repeat, by exposing the flaws of a humanism decidedly unable to establish the exercise of virtue among men, that Rousseau's thinking can help us to reject an illusion whose lethal effects we can observe in ourselves and on ourselves. For is it not the myth of the exclusive dignity of human nature, which subjected nature itself to a first mutilation, one from which other mutilations were inevitably to ensue? We started by cutting man off from nature and establishing him in an absolute reign. (*Structural Anthropology* 40–41; qtd. in Fontenay, *Le Silence des bêtes* 47)

Lévi-Strauss echoes another iconoclastic thinker, Nietzsche, who in *The Anti-Christ* wrote of "the vanity that man is the great secret objective of animal evolution. Man is absolutely not the crown of creation: every creature stands beside him at the same stage of perfection" (136; qtd. in Fontenay, *Without Offending Humans* 35).

A fundamental difference is apparent between Lévi-Strauss's thought and the existentialism of Vercors, Camus, and the Sartre of *Existentialism Is a Humanism*. The same crisis of "extermination, massacre, and torture" that leads to Lévi-Strauss's famously pessimistic view of humans inspires these existentialists to a relatively optimistic humanism based on a reaffirmation of human dignity. Much has been written of the contradictions between Lévi-Strauss's structuralism (analytical) and Sartre's existentialism (dialectical), which Lévi-Strauss himself discusses in the last chapter of *The Savage Mind*. Philippe Cabestan summarizes their differences as follows:

Invoking the structural and rational character of social phenomena, Lévi-Strauss envisages the possibility of being able to describe them in mathematical terms. Thus he rejects subjectivism as the primary attribute of the *cogito*, and refuses the Sartrian critique of analytical reason in the name of a dialectical reason founded on *praxis*. (287)

You Shall Know Them reiterates many of the thoughts presented by Camus in his "Human Crisis"[20] lecture at Columbia University in March 1946. Camus and Vercors, both veterans of the French resistance, were acquainted. Justin O'Brien,[21] a French professor at Columbia, wrote at the time how "Vercors has praised his young friend [Camus] in New York, Chicago, and San Francisco" (Hawes 101). At Columbia, the two men were together, and shared the stage. Existentialism was in the air, American intellectuals were reading Sartre, who had been in New York for over a year, writing for Camus's *Combat*. Just a month earlier Hannah Arendt had introduced many Americans to Camus, Sartre, and French existentialism in an article in *The Nation*. She underscored the rebellious nature of existentialism: "first, the rigorous repudiation of what they call the *esprit sérieux* [bourgeois respectability]; and, second, the angry refusal to accept the world as it is as the natural, predestined milieu of man" ("French Existentialism" 226). Both lines of rebellion relate to human dignity. Sartre, for example, in *Nausea*, ridicules *l'esprit sérieux*—"the hollow dignity which grows out of identifying oneself with one's function"—"in a delightful description of a gallery of portraits of the town's respectable citizens, the bastards [*les salauds*]" (226). And Camus, in *The Myth of Sisyphus*, admires the "proud defiance" of Sisyphus as he trudges down the hill towards his infernal rock; this hero of the absurd illustrates "that reason and human

---

20 The Columbia lecture, delivered in French, was entitled "La Crise de l'homme." According to Elizabeth Hawes, the original text was lost, and the English translation published in *Twice a Year* (Fall–Winter 1946–47) "serves as the historical record" (102). Recently, however, Yale University's Alice Kaplan discovered Camus's long-lost French manuscript in Yale's Beinecke Rare Book and Manuscript Library (see Schuessler).

21 In 1955, Justin O'Brien would translate Camus's *Le Mythe de Sisyphe. Essai sur l'absurde* (1942). References to the absurd pervade "The Human Crisis": "Absurd" is the qualifier that Camus uses early in the lecture to describe the world his generation has inherited from its elders.

dignity, in spite of their senselessness, remain the supreme values" (227).[22]

Like Vercors in *You Shall Know Them*, in his "Human Crisis" lecture Camus attempts to rehabilitate the concept of human dignity, annihilated by war. Morality has become a "monstrous hypocrisy" (20), values have disappeared. The worst of the monsters are the former SS officers, who "were no longer men," acting on instinct like passionless beasts or "like a mathematical theorem" (23), turning humans into zeros, and mass murder into an abstraction.[23] As I noted earlier, Hannah Arendt, in *The Origins of Totalitarianism*, would echo Camus a few years later when she described the Nazi death camps as meticulously calculated by the SS to destroy human values, individuality, and dignity. Like Arendt, and like Vercors and Rousseau, Camus regrets the "perversion of values" whereby a person "is judged today not in terms of human dignity but in terms of success" (22)—in other words, by the "law of the strongest." Even with Hitler dead, "the poison is not gone" (22).[24] Values and beliefs have vanished, replaced by a "cult of efficiency" (24), and the world after the war continues to be a world of "essential absurdity" (27):

22 Of the absurd man, exemplified by the conqueror, the actor, or the character Don Juan, Camus writes: "There is ... a metaphysical honor in enduring the world's absurdity. Conquest or play-acting, multiple loves, absurd revolt are tributes that man pays to his dignity in a campaign in which he is defeated in advance" (*Myth of Sisyphus* 93). Analyzing "absurd creation" (93–118), Camus praises the work of an absurd writer like Dostoyevsky (or Kafka, Melville ...): "Of all the schools of patience and lucidity, creation is the most effective. It is also the staggering evidence of man's sole dignity: the dogged revolt against his condition, perseverance in an effort considered sterile" (115).
23 One might say that since Descartes at least, France has been plagued by a philosophical sickness called abstraction. Camus sees abstraction as an obstacle to happiness, and fights against it, much like his hero Dr. Rieux battles the plague: "Rieux ... knew that sometimes abstraction may become stronger than happiness, and that then, and only then, should one take it into account. ... In this way, and at a different level, he would follow the sort of dreary struggle between the happiness of each individual and the abstractions of the plague" (*The Plague* 71).
24 Vercors, in *Sens et non-sens de l'Histoire* (Galilée, 1978), would use the same metaphor to describe Nazism after the end of the war: "Morte la bête, mais non mort le venin" ("The beast is dead, but the venom remains") (qtd. in Gibert-Joly 213).

Thus the world remains in the hands of the power-seekers, and finally, is ruled by terror. For if nothing is true or false, good or bad, if the only value is that of efficiency, then the only rule to follow is the one enjoining me to be the most efficient, that is to say, the strongest. The world is no longer divided into the just and the unjust, but into masters and slaves. He is right who dominates. (25)

Camus's essay is not totally pessimistic. Like Frances at the end of *You Shall Know Them*, Camus imagines a ray of hope for humanity, thanks to the enduring dignity of people who revolt against evil. He is full of admiration, for example, for the American soldiers who died "on the soil of the Ardennes, which until then [they] had never seen. And even this was absurd, mad, unthinkable, or almost so. But at the same time there was in this absurdity the lesson that we were caught in a collective tragedy the stake of which was a common dignity, a communion of men which it was important to defend and sustain" (27–28).

Like Camus, Vercors—as we have seen—equates humanity with dignity. Unlike most ecocritics and environmental philosophers today, he maintains a clear division between animals and humans. Animals belong to nature, and must passively submit to it, whereas the dignity of thinking humans leads them to actively question nature. The birth of *Homo sapiens* involved a traumatic "wrenching away" from nature:

> Intimately bound up with nature, the animal cannot question it. … The animal is *one* with nature, while man and nature make *two*. To pass from passive unconsciousness to questioning consciousness, there had to be that schism, that divorce, there had to be that wrenching away [*arrachement*] from nature. Is that not precisely the borderline? Animal before the wrench, man after it? Denatured animals,[25] that's what we are. (Vercors, *You Shall Know Them* 224–25)

For Vercors, defining human beings merely by their possession of a spirit of religion is incomplete and unsatisfactory; "the wrench, the refusal, the fight, the denature" (247) is the key to understanding humans. His idea of the evolution from animal nature to human "denature" mirrors

---

25 This passage gives the novel its French title: *Les Animaux dénaturés*.

the verticality of Aristotle's ladder of life, or Great Chain of Being. From antiquity through modernism, the place of humans has mostly been separate from and superior to nature. The denatured animal has lifted itself above nature to a position of dominance, but in so doing it is alone and terrified, forced to invent a "sur-nature" of myths and religions: supernatural beings who might provide answers to "those terrified questions" (225) about its existence. Consequently, only after acknowledging the *arrachement* of humans from nature can one say that we are defined by our possession of a "spirit of religion."

Vercors has thus given his answer to a question that years later would become central to ecocritics, that of *arrachement* versus *attachement*: are human beings truly divorced from nature, or must they be considered one with nature? Vercors's description of the "schism" between humans and nature typifies the modernist point of view, still held by some philosophers like Luc Ferry, who criticizes what he considers the antihumanism of deep ecologists:

> [T]he hatred of the *artifice* connected with our civilization of rootlessness is also a *hatred of humans as such*. For man is the antinatural being par excellence. This is even what distinguishes him from other beings, including those who seem the closest to him: animals. This is how he escapes natural cycles, how he attains the realm of culture, and the sphere of morality, which presupposes living in accordance with laws and not just with nature. (xxviii; emphasis original)

This "great divide" (Larrère and Larrère, *Du bon usage* 154) separating humans from nature, of which we are moreover the "masters and possessors" (Descartes, *Discourse on the Method*, part 6, p. 119), is being questioned by contemporary environmental philosophers. Larrère and Larrère, for example, criticize Ferry for his view that man "affirms his morality by tearing himself away [*s'arrachant*] from nature," which is but "a means subjugated to human ends" (8). They insist on the "hybrid" quality of nature (160), now rarely untouched by the hand of humans. Thus the dichotomy between "artificial" and "natural" no longer holds sway:

> One can no longer conceive of the exteriority of man and nature. Men and their aptitudes, societies and their activities, humanity itself are all in continuity with nature. Societies ... exist in a

nature that they transform and on which they depend: they live in nature. ... This nature is even less outside of us as it includes our technical works. Not only are these hybrid objects that activate natural processes, but, moreover, all the products we make, all the by-products we discard, have a natural future that we do not control. (162–63)

For better or worse, nature has become "technonature" (159, 169), indelibly marked by human technology. We can only hope that, as J. Baird Callicott optimistically writes, "appropriate" and "environmentally benign" technology holds sway in our changing concept of nature, so "that we may become good, law-abiding citizens of the world rather than brutal and ultimately self-defeating conquistadors" ("Role of Technology" 69, 78).

Larrère and Larrère's critique of Ferry recalls Bruno Latour's scathing review—"Arrachement ou attachement à la nature?"—of Ferry's *New Ecological Order*. Latour criticizes this contemporary philosopher for stubbornly sticking to such "pillars of modernism" as "the secular spirit, man's centrality, the antinatural being that is the Sartrian man" (16). Latour notes that Ferry uses the word "arrachement" around 50 times in his essay (17), underscoring his belief that humanity is divorced from nature. Mired in this vision of modernist humanism, Ferry refuses to recognize any originality in ecological thought. As we saw above in the Introduction, he reduces ecology to examples from a ridiculous or dangerous past: thus he compares animal rights activists to early Europeans who gave insects, rats, and other animals legal status in absurd animal trials; and he links deep ecologists to the brutally antihumanist Nazi Party, whose sweeping environmental reforms did not preclude them from committing monstrous crimes against humanity.

Luc Ferry's neo-humanism is out of step with the ecocentric world view held by most contemporary environmental philosophers.[26] But one can understand Vercors's similarly anthropocentric mindset which,

---

26 Ferry is not alone. Matthew Calarco, Peter Atterton, and the other contributors to *Animal Philosophy* criticize—besides Ferry—such eminent Continental philosophers as Heidegger, Levinas, Foucault, and Deleuze for their failure to transcend the modernist concept of the superiority of humans over animals. A notable exception is Derrida, who, in *The Animal That Therefore I Am*, is led by the gaze of a cat to explore what Heidegger called the "abyss of essence" ("Letter on Humanism," 1946–47; qtd. in David Farrell Krell,

in the wake of the human crisis of world war, is sincere, appropriate, and in accordance with Camus's vision of the essential dignity of the human race. The entire second half of the novel focuses on the attempt to determine whether the tropis are or are not human, a determination that hinges on agreeing to a universal definition of humanity's essence. Douglas Templemore's admirable crusade to save the tropis can only be successful if they are declared intellectually superior to other primates and given the ostensibly noble status of human beings, creatures of dignity, a rank earned through pain and suffering. There is no question of animal rights, only human rights.

Yet *You Shall Know Them* is important to ecocritics because it considers some fundamental questions that they are struggling to answer: What does it mean to be human? Where is the boundary between *Homo sapiens* and other animals? Is it true, as Matthew Calarco—following Jacques Derrida and Élisabeth de Fontenay—maintains, that "the human-animal distinction can no longer and ought no longer to be maintained" (*Zoographies* 3)? Is there a great divide, a divorce between humans and animals (or humans and nature), or does nature encompass all living beings, including humans? Although many contemporary ecocritics might disapprove of Vercors's humanism, doing so would be to ignore the context in which Vercors was writing in the late forties and early fifties. If many writers today are preoccupied by ecological themes, it is because in the twenty-first century we are experiencing an unprecedented environmental crisis. It is true that the Second World War was an ecological disaster (most tragically in the atomic bombings of Hiroshima and Nagasaki), but it was first and foremost a "human crisis," as Camus forcefully states in his Columbia lecture. When Camus and Vercors are addressing their Columbia audience, Europe is still trying to recover from the most devastating catastrophe in its history. The "poison" of the war endures, declares Camus, and with it the loss of human dignity ("Human Crisis" 22). Vercors, with other engaged authors, is working to restore dignity, by making it one of the cornerstones of the human.

You Shall Know Them appeals to the humanism that Sartre put forward in his *Existentialism Is a Humanism* (given as a lecture in Paris

Derrida and our Animal Others 32) between animals and humans that is key to Vercors's novel.

Vercors's You Shall Know Them *(Les Animaux dénaturés)* 117

in October 1945, then published in 1946).[27] Sartre denounced one type of humanism: the one "that takes man as an end and as the supreme value" (*Existentialism Is a Humanism* 51); this "cult of humanity leads ultimately ... to fascism" (52). This is the "shameless humanism" derived from the Judeo-Christian tradition and Cartesianism, condemned also by Lévi-Strauss as logically leading to colonialism, fascism, and the death camps ("L'idéologie marxiste" 14).[28] Instead, "existentialist humanism" (Sartre, *Existentialism Is a Humanism* 53), in a world without God, holds that humans are always transcending themselves:

> This is humanism because we remind man that there is no legislator other than himself and that he must, in his abandoned state, make his own choices, and also because we show that it is not by turning inward, but by constantly seeking a goal

---

27 This text caused quite a stir among Sartre enthusiasts, many of whom felt betrayed, because the philosopher had previously been a staunch critic of humanism. Take, for example, his mockery of the humanist Self-Taught Man in *Nausea*. The narrator Roquentin disdains radical humanists, leftist humanists, as well as the "beautiful fairy tale" of Catholic humanists. He also disparages
> the humanist philosopher who bends over his brothers like a wise elder brother who has a sense of his responsibilities; the humanist who loves men as they are, the humanist who loves men as they ought to be, the one who wants to save them with their consent and the one who will save them in spite of themselves, the one who wants to create new myths, and the one who is satisfied with the old ones, the one who loves death in man, the one who loves life in man, the happy humanist who always has the right word to make people laugh, the sober humanist whom you meet especially at funerals or wakes. They all hate each other: as individuals, naturally not as men. (*Nausea* 117)

See Christophe Perrin's "Sartre ou la fausse question de l'humanisme" for an analysis of Sartre's complicated relationship with humanism.

28 Even Voltaire exhibited this "cult of humanity." Hannah Arendt quotes excerpts of his article entitled "Chain of Created Beings" in the *Philosophical Dictionary*:
> At first, our imagination is pleased at the imperceptible transition of crude matter to organized matter, of plants to zoophytes, of these zoophytes to animals, of these to man, of man to spirits, of these spirits clothed with a small aerial body to immaterial substances; and ... to God Himself. ... But the most perfect spirit created by the Supreme Being, can he become God? Is there not an infinity between God and him? ... Is there not obviously a void between the monkey and man? (*Totalitarianism* 179 n. 52)

outside of himself in the form of liberation, or of some special achievement, that man will realize himself as truly human. (53)

This is the kind of humanism embraced by Vercors, whose career was devoted to refuting the "law of the strongest" and protecting the weak. This was his "special achievement," and also that of his protagonist Douglas Templemore, who risked his life to free the tropis. Moreover, like Sartre and Camus, Vercors believes that a fundamental quality of human beings is *rebellion*. Sartre advocates rebellion against *l'esprit sérieux*; Camus's Sisyphus rebels against the absurdity of the human condition. For Vercors, rebellion is even more essential to the human race. We dare to interrogate nature, and this is what distinguishes humans from early hominids. Nathalie Gibert-Joly writes that for Vercors, "the essence of the human lies in rebellion" (221), the "questioning consciousness" (Vercors, *You Shall Know Them* 224) that refuses to submit to nature. It is the very definition of humans that Vercors proposes in his 1949 essay, "La Sédition humaine":

> One fine day, the self-consciousness of the anthropoid woke up to its condition. One fine day, a furtive question flashed through its dark brain. ... What we call "man" is this self-consciousness that revolts against its merciless and deceitful destiny. (29, 31; qtd. in Gibert-Joly 216, 218)

Vercors's humanist task in *You Shall Know Them* is to combat imperialism, racism, and the staggering cruelty that he witnessed during the war.[29] His theory that rebellion is the common trait of

---

[29] The novel would thus lend itself to a postcolonial ecocritical reading, in the spirit of "the burgeoning alliance between postcolonial and environmental studies" (Huggan and Tiffin 2). New Guinea, where the English scientists discover the tropis, is an immense island with a staggering biodiversity. The indigenous population suffered first from European imperialism in the nineteenth century (the territory was divided among the Netherlands, Germany, and Great Britain), and then the Japanese invasion of 1942. Huggan and Tiffin note that a primary interest of postcolonial ecocriticism is the "vilification of designated 'others' ... metaphorised as a question of civilisation versus savagery, human versus animal." Given the association between humans and animals, there is an "inextricable link between racism and speciesism" (18). More fundamental is the refusal of fixed species boundaries (135). Postcolonial ecocritics study how "continuing human inequalities" are the legacy of colonialism and believe that "the very category of the *human*, in relation to animals and environment,

human beings "maintained the unity of the human species, seriously threatened by Nazism" (Gibert-Joly 218). For the concentration camps crushed all possibility of rebellion, destroying, as Hannah Arendt has shown, all that was human in their victims: morality, individuality, legality (*Totalitarianism* 452–53), attempting "to change man into a beast" (179). Lévi-Strauss states that the same attitude that led humans to declare themselves superior to other living creatures led to discrimination and racism within humanity.

Vercors's humanism is a dignified response to the murderous antihumanism of the Third Reich. Yet one could imagine that were he writing today he might reverse the ending of *You Shall Know Them*, and have the tropis declared nonhumans, but as such still worthy of the respect, dignity, and compassion called for by Derrida, Fontenay, and other animal studies scholars who have worked to finally escape "the metaphysical tradition of the human exception" (Fontenay, *Without Offending Humans* 20). Reading Vercors through the lens of contemporary animal studies might well lead one to regret his definition of humans as denatured animals, and his adherence to what Lévi-Strauss condemns as "the myth of the exclusive dignity of human nature, which subjected nature itself to a first mutilation" (*Structural Anthropology* 41). This "implicit anthropocentrism," Calarco points out, is a "blind spot" of the Continental philosophical tradition (*Zoographies* 13). Yet a humanism of the type advocated by Vercors, Camus,[30] and

---

must also be brought under scrutiny" (18). We have seen that imperialism and its associated racism, and the porousness of the human-animal boundary, are essential concerns of *You Shall Know Them*.

30 It must be noted that, like Sartre, Camus is not what one would call a traditional humanist. Both philosophers denounce the selfish humanism that arrogantly glorifies human exception. When the word "plague" is spoken for the first time in Oran, the citizens—humanists all—cannot believe that such a catastrophe could befall them:

> When war breaks out people say: "It won't last, it's too stupid." And war is certainly too stupid, but that doesn't prevent it from lasting. Stupidity always carries doggedly on, as people would notice if they were not always thinking about themselves. In this respect, the citizens of Oran were like the rest of the world, they thought about themselves; in other words, they were humanists: they did not believe in pestilence. A pestilence does not have human dimensions, so people tell themselves that it is unreal, that it is a bad dream which will end. But it does not always end and, from one bad dream to the next, it is people who end, humanists first of all because

Sartre does not entail a lack of esteem and sensitivity towards animals. Even Fontenay, one of France's most eloquent defenders of animals, insists that her work "sketches out a humanism that is ... uncompromising" (*Without Offending Humans* xii).[31] This is evident throughout *Le Silence des bêtes*, where, like Vercors, she dares to associate the plight of voiceless creatures and the crimes committed by the Nazis. On the first page, she evokes the death camps to which Jews were led like "sheep to the slaughterhouse," then insists that her defense of beasts is not antihumanist: "Conducting a critique of a humanist, subjectivist, and predatory metaphysics is not an offense against the human" (*Le Silence des bêtes* 13). Later, towards the end of her essay, she compares the mute incomprehension of prisoners entering the death camps to the silence of the beasts:

> We know that the great majority of those who, getting off the trains and finding themselves on the ramps of the death camps, did not speak German, did not understand these words that were not spoken to them like human words, but rained down on them in screaming rage. Now, to be subjected to a language that is no longer made of words but only of cries of hate, ... is that not precisely the destiny of so many animals? (747)[32]

> they have not prepared themselves. The people of our town were no more guilty than anyone else, they merely forgot to be modest and thought that everything was still possible for them, which implied that pestilence was impossible. (Camus, *The Plague* 30)

A year after the publication of *The Plague*, Camus was invited to St. Dominic monastery on the rue Latour-Maubourg in Paris to speak on the subject of what non-believers expect of Christians. Camus the atheist points out his differences with traditional Christian humanism:

> If Christianity is pessimistic as to man, it is optimistic as to human destiny. Well, I can say that, pessimistic as to human destiny, I am optimistic as to man. And not in the name of a humanism that always seemed to me to fall short, but in the name of an ignorance that tries to negate nothing. (*Resistance, Rebellion, and Death* 73)

31 Fontenay rejects the antihumanism of Peter Singer's utilitarianism, for example, criticizing Singer's "extremist hypothesis" and his "lack of civility" (*Without Offending Humans* 53, 57).

32 Derrida too compares the Holocaust to the "annihilation" of certain animals, killed for food or for science: "there are also animal genocides: the number of species endangered because of man takes one's breath away" (*The Animal That Therefore I Am* 26).

Existentialist humanism is not incompatible with environmental ethics. Both call for humility in the face of the world and nature, whereby "man, beginning by respecting all forms of life outside of his own, would be sheltered from the risk of not respecting all forms of life within humanity itself" (Lévi-Strauss, "L'idéologie marxiste" 14). Vercors has done just that in *You Shall Know Them*. A fine example of *littérature engagée*, it explores that unsettled border between humans and animals, and is first and foremost a plea for justice for all living beings.

Chapter 5

Marginality and Animality: Olivia Rosenthal's *Que font les rennes après Noël?*

> The possibility of pogroms is decided in the moment when the gaze of a fatally-wounded animal falls on a human being. The defiance with which he repels this gaze—"after all, it's only an animal"—reappears irresistibly in cruelties done to human beings, the perpetrators having again and again to reassure themselves that it is "only an animal," because they could never fully believe this even of animals.
>
> —Theodor Adorno, *Minima Moralia: Reflections on a Damaged Life* 68

Olivia Rosenthal has a knack for finding strange and troubling titles (Brendlé 16), such as *Mécanismes de survie en milieu hostile* (Survival Mechanisms in Hostile Territory), her 2014 meditation on death and mourning. None is stranger than *Que font les rennes après Noël?* (What Do Reindeer Do after Christmas?). A little girl whose Jewish family celebrates Christmas to better assimilate to French society, the narrator—obsessed with animals—waits in vain for a Christmas pet, and plots how she might leave her family for hyperborean Eurasia, to roam with Santa's reindeer. She dreams of running with them on the frozen taiga of Finland and Russia after their Christmas labors are through. Her dreams, alas, quickly turn to disenchantment. The only pet she ever receives from her parents is a caged canary, and she is much more intrigued by its death than by its short life. Little by little she learns the truth about reindeer:

You know that reindeer are now raised on farms, that their

numbers are known and registered, that they have had to acclimate to a life in humid, temperate zones, that they can no longer migrate to the East, that there are slaughtering quotas, that their meat is prized, and that one day you might even have eaten some. (Rosenthal, *Que font les rennes après Noël?* 176–77)

The narrator, 44 years old at the end of the novel, closes her story by coming to terms with her disenchantment: "you accept the idea that reindeer are transported in refrigerated trucks, you don't believe in Santa Claus, you are not following his sleigh; age has freed you" (211).

After the odd title, what next strikes the reader is the unconventional narrative structure of the novel. The little girl's narration is in the second person, which is unsettling enough. But the narrating "you" is written as the formal *vous*, hardly appropriate for a preschooler, or, for that matter, any twenty-first-century French person speaking about herself. Rosenthal thus creates a distance between the narrator and her reader, as well as between the narrator and her world, underscoring her self-conception as a misfit. The *vous* is also "disconcerting," as Joseph Mai contends, because it breaks the normal autobiographical pact between author and reader: "If autobiography suggests a discovery or an avowal of one's *self*, the second-person formal pronoun suggests a distance, between Rosenthal and the text just as between the narrator and the character, even though these entities are all supposedly the same 'person' at some level" (Mai 61).

Alternating paragraphs with "you" is a second narrator, "I," a series of professional men who work in some capacity with animals. It is a familiar style to readers of Rosenthal, who also employed this "polyphonic" structure (Rosenthal, interview by Fiolof) in *On n'est pas là pour disparaître* (2007), a novel about a man suffering from Alzheimer's disease. In *Que font les rennes après Noël?*, switching narrators serves to demonstrate the extent to which the narrator feels imprisoned by the expectations of her family and French society; her destiny seems as bleak as that of animals in zoos, abattoirs, and research labs. As a child, she is the property of her parents, just as domesticated animals are the property of their human masters. The novel thus asks questions similar to those posed by Vercors: What is a human? What is an animal? How do we define the porous borderline between them?

Que font les rennes après Noël? is thus a double novel. The "you" voice has a childlike quality in the beginning, before the narrator grows up.

Readers almost feel as if they are in a fairy-tale world of Santa Claus, reindeer, toys, and family gatherings. The alternating "I" voices are based on Rosenthal's interviews with a veterinarian, a zookeeper, laboratory researchers, a butcher, a wolf trainer, and a stock farmer. She explains that

> the interview helps avoid popular misconceptions, and gets us into the thickness, complexity, and ambivalence of the real. This choice—letting the voices of people in the profession be heard—also helps show that fiction is always securely attached to the real. There is no gap separating them: there is some fiction in the real, and vice versa. (Rosenthal, interview by Fiolof)

These adult voices shatter the little girl's fairy-tale world with the brutal, clinical naturalism (in the Zolian sense) of the animal professions.

Marginality and Animality

Little by little we come to understand that the girl narrator is indeed a misfit. She is disgusted by dolls and would much rather play Cowboys and Indians. She does not have many friends. The narrator's marginality is exemplified by her reactions to films she sees with her mother, the most important of which are *Rosemary's Baby* (1968), *King Kong* (1933), and *Cat People* (1942).

As a young girl, she is haunted by *Rosemary's Baby*. For some reason, she has always been told that her mother saw the film while pregnant with her. When she sees the film herself, she is disturbed by "the terrible anguish [her mother] must have experienced, expecting a baby that could be born a human or a beast" (Rosenthal, *Que font les rennes après Noël?* 16). Meanwhile, in alternating paragraphs, a wolf trainer is discussing strange beasts of another sort, feline hybrids bred in captivity—"tigons, leopons, pumapards" (13)—and commenting on their "mental troubles" (14). The little girl is obviously worried that she might also be a monstrous hybrid, a captive in her home. Later, she finds out that her birth could not have been affected by her mother's nightmares about *Rosemary's Baby*; she was born in 1965, and the film only appeared in 1968. But the psychological damage has been done: she wonders why her parents lied to her (34). *Rosemary's Baby* will always haunt her, and she will never have—or want to have—a child (176–77).

King Kong convinces the narrator that she is different from other girls. Sitting next to her mother at the movies, she doesn't dare ask if she should identify with Ann Darrow (played by Fay Wray), the boyfriend, or the gorilla. Finally, she realizes that she has nothing in common with perfect blonds, nor with their boyfriends. She identifies with the gorilla, who like her is uneasy in human society, unsure about whom to love.

Depicting "our fantasized relationship with animals: repugnance, desire, fear, and fascination all at once" (89), *King Kong* also brings attention to the dangers of humans altering the behavior of great apes. Contact with humans led to the spectacular demise of King Kong. In a less dramatic manner, the veterinary assistant declares that "if you want an orangutan to stay an orangutan, you interfere as little as possible, or else you humanize it" (88); "captivity has direct and irreversible consequences on animal behavior" (90).

Cat People is the story of beautiful Irena Dubrovna, a Serbian fashion designer living in New York, who falls in love with Oliver Reed, an engineer. They meet at the zoo, where Irena is sketching a black panther, pacing in his cage. After a short courtship, Irena and Oliver marry, despite Irena's conviction that she descends from survivors of the cat people, cursed devil worshippers and witches who were driven from her Serbian village in the sixteenth century. Irena's very practical husband does not believe the legend that she fears is true: that a cat woman will turn into a panther if aroused by love, anger, or jealousy, and kill the object of her passion. She thus refuses to make love with her husband, opening the door to a love triangle involving Oliver's coworker. Irena does metamorphose into a black panther, killing her psychiatrist, but sparing Oliver and Alice. Then, threatened with internment in a mental hospital, she walks to the zoo and ostensibly commits suicide, unlocking the cage of the panther, who kills her.

The narrator of *Que font les rennes après Noël?* is now about 18, and she describes *Cat People* as "a film that enlightens you once and for all on your sexuality, a black-and-white film, mysterious, dazzling, intriguing, and pathetic" (119). Once again, after identifying with the devil's spawn and a giant gorilla in the previous films, she sympathizes with the monstrous, antisocial character, Irena. We read in a paragraph narrated by a researcher inoculating lab animals with deadly diseases, that the animal must be well cared-for, "so that it calmly develops its pathology." And so our primary narrator "calmly develops [her] pathology" (133), which we can interpret as her sexual orientation or, more generally, what she repeatedly calls her "betrayal" or her "emancipation."

Cat People confirms the narrator's marginality. Even though she will complete her studies, get a responsible job, and marry, she will always feel stifled, out of her element, like an animal in a zoo. "You don't have any friends" (117), she writes. "You are contaminated" (131–32). "You feel like Irena Dubrovna, incapable of knowing who you are. You are caught in a trap" (139). Like Irena, she awaits her inevitable metamorphosis: "You are … with Irena; you think of her fear, her fear of becoming the predator of the man she loves" (161). The narrator will eventually begin a love affair with a woman and divorce her husband. She is more fortunate than Irena Dubrovna: her metamorphosis and emancipation will not be fatal. On the contrary, her lesbian affairs bring her the frenetic pleasure she could never share with her husband: "Emancipation is coming in ways you had never imagined" (198).

In the last few pages (206–11), the second- and first-person narrators finally meet. "You" visits "I" in his butcher's shop; he is eager to show her the calf he will kill for Christmas dinner. The lessons she learns from him confirm that she has, after much doubt, made the correct choices in her life. The highest quality beef comes from cows who have not had calves; females are tastier than males; veal tastes better if the calf has not been in constant company with its mother; after the animal is butchered, the meat must "relax" for some time to improve the taste. "You," always a lover of animals, is content that cows have blessed her life decisions: not to have a baby, to prefer women to men, to have become independent from her mother, and to have finally learned how to relax. She is especially happy to learn that farm families prefer to eat their own cows rather than animals they don't know. "We eat with more appetite and pleasure the ones we love" (210). "You," like all humans, is an animal, and like Irena Dubrovna, she has been following her instincts. At the end of the novel, she is living her own life instead of the life her mother wanted for her: "You choose to enter into your own body and stay there forever. You choose to betray your mother so as not to betray yourself. You awaken" (210).

The double narration of *Que font les rennes après Noël?* illustrates in a striking manner the unstable boundary between humans and animals. Again, Mai employs the term "disconcerting" to describe how the novel "deflate[s] distinctions that anthropocentrism has erected between animals and humans, making them eerily alike while leaving them their specificity" (58). It is this unsteadiness of the human-animal continuum that Rosenthal wants to explore:

> What interested me here was, among other things, the question of the borders between man and animal, instinct and reason, nature and culture, borders which we like to pretend are clear, strict, and neat. In fact, when we begin to look at the animal world in detail, we see that these distinctions and oppositions are convenient, but they are not really clear at all. And when these distinctions become blurred, all our reference points fail. Perhaps animality unsettles our humanity. This is what fascinates me about the animal question. (interview by Fiolof)

It is through the interlacement of the primary narrator and the five secondary narrators—a wolf trainer, a zookeeper, a researcher, a stock farmer, and a butcher—that Rosenthal explores important problems in the human-animal relationship.

The Wolf Trainer

In her excellent review of the novel, Francine de Martinoir remarks that

> the parallel lives of the little girl and animals are first of all characterized by confinement. Animals are prisoners of zoos, cumbersome rules and decrees, breeding farms and slaughter-houses; as for the girl, she is trapped in networks of codes imposed on her: language, decorum, and customs that she figures out very early to be the conditions of social integration. (n. pag.)

Indeed, "confinement" is a term that applies to animals in several ways. In grammatical terms, animals are confined to the objective case, as is nature in general. Despite progress in French civil law,[1] animals are not legal subjects. Confinement is the opposite of liberation. The narrator

---

1 See the discussion above in the Introduction concerning the law of January 2015, recognizing animals as "sentient living beings."

is liberated by the end of the novel, but the animals are not, despite decades of effort from advocates like Peter Singer.

A wolf trainer is the novel's opening secondary narrator. Mocking the complicated laws governing interactions between humans and wild animals, he states that before being qualified to legally train an animal, "one must consult the laws, codes, decrees, orders" that distinguish the various species, protected or not, endangered or not, dangerous or not (Rosenthal, *Que font les rennes après Noël?* 15). He then reflects on what it means to love an animal. Could humans love animals without the zoos that make it possible to approach them? Can we love an animal that exists only in our imagination? He concludes that everyone loves animals except the professionals who work with them: "It's only those who use them, live from them, raise them, capture them, sell them, hunt them, kill them, who don't speak about love. Love, in the case of animals, is a luxury" (17).

As we have seen, the primary narrator has a conflictual relationship with her mother: she loves her but realizes that eventually she must seek independence. In turn, the wolf trainer stresses the importance of minimizing the time a young animal spends with its mother: "Every trainer starts his career by separating newborns from their mother" (49). Perhaps in order to ease his conscience, he wonders if "independence" might be a more accurate term than "abandonment" when referring to the experience of the newborns. In any case, he believes that, regarding the capture of wild animals, the law is on his side. The property of no one, wild animals fall under the law of the first occupant, a law of "natural reason," according to the ancient Code of Justinian.[2]

The wolf trainer explains how the French are planning to reintroduce wolves to the cities they once terrorized.[3] Some wolf habitats will be built around old castles, with the wolves safely contained in what used

---

[2] As we saw in Chapter 4, Rousseau, in Book I, ch. 9 of the *Social Contract*, contrasted the cruelty of the law of the strongest with the legitimacy of the right of the first occupant. According to the laws of Justinian I (Byzantine emperor from 527 to 565), "[w]ild animals, birds, and fish, that is to say all the creatures which the land, the sea, and the sky produce, as soon as they are caught by any one become at once the property of their captor by the law of nations; for natural reason admits the title of the first occupant to that which previously had no owner" (*Humanistic Texts* n. pag.).
[3] Joseph Mai explains that Rosenthal's novel began as a text she was commissioned to write for the opening of a wolf installation in Nantes.

to be moats. The narrator ironically states that "housing wolves in the city and in castles reminds us of our history" (32). Obviously, this project is for humans, and does nothing to benefit wolves. Wildness will be bred out of the wolves so they will not threaten visitors. The wolves will be specimens not found in nature: sterilized and transformed from predators into scavengers, dining on vitamin-stuffed hamburger meat rather than live prey. They will be microchipped, and under constant video surveillance.

In order to demonstrate differing viewpoints regarding the relationship between wolves and humans, Rosenthal constantly plays on the ancient "man is wolf to man" maxim (*homo homini lupus est*), first credited to the Roman comic writer Plautus, early in the second century BC. The adage suggests that humans are their own worst enemies, victims of their own aggressiveness and lack of scruples, but Rosenthal turns it inside out. To show how we must protect wolves from themselves, the wolf trainer says: "The wolf is the enemy of the wolf" (34). After "proving" that wolves are better off in captivity than in the wild, he declares: "Man is not the enemy of the wolf" (36). Finally, this world of wolf commercialization proves that wolves are mere merchandise, of which the human is "master and possessor" (52). When all is said and done, animals do not really count: "Man is man for man" (48).

The Zookeeper

The theme of confinement also dominates the discourse of the zookeeper. After he describes the Vincennes Zoo in Paris, one of the oldest in Europe,[4] the little girl realizes that "The first time you saw a wild animal, it was an animal in captivity" (65). She finds out that reindeer are often captives, too, moved to snowless climates far from

---

4 The Vincennes Zoo opened in 1934. It was closed for extensive renovations between 2008 and 2014, and now features five different biozones. The zoo thus presents animals in as close to their natural environment as possible, unlike the small Ménagerie du Jardin des Plantes (open since 1794). For a "factional" treatment of the Ménagerie, see Stéphane Audeguy's *Histoire du lion Personne* (Seuil, 2016), which traces the epic journey of a lion from Senegal to Paris during the late eighteenth century.

their natural habitat. The keeper stresses that zoo animals must always be visible and draws a parallel between zoos and Jeremy Bentham's panopticon prison, first proposed in 1787. Prisoners could at any moment be observed by a guard in a central tower, around which the cells were built in a circle. Lighting would ensure that the guard could see the prisoners without being seen by them. Thus, they always knew that the guard might be watching them, but never knew if he actually was. Foucault devotes a chapter of *Discipline and Punish* to "Panopticism," and summarizes its function as follows:

> Hence the major effect of the Panopticon: to induce in the inmate a state of conscious and permanent visibility that assures the automatic functioning of power. So to arrange things that the surveillance is permanent in its effects, even if it is discontinuous in its action; that the perfection of power should tend to render its actual exercise unnecessary ... . It is an important mechanism, for it automatizes and disindividualizes power. Power has its principle not so much in a person as in a certain concerted distribution of bodies, surfaces, lights, gazes. (201–02)

The effect of Rosenthal's comparison of security systems in zoos to the panopticon is disturbing. The panopticon guard sees without being seen, much like the surveillance cameras that proliferate in public places today. The prisoner is depersonalized; he has no privacy, and no human face to put on the guard. If zoo animals cannot be depersonalized, they are certainly de-animalized, constantly under human observation through microchipping and video technology. Traditional zoos have no hidden corners to which the animals can escape, since visitors become annoyed if they cannot see them. Critiquing this lack of privacy, Rosenthal quotes verbatim Foucault's notion of panoptic "permanent visibility": "The spectacle and the necessity to attract the public required permanent visibility. The principal actors didn't even have the right to get away for a moment of privacy, alone by themselves" (Rosenthal, *Que font les rennes après Noël?* 71). And animals do need privacy, as the British naturalist David Attenborough made clear to the *Guardian*, saying that an escape attempt of a gorilla from a London zoo was "hardly surprising": "Sometimes visitors to zoos are not respectful and they start shrieking or waving their arms in order to get the poor gorilla to do something. They are not just animals. They are related to us. They value their privacy. Just imagine what it's like to be there" (Attenborough n. pag.). And Rosenthal's narrator does just that. Like a zoo animal, she feels like she is constantly being watched by her parents, and she especially resents her father's "repeated incursions" (*Que font les rennes après Noël?* 70) into her room.

Animal philosophers, of course, remember Jeremy Bentham (1748–1832) for much more than his rather sinister panopticon. Rosenthal mentions the major contribution made to animal ethics by the founder of utilitarianism, found in a footnote in chapter 17 of *An Introduction to the Principles of Morals and Legislation* (1789), in which he compares cruelty towards animals to slavery:

> The French have already discovered that the blackness of the skin is no reason why a human being should be abandoned without redress to the whims of a tormentor. Perhaps it will some day be recognised that the number of legs, the hairiness of the skin, or the possession of a tail, are equally insufficient reasons for abandoning to the same fate a creature that can *feel*? What else could be used to draw the line? Is it the faculty of reason or the possession of language? But a full-grown horse or dog is incomparably more rational and conversable than an infant of a day, or a week, or even a month old. Even if that were not so, what difference would that make? The question is not *Can they reason?* or *Can they talk?* but *Can they suffer?* (143–44; emphasis original)

Bentham's argument contradicts long-held views on animals in the Christian and Cartesian traditions, in which animals, lacking the ability to reason or speak, were not considered to have a conscience. Christians believed that evil and suffering are our lot bequeathed by Adam and Eve's original sin. But why would a good God let innocent animals suffer? Peter Singer—evoking the writings of Descartes's disciple Pierre Bayle (1647–1706)—suggests that Descartes found a convenient answer to this conundrum by declaring that in fact animals do not suffer, since they do not possess consciousness (that is, "mind," or "cogito"), as do humans, whose suffering is a punishment for Adam and Eve's transgression ("Les animaux libérés" 24–25). Discussions of animal ethics can be found in Greek and Roman antiquity (Singer references Plutarch and Porphyry), but during 16 centuries of Christianity the subject was not broached until Montaigne finally broke the silence, followed by the Enlightenment thinker Hume, and later Bentham.

Singer summarizes the Western attitude towards animals as follows: "It was as if, with the Christianization of Europe, a deafening silence had surrounded the question of animal ethics in the West, while in the East, in part because of its Buddhist tradition, thinking on this subject flourished" (31).[5] The phrase "deafening silence" is well-chosen, evoking the mutism of animals that since time immemorial has been a major reason to consider them inferior to humans. Like Montaigne, Hume, and Bentham, and contemporary philosophers like Singer and Élisabeth de Fontenay, author of *Le Silence des bêtes*, Rosenthal seeks to reverse this injustice. For far too long animals have been victimized by a "silence, a suffering long accepted in the name of a facile Cartesianism, whereas today, the concepts of 'animal-machines' and absolute separation between body and thought seem singularly simplistic" (Martinoir n. pag.).

What becomes evident from the zookeeper's monologue is the "absurdity" of the existence of animals in captivity (Rosenthal, *Que font les rennes après Noël?* 81). In the wild, animals are constantly active, searching for food, defending themselves, and hiding from predators. In a zoo, their life has no objectives, activity is reduced to near zero: "A bear that usually spends eight hours per day looking for food finishes its dinner in ten minutes" (79). So, in addition to lack of privacy, zoo animals suffer from boredom. Some pace eternally, like the black panther in *Cat People*. Other symptoms of what is now called "zoochosis," include rocking (apes), overgrooming and self-mutilation (apes, bears, parrots, and felines), coprophilia and coprophagia (primates) ("Zoochosis" n. pag.). The symptoms of Rosenthal's narrator are not as dramatic but, like a teenage Baudelaire, she does suffer from the monstrousness of boredom,[6] especially the days she is not in school. She declares that "ennui is worse than anything, worse than death" (*Que font les rennes après Noël?* 80). To pass the time, she watches films about animals in the wild, which seem to legitimize her nascent feeling that she will never conform to accepted social and sexual standards: "Males do not necessarily fight over mounting the female; females don't necessarily

---

5 For further analysis of Bentham and animal ethics, see Peter Singer, "All Animals are Equal," and Tristan Garcia, *Nous, animaux et humains. Actualité de Jeremy Bentham*.
6 Ennui is the "refined monster" of the prologue to *Les Fleurs du mal*, "Au lecteur" ("To the Reader").

fight over choosing the male; males are not always dominant; females aren't always dominated" (75). One documentary in particular, by Frédéric Rossif, affects her profoundly. She does not name the film, but it is undoubtedly Rossif's masterpiece from 1976, *La Fête Sauvage* (*The Wild Nation*). It is through this documentary that she not only discovers sex, but also its close association with death. Eros and Thanatos are as inseparable in the wild kingdom as they are in the realm of the human:[7]

> You learned about killing and copulating at the same time, and for the first time you saw the actions, the movements, the cries, the rhythms. Desire and death were exposed in front of you before you could possibly analyze and decipher the fantastic and lasting effect of these images on your unconscious. Your mother was truly sorry. (77)[8]

The zookeeper speaks of the importance of captive animals "imprinting" on their human handlers, that is, habituating the young animal to the presence of humans. Imprinted animals become artifacts fashioned by humans and can lose their natural instincts. For example, a female orangutan may have to be aided by "educational" films to relearn how to raise her baby. Imprinted animals have little chance of surviving in the wild, so they cannot be returned to their natural environment. However, they are prized by unscrupulous hunting reserves, because their trusting nature makes them less wary of humans, and easier to kill (101–02). Zoos may save some species from extinction, but they significantly change the animals. "Living animals will soon be museum pieces" (94).

The narrator is going through the imprinting experience with her parents. She alternates between rebelling against them and accepting their will, which she finally does, for example, by leaving her bedroom door open and relinquishing all privacy. She fails miserably in attempts to kiss her new boyfriend, because, like a zoo animal, she has lost the

---

[7] Gilbert Durand quotes the psychoanalyst Marie Bonaparte, who illustrates the inseparability of sex and death by saying that "one of the most constant features of Eros is that he drags his brother Thanatos along behind him" (Durand 189).

[8] About his documentary, Rossif says: "It's a film, it's a dream; let's take a long journey through thousands of years of our existence, to see again how animals express the fundamental drives of love, play, death, and dream" (Bitoun n. pag.).

instincts of her species. She abandons her true nature in order to make peace with her parents, finally admitting that "you are imprinted" (97).

The zookeeper spends a considerable amount of time describing methods of euthanasia: how to ensure that the "gentle death" (113) is indeed gentle. Carbon dioxide or carbon monoxide—released into a small gas chamber[9]—are his preferred methods for smaller animals. In "Les animaux libérés," Peter Singer states that euthanasia is the only area in which animals are treated more fairly than humans (27–28). Animal euthanasia is totally accepted, whereas human euthanasia rarely is, due to our supposedly sacrosanct nature. Rosenthal broaches this sensitive subject indirectly. The zookeeper's descriptions of euthanasia methods alternate with the primary narrator's worries about her boyfriend, a foreigner who does not speak French well, and whom she hides from her parents. The boyfriend, known only as "the young man whom you love" (107, 109, 113, 114), is, like the narrator, a marginal character: he lives far from his family, does not do well in school, and eventually abandons his studies. The narrator's descriptions of the young man are interspersed with images of hunting: he thus resembles an "exotic" (109) wild animal that she yearns to capture. Finally, she learns that he has hung himself. The reader, weaving through Rosenthal's double narrative structure, is left to wonder if this man's suicide is for her a form of euthanasia.

The Researcher

The theme of contamination dominates this section. The secondary narrator is a medical researcher who conducts experiments on various species of animals, infecting them with diseases in the hope of finding a cure. Thus, the animals are deliberately contaminated. Yet contamination then becomes the greatest threat to the success of the

---

9 The zookeeper is quick to add that the term "gas chamber" is not used, "because it's nothing, it's just a box where we put the rats and when it's ready we hook up the pipe, open the gas, count to 15; we wait a bit, nothing's moving, it's done, we empty them out" (Rosenthal, *Que font les rennes après Noël?* 115). The unfortunate association of the gas chamber and rats in the zookeeper's discourse recalls the identification of Jews and rats in Nazi propaganda, as we will see later in this chapter.

experiments. Infecting animals with Parkinson's or multiple sclerosis "doesn't mean that we mistreat animals. We perform surgeries under exactly the same conditions as human surgeries; ... we give them analgesics and antibiotics; we pay close attention to the materials we use because, in order to obtain good scientific results, the animal must be maintained in good condition, it must wake up gradually, it must not suffer, it must not get an infection" (133).

There are four types of laboratories, rated according to the level of the pathogen given to the animals. Group 4 contains the most dangerous biological agents, and these labs must especially be protected from contamination. According to the researcher, "anthropomorphic projection" (130) must be avoided; a strict, impassable boundary between humans and animals must be respected: "To successfully protect against the dangers of contamination created by inoculating laboratory animals with serious illnesses, one must be certain that the mental and psychological barrier between men and beasts are not crossed" (132). The primary narrator is, however, crossing this boundary, like the HIV virus that passes from chimpanzees to humans (136), or like Irena in *Cat People*, who feels more and more contaminated by the feline curse of her village. The narrator repeats twice: "You are contaminated" (131, 132). Like a laboratory animal, she suffers: "You are dazed, stunned, inattentive, distracted, absent, deaf, and blind. You are forgetting yourself" (132).

Rosenthal continues to discuss euthanasia in this part of the novel. We may give an animal a horrible disease, like liver cancer, rationalizes the researcher, but "on the other hand, we can give it a gentle death" (162), referring to the etymological meaning of euthanasia (*eu* + *thanatos*). The researcher echoes the sentiments of Peter Singer, quoted above, asserting that euthanasia is the one area where animals are luckier than humans:

> Animals, even if they don't express their wish for it, can benefit from euthanasia. Humans, on the other hand, even if they do express their wish for it, never have the right to such a treatment. So for a human to ask for euthanasia is useless; it's better to be quiet, like an animal. Keeping the border between humans and animals intact leads to terrible contradictions. (162)

Again, the researcher stresses that successful experimentation on animals depends on refusing to question the human-animal borderline, and the rigidity of the subject-object divide. This is exactly what Rosenthal and animal rights philosophers are doing.

The researcher goes on to discuss methods of animal euthanasia with which he is familiar: inhalants (halothane, for example), cerebral rupture, decapitation by "specially conceived guillotines" (164), blow to the head (used for small and young animals), and intravenous anesthetic (using barbiturates like sodium pentobarbital). Despite his defense of "gentle death," he is bothered by its pervasive use. Animals can be euthanized on the spot if they are hurt, psychologically or physically, or even because of transportation delays or other transportation problems (163). He cannot—despite his dedication to science—put an animal to death without regret: "The killer spends his time consoling himself for killing" (164).

Finally, Rosenthal discusses the female narrator's Oedipus complex. Normally, one would expect a young girl to go through what Jung called the Electra complex, desire for the father coupled with hatred for the rival mother. Earlier in the novel, however, she experiences the kinds of feelings that Freud observed in young boys: desire for the mother and hatred for the father, perceived as a rival: "You recognize the mother in your mother, in your father the rival and the enemy" (92). Once more, the girl who prefers cowboys to dolls shows herself to be atypical. At this point in the novel, obsessed by her love for animals and the film *Cat People*, she feels like Irena Dubrovna, unable to distinguish between her human desire and her animal desire (164). Her Oedipal musings mirror one of the researcher's anecdotes that makes us wonder if chickens read Sophocles and Freud. He speaks of the importance of "imprinting," which in the wild means that a hatchling must immediately learn to follow its mother, "or else it will be killed and eaten by birds of prey or foxes" (158). Chicks in captivity, however, are taught to follow colored balls rather than their mother. So male chicks, upon reaching adulthood, will try to copulate with colored balls rather than another bird. "Based on that, declares the researcher, eminent psychologists have stated that similar behavior could be observed in men who sometimes attempt to copulate, not exactly with their mother, but with a woman who resembles her" (159).

As for the narrator, she wonders why the story says nothing about female chicks in the wild, who must learn to follow their mother just as males do. And as much as she longs to escape the control of her mother, she does not think that colored balls will do the trick: "In spite of your desire to leave the family fold, learning to follow rolling balls instead of your mother doesn't seem to be an experiment worth trying. You must find another way to separate from your mother" (159).

The Stock Farmer and the Butcher

In the last 40 pages of the novel, the female narrator's voice alternates with those of a farmer who raises chickens and pigs, and then a butcher who has also worked in an abattoir. The controversial nature of the meat industry is thus front and center. Rosenthal plays on the term *élevage* ("raising" or "breeding," for both animals and humans). The female narrator claims that she is "well-bred" ("bien élevée," 172, 180), and wishes to remain so; at present she has not yet metamorphosed into the person who will betray both her mother and her husband. Reflections on good and bad breeding continue. We learn that French poultry breeders have four possible methods for raising their birds: battery cages[10] (code 3); indoors (code 2); free range (code 1); organic (code 0). The narrator remarks that the code numbers are inversely proportional to the well-being of the animals, while being proportional to the profitability of the enterprise. And the code leaves no room for better treatment of the birds (supposing that code -1 or -2 are not possible); however, the possibility of a code 4 or 5 leads one to wonder if even worse methods than battery cages might be invented someday.

A remark on the famous virility of roosters, who should have seven or eight hens lest he wear them out, leads the narrator to think about her husband: "You don't like the violence of his desire, you don't like how it transforms him, you feel like you are making love with someone else" (174–75). Once again, Rosenthal illustrates the proximity of

---

10   Although the European Union banned battery cages for laying hens in 2012, the practice still continues. In January 2017 *Le Monde* reported that, in part due to videos exposing the terrible living conditions for hens in battery cages, large egg distributors, hotels, and restaurants are demanding that the cages be outlawed. This would have an enormous impact on French agriculture, the leading producer of eggs in Europe. According to *Le Monde*, "68 percent of the 47 million laying hens are today raised in cages, versus 25 percent in buildings with outdoor access, and 7 percent indoors without outdoor access" (Garric n. pag.). Battery cages are still legal in most of the United States.

violence and eroticism,[11] which the narrator learned from watching films like *Cat People* and *The Wild Nation*. She doesn't like the transformation of her husband when he becomes her lover, yet she awaits her own metamorphosis: "you are not violent, you are not passionate, you are not transformed. Your metamorphosis has not yet occurred" (175).

The last secondary narrator is the most unsettling. He is a butcher who has also worked in an abattoir. He declares that he "wanted to be a butcher because I felt like killing. Maybe that scared me at first, but at the same time I liked the idea; I wanted to become a butcher so I could kill animals" (197).

The butcher complains about "traceability" rules, by which the origin of meat must be known: "We don't need that, and if they continue with their damned regulations, we'll be out of a job" (203). He seems a bit unsure of the efficacy of his abattoir, because he feels the necessity to repeat three times that, usually, everything works fine (192, 193, 195). Yet he is proud of his work, because "it's physical work; it takes a man to kill" (206). Upon hearing that, the narrator is relieved to know that men, not women, are the ones who do the killing in the abattoir.

During these last few pages, the narrator finally leaves her husband and, as I discussed earlier, is liberated. Her emancipation is influenced by her continual identification with animals, which peaks during her discussions with the butcher, when she realizes how much she has in common with his calves and cows. This, along with earlier remarks that seem to identify the narrator as descended from German Jews, leads us to ponder the connection between the modern meat industry and the Holocaust.

---

11 In an earlier novel, *Puisque nous sommes vivants* (Because We Live), sex and death are tragically and inextricably intertwined: Rosenthal uses "a pitiless expression to explain the amatory and erotic emancipation of her heroine and narrator. ... To describe the mixture of independence and alienation that upsets her, she says that she approaches her desire 'like an animal to the abattoir'" (Brendlé 17). One could say that the narrator of *Que font les rennes après Noël?* has similar feelings about heterosexual relations.

140   *Ecocritics and Ecoskeptics*

Eternal Treblinka

We have seen how the narration of *Que font les rennes après Noël?* alternates between the angst-ridden female protagonist and several men who work in various capacities with animals: in zoos, research laboratories, farms, butcher shops, and slaughterhouses. One effect of the multiple narrators is to bring into focus the damage that the "law of the strongest" does to all creatures, animal and human. Rosenthal would seem to concur with Élisabeth de Fontenay and Jacques Derrida (see Chapter 4 above) that there is indeed a link between the human tragedy of the Holocaust and the animal tragedy of the abattoir.

Early in the novel, the narrator, still a young girl, recounts how her father repeatedly tells her the story of "The Pied Piper of Hamelin," a medieval German tale about a piper who, playing his magical music, lures all the rats of the city into the river, where they drown. Only later does she learn the dark conclusion of the story, never mentioned by her father: When the townspeople refuse to pay the piper for his services, he enacts revenge by luring about one hundred children out of town in the same manner, and they are never seen again. Even before she learns the end of the story, her father's telling of "The Pied Piper" makes the narrator feels uneasy: "Maybe it's because, at the end of the tale, he always sings a little rhyme in German, and you don't understand a word. Maybe it's because you wonder why your father speaks German. Maybe, finally, because part of the story is missing" (31).

After hinting that the family may have German origins, the narrator reveals that they are also Jewish, and probably Polish. In a comical scene, she describes her "calm and extremely discreet" grandmother, who manifests uncharacteristic violence as, squirting blood on the walls, she hammers to death live carps swimming in the bathtub. She is about to prepare her Polish specialty, "that bland and slightly sweet dish that you detest, and that is called, with a mixture of disgust and community pride, 'Jewish carp' [*la carpe à la juive*]" (39).[12] The family's

---

12   Even though the grandmother does not appear to be a talented cook, devotees of Marcel Proust will see a resemblance between her and Françoise, Aunt Léonie's faithful, devoted cook. In a scene from *Combray*, in which she is preparing one of her wonderful dinners, Marcel, like Rosenthal's narrator, learns that cooking can bring out one's hidden savagery:

Jewish heritage is confirmed a few pages later, when the narrator states that "your mother decided that the integration of Jewish families to the French nation starts with the celebration of Christmas" (41). An interviewer in *Le Monde des Livres* observes that the narrator's family is based on the author's actual family. Commenting on the presence of death in Rosenthal's novels, in part due to the suicide of an older sister, he writes, quoting Rosenthal:

> There are other dead people too, less well-known, further in the past. From her father's family, who didn't want to leave Nazi Germany in 1933: "They were Polish. They were deported as foreign Jews to the Warsaw ghetto, then to Auschwitz. I only heard bits and pieces of their story." (Houssin n. pag.)

In retrospect, "The Pied Piper" would be a disquieting tale for Polish Jews who survived the Holocaust. Researchers contend that there is probably some truth to the legend and have theorized that the piper might personify the *danse macabre* (dance of death), or perhaps represent a recruiter for a Children's Crusade. A leading theory, however, proposed by Jürgen Udolph, is that the disappearance of the children of Hamelin symbolizes a very real emigration that was taking place at the time, from Germany eastward towards Poland:

> [T]he most widely accepted theory links the loss of the children to a 13th century migration from the Hamelin area eastwards.
>
> Professor Juergen Udolph speculates that, with new lands to settle, feudal barons sent a brightly coloured "recruiter" into Hamelin with a pipe and a drum to draw the young away.
>
> "He said—You have a new chance in a new land. Please, come with me."

> I saw her in the scullery which opened on to the back yard, in the process of killing a chicken which, by its desperate and quite natural resistance, accompanied by Françoise, beside herself with rage as she attempted to slit its throat beneath the ear, with shrill cries of "Filthy creature! Filthy creature!," made the saintly meekness and unction of our servant rather less prominent than it would do, next day at dinner, when it made its appearance in a skin gold-embroidered like a chasuble, and its precious juice was poured out drop by drop as from a pyx. When it was dead Françoise mopped up its streaming blood, which did not, however, drown her rancour, for she gave vent to another burst of rage, and, gazing down at the carcass of her enemy, uttered a final "Filthy creature!" (Proust 132)

> Whatever the truth of the story, experts in myth and fairytale believe it reflects our preoccupation with the fear of losing children—whether to a stranger, or to death. (Pearson n. pag.)

The silence of the narrator's father regarding the seduction of Hamelin's children by the Pied Piper could indicate his painful memory of other Jewish children like him in Poland of the 1930s, marched off to the death camps never to return. One of the most horrific aspects of the Holocaust was, of course, the number of victims who were children.[13] Wolfgang Mieder reports that in both literary and cultural texts, Hitler "to this day is referred to as an evil Pied Piper" (19). For example, in 1941, Bertolt Brecht, from the safety of exile, published "The True Story About the Pied Piper of Hamelin," a poem that depicts Hitler as a piper who initially enthralls the German people. Each stanza ends with a variation of "He piped nicely. He piped long. It was a marvelous song" (qtd. in Mieder 104–05). But as "he tries to deceive people, he is driven to madness by his own music (power), leading everybody back to Hamelin, his death, and the end of Germany's pact with the devil" (Mieder 102). Mieder also reprints a 1934 British anti-Nazi caricature entitled "The Crazy Piper," which portrays Hitler as a piper leading out of a medieval town a procession of glassy-eyed children shouting *Heil! Heil! Heil!*.

Another troubling aspect of the Pied Piper story as it relates to the Holocaust is the specter of rats. Comparing Jews to rats was common in Nazi propaganda, most notoriously in the 1940 film *Der Ewige Jude (The Eternal Jew)*,[14] produced by Minister of Propaganda Joseph Goebbels and filmed in the Jewish ghettos of Nazi-occupied Poland. In *The Eternal Jew*,

> Jews are equated with rats—a menace of restless parasites that

---

13 Non-Jewish children were victims as well. The military pageantry of the Third Reich, with its uniforms, flags, light shows, and fanfares, was extremely attractive to them. This phenomenon is excruciatingly illustrated by Michel Tournier in *The Ogre* which, inspired by Goethe's haunting poem "The Erl-King," depicts how *Jungmänner* were seduced by the ogre that was Nazism into joining *Napolas*, or elite Nazi training schools, where they mostly ended up as cannon fodder for Allied artillery.
14 More recently, in a chilling scene at the beginning of the 2009 film *Inglourious Basterds*, the SS Colonel Landa compares Jews hiding in the basement of a French farmhouse to rats.

spread disease and bring ruin. ... The film argues that Jews are criminals; that they have no soul; that they are different in every way; that killing them is not a crime, but a necessity—just as killing rats is a necessity to preserve health and cleanliness. (Barsam 205)[15]

While the camera focuses on swarms of rats, a narrator explains:

Wherever rats appear they bring ruin, by destroying mankind's goods and foodstuffs. In this way, they spread disease, plague, leprosy, typhoid fever, cholera, dysentery, and so on. They are cunning, cowardly, and cruel, and are found mostly in large packs. Among the animals, they represent the rudiment of an insidious and underground destruction, just like the Jews among human beings.[16] (D. L. Smith 139)

Charles Patterson dedicates *Eternal Treblinka: Our Treatment of Animals and the Holocaust* to Isaac Bashevis Singer, and opens his essay with this epigraph from the Jewish-American Nobel Laureate:

They have convinced themselves that man, the worst transgressor of all the species, is the crown of creation. All other creatures were created merely to provide him with food, pelts, to be

---

15 The United States was not above using similar propaganda tactics during World War II. In 1943 *Time* published an aircraft advertisement depicting an American fighter pilot as the "Pied Piper of the Pacific," who "destroys the [Japanese] rats which threatened to overrun civilization" (Mieder 20).

16 Rats are not the only animals to be compared to Jews in anti-Semitic literature. Charles Patterson traces the "practice of vilifying Jews as animals" (44) back to Christian writers of the fourth century. He writes that the Nazis' "favorite epithets were 'pig,' 'Jew-pig,' 'swine,' and *Saujuden* ('Jewish swine')" (46–47). I have described elsewhere (see J. Krell, *The Ogre's Progress* 45–46) the research of Gérard Macé, who, in *Le Goût de l'homme* (The Taste of Man), describes the assimilation of Jews to pigs, and to cannibalism as well, in the writings of the Roman poet Juvenal. He also cites examples from the Gospels and European folktales in which Jews and pigs are quite interchangeable. He concludes his essay on the subject with this comment on the deep roots of the Holocaust in both Christianity and classical polytheism: "[N]azism was not an accident of history: For the murder—so well prepared—to be accomplished on such a large scale, an insanity had to assume unknowingly two thousand years of Christianity, and at the same time detach itself from it to identify with the pagan world" (Macé 68–69).

tormented, exterminated. In relation to them, all people are Nazis; for the animals it is an eternal Treblinka. (vii)

As Hannah Arendt denounced the "law of the strongest"—policies that led to imperialism, racism, the domination of the poor and weak, and totalitarianism (see Chapter 4 above)—so Patterson decries "the great divide between man and other animals and man's might-makes-right attitude toward others—what Montaigne called human arrogance and Freud called human megalomania" (3–4). The development of language by humans allowed them—as Élisabeth de Fontenay has shown—"to exploit the earth's voiceless inhabitants" (6). The domestication and exploitation of animals "opened the door to similar ways of treating other human beings, thus paving the way for such atrocities as human slavery and the Holocaust" (12).

Patterson, quoting the artist Judy Chicago, maintains that it is the work of "processing" that links the Holocaust to our slaughtering of animals for food: "When she visited Auschwitz and saw a scale model of one of the four crematoria, she realized 'they were actually giant processing plants—except that instead of processing pigs they processed people who had been defined as pigs'" (49). And America played its role in the Holocaust. Patterson states that, after "meatpackers introduced the conveyor belt to increase the speed and efficiency of the nation's first mass-production industry" (57), "assembly-line slaughter crossed the Atlantic Ocean and found fertile soil in Nazi Germany" (53). He quotes the protagonist of J. M. Coetzee's novella *The Lives of Animals*, who states: "Chicago showed us the way; it was from the Chicago stockyards that the Nazis learned how to process bodies" (53; qtd. in Patterson 72). Patterson maintains that Henry Ford bears some responsibility for the brutal efficiency of death camps like Treblinka; Ford's "impact on the twentieth century began, metaphorically speaking, at an American slaughterhouse and ended at Auschwitz" (72). He explains that Ford's ideas for assembly line automobile production and division of labor were inspired by a visit to a Chicago slaughterhouse. Ford thus "made his own special contribution to the slaughter of people in Europe. Not only did he develop the assembly-line method the Germans used to kill Jews, but he launched a vicious anti-Semitic campaign" (73) in the United States, and thus earned the admiration of Adolf Hitler, who reportedly kept a life-sized portrait of Ford in his office (75).

Olivia Rosenthal's Que font les rennes après Noël? 145

References that Patterson makes to Austrian and German animal rights activists recall two secondary narrators in *Que font les rennes après Noël?*: the researcher and the butcher. The Austrian, Helmut Kaplan, agrees with Isaac Bashevis Singer that humans are Nazis to animals:

> If you don't believe it, then you should read reports of the experiments the Nazis carried out in their research labs on Jews, and then read reports on the experiments done today with animals. Then you'll lose your blindfold: the parallels are plain to see. Everything the Nazis did to Jews we are today practicing on animals. (qtd. in Patterson 221)

Kaplan's statement directly contradicts Rosenthal's researcher, who insists that the borderline between humans and animals must be strictly observed; this would belie any comparison between experiments on humans and experiments on animals. The researcher describes the horrible diseases he inflicts on animals, but says that he and his colleagues cannot empathize with them: "Scientific research requires a suspension of judgment" (Rosenthal, *Que font les rennes après Noël?* 154). One could argue that this suspension of judgment is akin to how the killers in the death camps anesthetized themselves to violence by denying the individuality of the prisoners they murdered. For Arendt this was "total domination"; for Camus, "abstraction" (see Chapter 4 above).

The German activist mentioned by Patterson, Christa Blanke, recounts the striking similarities between the transportation of animals to the slaughterhouse and of victims to the death camps. Blanke states: "Animals in transport go through tremendous suffering similar to what the Jews suffered when they were transported to the Nazi camps" (Patterson 223). Often prisoners were taken to concentration camps via the same infrastructure used to transport animals to the slaughterhouse: rounded up in cattle pens, transported in cattle cars along special slaughterhouse rail routes.[17] Blanke is struck by the Nazi

---

17 In *Balkan Ghosts*, Robert D. Kaplan tells of a grisly incident that took place on 22 January 1941, during the Romanian Holocaust. A Bucharest slaughterhouse was the site of the murder of 200 Jewish men, women, and children, perpetrated by the Legionnaires of the Archangel Michael:

> They made the victims, all Jews, strip naked in the freezing dark and get down on all fours on the conveyor ramp. Whining in terror, the Jews were driven through all the automated stages of slaughter. Blood gushing from decapitated and limbless torsos, the Legionnaires thrust each on a hook and

overtones that she hears in the language of the slaughterhouse, for example the division of the site into "pure" and "impure" zones (227). As Hannah Arendt noted that victims of the death camps were stripped of their individuality and killed by means of mechanized technology, so in the slaughterhouse "technical language depersonalizes victim and perpetrator—phrases like 'delivery of goods,' 'shipments,' 'special processing' of sick animals, 'procedures' of slaughtering, 'utilization' of hair, bones, skin" (228).

Rosenthal's butcher is characterized by this same lack of compassion, and a comparison to the SS officers in the death camps, described by Hannah Arendt, would not be far-fetched. We have already seen his disturbing reason for choosing a career in the abattoir and butcher shop: "I felt like killing" (Rosenthal, *Que font les rennes après Noël?* 197). He possesses a twisted sense of virility, when he claims that only a man can kill, and remembers with fondness the first time, at age 11, that he killed a pig: "He bled perfect" (198). He details each step in the killing process of the abattoir, passing from the "impure" to the "pure" zone, and admits: "I don't have a favorite job; I like them all" (201). He is enthusiastic about the efficiency of the process. If the first bullet doesn't kill the animal, a second shot is fired; the animal doesn't suffer, he claims. The assembly line chain is so fast-moving at his slaughterhouse that they could probably even kill more creatures than they already do: 400 per day, 58 per hour.

We close this chapter with a word of caution from Élisabeth de Fontenay regarding *Eternal Treblinka*. In Chapter 4 we noted her moving quotation from the end of *Le Silence des bêtes*, comparing the mutism of animals—at the root of their domination by humans—to the condition of prisoners as they stepped off the cattle cars at the death camps to the sounds of insults being hurled at them in a language they could not understand. And she is convinced that those who are cruel to animals will be cruel to humans: the quotation of Adorno—"after all, it's only an animal"—on this subject in the epigraph at the beginning of this chapter "has always kept vigil over [her] work" (Fontenay, "Les animaux considérés" 128). Yet this philosopher does have certain reservations

> stamped it: "fit for human consumption." The trunk of a five-year-old girl they hung upside down, "smeared with blood ... like a calf," according to an eyewitness the next morning. (xlvi)

I am grateful to Jack Hudson for this reference.

about *Eternal Treblinka*. She appreciates how Patterson has helped bring to light the horrible cruelties of the slaughterhouse process, and the direct connection between the assembly line process used in the Chicago stockyards and the one used in the death camps, as well as the influence of Henry Ford, whose virulent anti-Semitism cannot be denied: "So for Patterson there is not only analogy, but connection, between the deadly anti-Semitism and division of labor in the abattoirs" (164).

Fontenay, however, objects to Patterson's methodology. She is struck by the lack of a sense of history that many defenders of animal rights, including Patterson, display:

> I have many reservations, due to his lack of methodological precautions: the way he constructs an analogy between two vastly different time periods, one lasting for thousands of years, and one that is barely longer than four years; and the way he draws a parallel between a story of the battle to survive (hunting, stock raising, slaughter), and a story of pure racial hatred. (163)

The "means" of the abattoir and the Holocaust (transportation, killing) are undeniably similar. However, the "ends" are not:

> If we think about the question of the ends, which are that we raise and slaughter animals in order to eat them, then we must recognize that the comparison does not hold. For the goal of the Nazis was truly to achieve a radical elimination, which has nothing to do with satisfying a need for food and the stock-raising and slaughter that ensue. (165)

Part 3

Two Ecoskeptics:
The Humanist and the Humorist

In Globe we trust ... Liberty, Security, Prosperity.
—Jean-Christophe Rufin, *Globalia* 193

Liberty under a globe. iStock.com/Vadmary.

Chapter 6

Deep Ecology Gone Wrong: J.-C. Rufin's *Globalia* and *Le Parfum d'Adam*

> Let us therefore face the future with the salutary fear that keeps us vigilant and ready for battle, and not with the spineless and idle terror that afflicts and saps the heart.
>
> —Tocqueville, *Democracy in America*, vol. 2, part 4, ch. 7, p. 830

> There is no need to sympathize with democracies when they are faced with enemies. Enemies are their most precious allies.
>
> —Rufin, *La Dictature libérale* 282

Globalia

If one may call Jean-Christophe Rufin a "critic" of environmentalism, it is because his extraordinarily varied career as a neurologist, humanitarian, diplomat, and writer has given him the opportunity to view the topic in all its complexity. After finishing medical school, he began a humanitarian career that took him to trouble spots in South America, Africa, Asia, and Eastern Europe. He was an early member and then vice president of Doctors Without Borders (Médecins sans frontières), president of Action Against Hunger (Action contre la faim), and an administrator of the French Red Cross and Première Urgence. His diplomatic career took him to Senegal, where he was ambassador for three years. Author of many works of fiction and non-fiction, winner of numerous literary prizes, including the Prix Goncourt in 2001 for *Rouge Brésil* (*Brazil Red*), he was elected to the Académie française in 2008, becoming at the time its youngest member.

Globalia recounts the story of a dystopian future, when the earth is divided in two. Globalia is the sole national state, and the author makes it obvious that it is the United States gone terribly wrong: people speak *anglobal* (*anglais* + *global*), the currency is the *globar* (from "dollar"), and the national motto is written in English: "In Globe We Trust." The novel is a good example of what has come to be known as "ecotopian fiction." It describes an authoritarian country governed by ideals inspired by deep ecology, such as vegetarianism, the protection of forests and animals (trees are preserved because paper is no longer used; hunting is illegal, since human rights have been extended to animals), and zero population growth.[1] Standardization is enforced, difference is not tolerated in this immense monolithic state, covered by a series of domes which secure the borders and ensure perfect weather. Outside the domes are the savage "non-zones," home to warring tribes, mobsters, and terrorists, some real, some invented by the Globalian government, since every society—be it totalitarian or democratic—needs an outside source of fear, an enemy "other" to unite its citizens.[2]

This enemy will be Baïkal, the novel's protagonist. His very name—Baïkal is a Siberian lake, the oldest and deepest in the world—links him to nature, so it is not surprising that he is unhappy in the stifling atmosphere of Globalia. As punishment for attempting to escape to the other side of the globe surrounding Seattle, he is exiled in the non-zones to serve as a scapegoat, the photogenic face of terrorism, the "New Enemy" (Rufin, *Globalia* 304) of the people. Although he has absolutely no terroristic intentions, Baïkal is presented constantly as a terrorist leader on the ubiquitous Globalian video screens. In the

---

1 For more on the hypothetical link between environmentalism and tyranny, see the discussion of Luc Ferry's *The New Ecological Order* in the Introduction, and Iegor Gran's *L'Écologie en bas de chez moi* in Chapter 7, as well as my interview with Gran in the Appendix.
2 This is the thesis of Rufin's 1994 essay, *La Dictature libérale*, which we will study later in this chapter.

non-zones he befriends Fraiseur, whose given name is also his tribe's name, roughly translated as "machine operator." Like everyone in his tribe, Fraiseur wears a medal inscribed with the name of the urban paradise where the tribe's founder lived centuries ago: DETROIT. "It's the city, *the* city. *Our* city. It is the origin of all things" (220). The legendary ancestor was an automobile assembly line worker who over the centuries had been mythicized by his descendants into a sort of high priest of industry. Each morning, recounts Fraiseur, in this city near a lake as great as the sea, his forefather would enter a gigantic temple, dressed in a blue "ceremonial uniform" (221), to perform ritualistic gestures honoring the god whose name one must not pronounce: F-O-R-D.

Rust and Resistance in the Non-Zones

In Globalia, every 60 years the calendar starts over again. The government knows how dangerous the study of history can be, so the past must be forgotten: "a month seemed as long ago as a century" (221). The non-zones, however, are dotted with rusty remnants of our twentieth-century industrial society. Yet this rust is not merely junk. These ruins are undifferentiated from trees and stones in a hybrid nature[3] that serves as a remembrance of an idealized past, "fossils polished by time" (222). Among all this rust grows a resistance, fed by memories of better times, as the tribes of the non-zones plot a revolt against tyrannical Globalia.

"Material ecocriticism" (see Phillips and Sullivan) has shown that the study of "messy matter" (Phillips and Sullivan 445) like rust can shed light on the health of both economies and ecologies. One cannot understand humans' place in the environment without knowing something about nonhuman "actors" and "material processes" (446) in nature. Moreover, some ecocritics are calling attention to the value of materials heretofore considered waste: processes of decomposition and aging can be positive. In an article entitled "Waste Treatment," Laura Call describes how in biogeochemical cycles, "microbes constantly

---

3 Hybrid nature is a "nature shaped by man," a "result of the interaction between natural processes and human activities" (Larrère and Larrère, *Du bon usage* 258).

compose, decompose, and recompose all matter, so there is no physical waste. ... Materials that we might refer to as waste, from water bottles to bodies, are in fact resources that microbes use for their metabolic processes" (147).

Rust is not decomposition, but like decomposition, its connotation is largely negative. Rust is iron oxide, the compound that results when two elements, iron and oxygen, are exposed to moisture. Like oxygen, rust is an ambivalent substance, in both a real and metaphorical sense. The economic consequences of rust are disastrous; per one estimate, corrosion costs about $300 billion in damage each year in the United States alone (Kanegsberg n. pag.). A quick look at the *OED* reveals rust's negative metaphorical connotation: it may imply moral and physical decay, neglect, ruin, aging, impairment of the mind or body due to inactivity; it used to be synonymous with malice or rancor. In *Rust: The Longest War*, Jonathan Waldman writes that "[r]ust represents the disordering of the modern, and it reveals many of our vices: greed, pride, arrogance, impatience, and sloth. It reveals the potency of our foresight, the weakness of our hubris, our grasp of risk, and our understanding of the role we fill in the world" (10).

There is a positive side to rust, however. Growing up in Pittsburgh, I was quite excited when in 1971 the U.S. Steel tower was completed, and my father's engineering department could move in. He explained to me that the building—at the time the tallest between New York and Chicago—was coated with COR-TEN steel, a corrosion-resistant steel made right down the Monongahela River in Pittsburgh. COR-TEN provided what was essentially a protective coating of non-penetrating rust: as the building weathered, it slowly changed from a gleaming black skyscraper to a reddish rusty tower that would never need painting. Waldman recounts that the weathered steel unfortunately had unplanned consequences: nearby sidewalks and buildings became spotted with unsightly rust and had to be scrubbed. Still, the U.S. Steel tower was an architectural marvel in the heart of the rust belt that showcased a positive use of rust, and COR-TEN has shown its artistic value in the many outdoor sculptures that have been created from it.

As for oxygen, its ambivalence is quite fascinating, disconcerting even. Ozone (O_3) is invaluable in the upper atmosphere as a shield against the sun's ultraviolet rays, yet when found close to the earth—often in automobile emissions—it is a pollutant. Dioxygen (O_2) is vital to animal life as the element of respiration, but dangerous because of its combustibility. We cannot live without oxygen, and free radicals containing it are crucial to cell signaling in our bodies; yet these same free radicals might also speed the aging process, and contribute to diseases like Alzheimer's and Parkinson's, so we combat this nasty oxygen with "antioxidants" like vitamins A and C. Scientists call this the "oxygen paradox" (Butnariu n. pag.).

A fascinating literary example of the oxygen paradox can be found in the mystical philosophy of the early German romantic Novalis (1772–1801).[4] Novalis studied geology at a mining academy in Saxony and worked for a short time at the salt mines. Rocks, metals, and chemistry are linked in his peculiar conception of good and evil. Oxygen and respiration must have been constantly on his mind: his fiancée Sophie succumbed to tuberculosis at the age of 15, and he would die of the same disease at 28, four years later. For Novalis, God and the devil are linked in the process of oxidation:

> God is of infinitely compact metal—the most corporeal and the heaviest of all beings.
> Oxidation comes from the devil.
> Life is a sickness of spirit, an activity born to undergo *passio* [literally, "a passionate deed"].
> Annihilation of air establishes the Kingdom of God. (2: 820; qtd. in D. Krell, *The Tragic Absolute* 60)

God is thus the heaviest of heavy metals, the noblest of noble metals. Like platinum, silver, and gold, God does not corrode. Novalis takes the oxygen paradox from chemistry and applies it to poetry. He states here that oxidation is diabolical, causing sickness and death, yet it is only by the "annihilation" of oxygen that we may die and join God, the ultimate antioxidant. Elsewhere Novalis wrote that *life*—not sickness—is "phlogistical," "the process of oxidation and combustion," and that *illness* is "antiphlogistical," "that is, anything that inhibits oxidation" (2: 818–19; qtd. in D. Krell, *The Tragic Absolute* 66). His lungs ravaged by tuberculosis, Novalis maintains that "Life is strengthened by means of death" (2: 756; qtd. in D. Krell, *The Tragic*

---

4 I am grateful to David Farrell Krell for sharing his notes on oxidation from Novalis. He analyzes these strange passages in two essays on German idealism, *Contagion* and *The Tragic Absolute*.

Absolute 68). Humans are corrosive light metals, suffering beings, and only in golden death will the corrosion stop.

Following Novalis, we might venture to say that humans have more in common than we thought with metals, corrosion, and chemical elements. Globalia's non-zones exemplify our "natured," rather than "denatured" state. In a 2008 article on Rufin's novel, Stephanie Posthumus remarked that the harsh non-zone landscapes are apt illustrations of the relatively recent change in the way we perceive nature ("L'exception écologiste française" 450). Baïkal, exiled to the non-zones, is walking with Fraiseur, who has never left the non-zones, towards a city where h-e hopes that a mafioso will help him contact his girlfriend Kate back in Globalia. The desolate and violent non-zones, reminiscent of the *Mad Max* films, abound with rusty objects: tools, vehicles of all kinds, poles, cars and rails from ancient railways, oil tanks. Vegetation has sprung up in and around the rust:

> They passed by an industrial complex in ruins, built along a stream deep in a valley. Seen from afar, the site looked like a monstrous neglected garden. Weeds and trees had completely covered an ancient combine. Like gigantic pumpkins ripening silently in the sun, old round tanks, orange with rust, were strewn about. Here and there some train rails were still visible. (Rufin, *Globalia* 143)

This amalgam of the artificial and the natural found in the non-zones is repeated throughout the novel. As Baïkal and Fraiseur approach the city, they observe people sleeping in makeshift shelters, constructed from both "natural materials, like branches, tree trunks, and piles of rocks, as well as debris obviously created by humans: wooden panels, rusted pieces of metal, and tires" (222). Later, Baïkal enters the village of the Déchus (the fallen ones), the tribe that hopes to lead a revolt against Globalia. As a Globalian, he is struck by the appearance of the houses:

> extreme imbrications of natural materials and manufactured objects. ... The houses were imbroglios of cut branches, clay and straw, and shale stones pulled out of the ground. But mixed in were hammered metal surfaces made from beer cans or oil containers, and metal window frames ripped from more

urban buildings. ... More surprising still were all the materials borrowed from cars. (341–42)

What most amazes Baïkal is that the people from the non-zones who see these hybrid constructions every day do not differentiate between their natural and artificial components. When Baïkal inquires about the rusty factory overgrown with weeds, Fraiseur does not comprehend his question, and finally responds:

> "I don't see what you are talking about."
> Baïkal thought at first that he was joking. Then he realized that in fact Fraiseur could not distinguish these relics in the landscape. For him, they were part of nature, like the trees or the rocks. ... Any discontinuity between these ruins and nature had been obliterated, to the point that they seemed a part of it. It took a considerable effort of the imagination to make a connection between these forms and any human intention, whereas they blended in quite naturally with the trees, brambles, and weeds, spontaneous products of the soil. (144)

This littered landscape, as ugly and uninviting as it is to the Globalian eye, is merely nature for those who live there. The rusty remnants of the past constitute yet another paradox. Given the non-zones' devotion to their history, one would think that the industrial ruins would stand out, recalling age-old glories. This is not the case, however. Memories distort the past: assembly line workers become high priests, cars and beer cans lose their human connection and are no longer differentiated from trees and stones: "Distorted, like a voice echoing off a mountainside, the ancient stories were immortalized in everyone's memory. But they were deformed, transformed, and embellished, and had but a remote connection to the present that, long, long ago, had created them" (222).

In the last decades of the twentieth century, philosophers like Michel Serres and Bruno Latour in France, and J. Baird Callicott in the United States, announced the end of *le grand partage* (Larrère and Larrère, *Du bon usage* 93; Patterson 3), "the great divide" that had always been taken for granted, wherein humanity was considered separate from and vastly superior to nature. But now humans are no longer regarded as denatured; they are a part of nature, for better or worse. "World-objects" (Serres, "Revisiting the Natural Contract) and "hybrid objects" (Larrère and Larrère, *Du bon usage* 163) populate the earth, from our domesticated dogs and cats to our cities to air and water pollution. Nature has become "socionature" or "technonature" (Larrère and Larrère, *Du bon usage* 158, 159), touched everywhere by human society and technology. The Cartesian and Newtonian mechanistic view of a nature without humans that characterized modernism is dead, and has been replaced by an organic, ever-changing nature in process (*natura naturans*)[5] that includes humans and hybrid objects. As Callicott wrote in 1992, "The old, mechanistic idea of nature is dying. We are witnessing the shift to a new idea, in which nature is seen as an organic system that includes human beings as one of its components rather than as brutal and ultimately self-defeating conquistadores" ("La Nature est Morte, vive la nature!" 16). Rufin's narrator, while observing "carcasses of cars, trucks, tractors, trailers, and cranes" (*Globalia* 255) lying in fields, is aware of the shift. These objects, he states, "belonged to that universe of machines that had once separated man from the rest of creation" (254).

In a chapter entitled "Is There a Nature After Modernism?," Catherine and Raphaël Larrère cite the example of rust to describe this "nature of artifice" (*Du bon usage* 158). For these scholars, rust and corrosion are prime illustrations of the assimilation of artifice and nature. They imagine a cast-iron pan forgotten in a field: "Six months later, it is rusted. Cast iron does not exist in nature; it is a new object but created from elements found in nature. Throw away the pan, and nature will take it back by means of corrosion" (159). Thus, nature is "enriched" (159) by human technology. Larrère and Larrère provide one more example that demonstrates how technology can also be at the mercy of corrosive nature. The countless ground wires from our appliances may cause "stray voltage" ("courants baladeurs"), uncontrolled electrical currents coursing through the moist ground, "leading to hydrolysis, which can corrode lead pipes" (159). Finally, Larrère and Larrère argue that "[e]verything that surrounds us, from the factory to the abandoned thicket between two grain fields, bears the mark of human activity, of some technological intervention. How to distinguish the natural from the artificial? The traces of this artificialization have become imperceptible" (*Du bon usage* 159). We are all

---

5   See Larrère and Larrère, *Du bon usage* 19, 71–81; Bennett 116–19.

like Fraiseur staring at the weed-covered ruins of a factory. What used to be called nature is no longer distinguishable from objects created by human society and technology.

Globalia underscores the positive aspect of the ambivalent compound we call rust. Like the COR-TEN steel covering Pittsburgh's U.S. Steel tower, rust symbolizes resistance, not to chemical corrosion, but to the political corrosion of Globalia's totalitarian government. Rust thrives in the vibrant non-zones, where humans live as an integral part of a changing, hybrid nature. Rust is nonexistent in the dystopia of artifice called Globalia, where nature has been practically eliminated. Metal cannot rust, because the authorities only allow rain one week each year; "good-weather cannons" ensure constant sunshine in this land without seasons (Rufin, *Globalia* 241, 249). And aging—the human version of rust—has been slowed to a minimum; cancer and Alzheimer's disease have been cured, multiple plastic surgeries and organ transplants extend life and keep people looking young. But Rufin shows that chaos, unpredictability, and change—characteristics of the non-zones—are important elements of real democracy. Like the nineteenth-century French political scientist Alexis de Tocqueville, Rufin wonders if a globalist and capitalist democracy like the United States carries within it the seeds of totalitarianism.

Tocqueville and the "tyranny of the majority"

When Alexis de Tocqueville spent nine months in the United States in 1831, the purpose of the young French magistrate's visit was to evaluate America's carceral system. This he did, but what he is most remembered for is his two-volume essay on American society and politics, *Democracy in America* (*De la démocratie en Amérique*, 1835 and 1840). While Tocqueville appreciated many aspects of America—decentralization, freedom of association, the religiosity of the populace—he was quite critical of others, especially the institution of slavery and the steady extermination of the Indians. The most celebrated sections of his essay discuss the dangers of what John Adams called the "tyranny of the majority,"[6] in which the self-interests of the majority take precedence

---

6 See Tocqueville's *Democracy in America*, vol. 1, part 2, ch. 7, "On the

over the common good, leading to oppression of minorities. Tocqueville feared that someday the United States might succumb to what he calls a "mild" dictatorship, like that of a parent whose offspring remain perpetual children (Tocqueville vol. 2, part 4, ch. 6, pp. 817, 818); the sovereign "does not break men's wills, but softens, bends, and guides them" (819). Tocqueville contrasts this new authoritarianism with the violent tyranny of ancient Rome:

> If despotism were to establish itself in today's democratic nations, it would probably have a different character. It would be more extensive and more mild, and it would degrade men without tormenting them. ... When I think of the petty passions of men today, of the softness of their mores, the extent of their enlightenment, the purity of their religion, and the mildness of their morality, of their laborious and orderly habits, and of the restraint that nearly all of them maintain in vice as well as in virtue, what I fear is not that they will find tyrants among their leaders but rather that they will find protectors.
>
> *I therefore believe that the kind of oppression that threatens democratic peoples is unlike any the world has seen before.* Our contemporaries will find no image of it in their memories. I search in vain for an expression that exactly reproduces my idea of it and captures it fully. The old words "despotism" and "tyranny" will not do. (Tocqueville, vol. 2, book 4, ch. 6, pp. 817–18; emphasis added)

Jean-Christophe Rufin begins his short afterword to *Globalia* with an epigraph quoting the sentence emphasized above. He imagines that if he were Baïkal, escape from Globalia would be his only option. Globalia incarnates the worst of Tocqueville's fears, "a democracy pushed to the limits of its dangers" (Rufin, *Globalia* 499). Interviewed at the novel's release in 2004, Rufin again cites Tocqueville's influence. *Globalia* he states, is based on two main ideas:

> First, to imagine a possible evolution of the North-South relationship, a subject I know well because, given my profession, I travel between rich and poor countries. Second, to explore the unforeseen side of democracies which, after their triumphs in the

Omnipotence of the Majority in the United States and its Effects," and vol. 2, part 4, ch. 6, "What Kind of Despotism Democratic Nations Have to Fear."

1990s, are beginning to reveal their totalitarian side, or at least are proving to be not as heavenly as was once thought. Tocqueville, in fact, had already explored this paradox of the evolution of democracies. (Rufin, "Rencontre avec Jean-Christophe Rufin")

Rufin's humanitarian career has made him an expert on globalization and the North-South divide. The economic gap between developed and developing countries grows ever wider, and in the novel it has become a physical barrier between the secure Globalia and the unsecured non-zones, most of which are located in the South. Indeed, Baïkal's adventures with Fraiseur, culminating in their participation with the Déchus in a failed revolt, take place in the northern part of South America, in today's Brazil and Suriname.[7] As today's South has been victimized by globalization, the non-zones are victims of Globalia-ization. They are forced to pollute their own lands in order to produce fuel for Globalia; they are subject to military incursions of Globalian forces; they live in a Babelian world as scattered tribes speaking many languages, so that a united revolution against Globalia is improbable; and, as we have seen, unlike Globalians they are masters of *bricolage*, obliged to recycle and reuse the rusty relics of ancient times. As Christian Moraru states in a review of the novel, "another, vernacular Babel is arising outside Globalia. Its community of linguistic and cultural *bricoleurs* recycles and reassembles almost everything—technologies, practices, discourses, idioms—that Globalia discards, renders obsolete" (253).

Rufin imagines that Tocqueville's dire prophecy has come true; the tyranny of the majority has come to pass. Free expression is touted as a right, but any critique of the government is repudiated by the majority. Any person who disagreed with government policy "was guilty of an aggression against everyone" (Rufin, *Globalia* 186). Yet, as Tocqueville predicted, Globalia's tyranny is relatively "mild," its tyrants more "protectors" than vicious despots. "Petty passions" govern the lives of Globalians: sports, games, and commercials are constantly televised; casual sex is encouraged, but love and marriage are not. Globalia calls itself "a universal and perfect democracy" (297), and its citizens believe this. However, the study of history and geography are considered

---

[7] At one point, the characters can see Paramaribo. The capital of Suriname seems to be one of the few Globalian cites in the South.

dangerous, as is reading of any kind, since these serious activities may lead one to be curious about freedoms enjoyed in the pre-Globalian world.

Globalia is what Michel Tournier would have called a "malignant inversion" (*Wind Spirit* 102) of contemporary America, where two minorities have metamorphosed into tyrannical majorities. First, seniors have grown from a minority (they constituted 15 percent of the United States' population in 2015) to an overwhelming majority. Rufin thus exaggerates the current demographic trend in developed countries, where the older population is increasing. In Globalia, life and "youth" are grotesquely extended through the common practices of plastic surgery and organ transplants. Young people are rare and despised in Globalia, where childbirth is discouraged, and the demographic objective is "mortality zero, fertility zero" (Rufin, *Globalia* 99). Youth is no longer the trend-setting class; its sole purpose is to mature, age, and keep the population steady, "or, per the ecological directives, slightly falling" (100). Having babies is no longer a privilege of the young; the average childbearing age is 61 (98). The young are viewed with suspicion and are considered unattractive. Baïkal's girlfriend Kate, beautiful by our standards, like "one of Raphaël's Madonnas" (Rufin, *Globalia* 105), is too natural to be beautiful. Like a classical *jardin à la française*, a Globalian becomes beautiful by challenging and controlling nature, not imitating it. Even Kate's mother is repulsed by her natural look, "the opposite of civilization, truly barbaric" (105). In this "perfect democracy," even beauty is democratic: "beauty had become an ideal accessible to all, with enough time and effort, thanks to makeup, surgery, and especially the tolerance that had displaced the standards of beauty towards maturity and the wealth that comes with it" (106). Moraru credits the fight against aging with the establishment of Globalia's form of government, a "gerontocratic oligarchy" (250).[8] The enigmatic Ron Altman—seemingly the only Globalian who

---

[8] Laura Call reminds us how aging, like other forms of decomposition, is culturally repugnant in our society: "Humans spend much of their time avoiding or actively fighting this process. ... We have esthetic and medical treatments for the signs of aging, funerals to mourn the dead ... . As for spaces, we have clinics, homes for the aging, funeral parlors" (147). Globalians spend even more time fighting old age, and with great success. They have inverted our relationship to age. The elderly are venerated, albeit at the price of mummifying and plasticizing bodies and faces.

allows himself to look his age—rules the country, advised by a handful of elderly industrial barons. The malignant inversion of a minority into a majority has had profound political consequences:

> At last, the aged or ageing body becomes the exclusive signifier of beauty, strength, competence, and power, with anti-young biases and policies taking the place of ageism. The descending political narrative is complete now that a minority's legitimate claim has been recognized as a right and has been made into a fashion standard and civility benchmark, then a prejudice, a privilege, and at last, a legally enforceable civic duty. (Moraru 251)

The second inversion of a minority occurs when environmentalism becomes the ruling creed of Globalia. As I noted earlier, certain tenets of Arne Naess's deep ecology, such as the necessity to reduce the human population, have been formalized and written into Globalian law.[9] Completely liberated, animals now have equal legal standing with humans. Vegetarianism is of course the rule, so when Baïkal finds himself among a horde of hungry non-zoners devouring a roasted sheep, he is revolted, yet intrigued by an enthusiasm and appreciation for food that he had never witnessed in Globalia:

> Baïkal was overpowered by a sense of disgust but at the same time he was fascinated by the scene. He had grown up in a world in which animals were worthy of the same respect as man. ... And yet, he was flooded by a dark, visceral joy, more authentic than any that he had ever experienced. ... The taste of the charred meat sickened him, and it was all he could do to keep from vomiting. (174)

Plants too are protected in Globalia. One can be punished for breaking a tree branch, so when Baïkal gathers wood to make a campfire in the non-zones, he feels that he is committing a crime: "The 'law of the protection of life' declared that the least of plants

---

[9] The reader might recall item five of Naess's deep ecology platform, quoted above in the Introduction: "The flourishing of human life and cultures is compatible with a substantial decrease of the human population. The flourishing of nonhuman life requires such a decrease" (Foundation for Deep Ecology n. pag.).

must be treated with respect. In that immense garden that Globalia had become, a tight guard kept watch over this potentially dangerous species: man. Fortunately, the whole society agreed that he must be controlled" (131). Globalia has recognized that the great predator must be contained.

If ecology is the social cohesive myth that holds this dictatorship together, it is also a subversive myth that threatens to tear it apart. Reading is a lost art in Globalia, yet there is a secret society that has saved books and will lend them to those who dare to read. This reading club is called Walden, and new members are given Henry David Thoreau's essay of the same name to begin their reading adventure. To Globalian readers, *Walden* is an absurd fiction; it takes a fantastic imagination to invent a character who lives in the woods, cuts down trees, and studies nature (185). Thoreau inspired modern environmentalism and many of the tenets upon which Globalia is based. However, the author of *Civil Disobedience* also provides a voice for those who protest when environmentalism goes too far and leads to tyranny.

Liberal Dictatorships and the Ecological Apocalypse

In 1994, Rufin published *La Dictature libérale. Le secret de la toute-puissance des démocraties au XXe siècle* (The Liberal Dictatorship: The Secret of the Omnipotence of Twentieth-Century Democracies). He writes that liberal democracies like the United States, far from being fragile, are dictatorships of freedom, political ogres who nourish themselves with the fear of perceived mortal enemies. During most of the twentieth century, the Soviet Union was that enemy, but since 1989 three other "new apocalyses" (Rufin, *Dictature libérale* 179–278) have raised their ugly heads to frighten and feed the ogre of capitalism: the environmentalism movement, the developing countries of the South, and an internal enemy, the have-nots ("les exclus") of society.

Rufin would doubtless have much to say about this third apocalypse, represented by the wave of right-wing populism that has swept across liberal Western democracies in the early twenty-first century. Ecology, however, is the enemy of democracy that most concerns us here, as it is the ideology that dominates the fictional universe of *Globalia*. How could environmentalism have metamorphosed into such a dystopic society? How could a movement so radically against Promethean progress and growth—economic and technological—take the reins of power in a dictatorship?

In *La Dictature libérale*, Rufin explains how environmentalism was a natural successor to Soviet communism as public enemy number one of democracy. The red and green apocalypses are both international movements, hostile to capitalism, and teleological. And the environmental movement had its own *Das Kapital*, *The Limits of Growth* (also known as *The Meadows Report*), published by The Club of Rome think tank in 1972. Studying five variables (world population, food production, industrial output, pollution, and non-renewable natural resource depletion), the report concluded that the planet could not support current rates of growth. "Thus begins the planetary crisis of the human species" (185): capitalism survived the red apocalypse, but could it survive the green?[10]

Rufin explains how the green apocalypse was ultimately tamed by liberal democracies. Following his logic, we see how ecology could actually become the "tyranny of the majority" that rules Globalia. Capitalism formed a three-part "pact" with militant environmentalism. First came the phase of "coexistence" (194) between industrial areas and areas of protected wilderness. But this "ghettoization of nature" (194) was unsatisfactory, because it did little to save the planet. Second, the idea of a "cultivated nature" (195), bucolic rural landscapes that prove that humans and nature can live in harmony, became part of the discussion. But this point of view is sadly nostalgic, turned towards the past rather than the future. Finally, the connotation of technology was completely reversed. It was now understood that technology not only destroyed nature, it could also preserve nature. The vicious circle—growth leading to technology leading to more growth—was redrawn into a "virtuous circle" (201) of environmental degradation leading to growth in the demand for green industry:

> New types of pollution are discovered? New techniques of environmental remediation are developed. Resources are becoming scarce and costly due to overuse? High prices encourage research and cheaper substitutes are discovered. Technology is

---

10 In *Écologiser l'homme* (Ecologize Man), Edgar Morin uses similar biblical vocabulary to describe *The Limits of Growth*: "Between 1969 and 1972, the ecological consciousness gives rise to a prophecy of apocalyptic colors" (34).

triggering new illnesses? It will find cures for other illnesses, and eventually for the new ones it has caused. (196)

"Realistic ecology" (202), supported by philosophers like Luc Ferry and Pascal Bruckner, accepting the democratic rules of the game and encouraging policies such as sustainable development, became the more influential school of ecology. "Utopian ecology" (204), including groups like Greenpeace, more radical and in line with Michel Serres's thinking, became a secondary (yet still important) adversary. Capitalists succeeded in completely inverting the sign of industry, from negative to positive: "The revolution has happened. Evil has become good, the diabolical genie of science and its lustful double, profit, are no longer just the origin of all evils, but the origin of all healing" (199). Technology is indeed the new *pharmakon*, Plato's concept of the substance that can both poison and heal.[11] Humans and technology have caused the mess that is the environmental crisis, and only humans and technology can clean it up. The remedy is in the poison ...

La Dictature libérale reads like a blueprint for Globalia. The green apocalypse has been met, conquered, and transformed into the law of the land, and has been replaced by a new apocalypse, the poor, barbaric[12] South, represented in the novel by the wasteland of the non-zones. As Ron Altman tells Baïkal,

> people need fear. ... In a free society, it is the only thing that holds people together. Without a threat, without an enemy, without fear, why obey, why work, why accept the order of things? Believe me, a good enemy is the key to a balanced society. (Rufin, *Globalia* 93)

One is reminded of another literary tyranny, ancient Argos of Sartre's *The Flies*, first presented in Paris in 1943, during the very

---

11 See Jacques Derrida's analysis of the *pharmakon* in "Plato's Pharmacy."
12 In 1991 (reedited in 2001), Rufin published *L'Empire et les Nouveaux Barbares* (The Empire and the New Barbarians). Using the metaphor of the Roman Empire and its conflicts with the "barbarian" tribes, Rufin states that the East-West conflict has been replaced by a North-South opposition. He compares the wealthy and powerful North to the Roman Empire, separated by a series of *limes* (borders) from the marginalized South: poor, barbaric, and potentially hostile. In *La Dictature libérale*, he describes the "apocalypse North/South" (213) in terms of the Robinson Crusoe myth of European dominance: "South: You Barbarian, Me Robinson."

real despotism of the Occupation. Jupiter's reign of terror only works because the citizens of Argos cooperate with him; they need the fear and guilt he instills. Orestes liberates the city from Jupiter's yoke because he realizes that he is free, and not subject to the whims of a god. Baïkal becomes another Orestes, in spite of himself. Exiled in the non-zones, he finally realizes that it is here, not in Globalia, that freedom is found. Unlike Oreste's painful triumph, Baïkal's revolt will be a personal success—he and Kate will apparently live happily ever after in the non-zones—but a political failure, because Globalia has quashed the rebellion and continues to thrive.

Le Parfum d'Adam

Rufin's second ecological novel takes place not in some dystopian future, but in the almost equally discouraging contemporary world. He continues his critique of deep or radical ecology, concentrating this time on the issue of ecoterrorism. Two American ex-CIA agents, Paul and Kerry, are persuaded by their former superior, now head of a private espionage firm, to come out of retirement in order to investigate an incident of ecoterrorism. As the investigation proceeds, what first looked like a simple attempt to free animals from a Polish lab by an animal liberation movement cell turns into a plot by a fictional terrorist organization, the New Predators, to infect the drinking water of Rio de Janeiro's largest *favela* with a deadly new and "improved" cholera bacteria. The New Predators are convinced that it is the poor countries of the South, rather than the rich industrial North, that bear responsibility for the environmental crisis. They share Arne Naess's concern with overpopulation and conclude that they must drastically reduce the population of the world's poor. As Ted Harrow, the brutal leader of the New Predators, explains: "Nature is not respect for life. It is the work of death. Each one kills and is killed. Equilibrium is the harmony of predators. Protecting nature means knowing who must be killed" (Rufin, *Parfum d'Adam* 312). The American agents discover that "for Harrow, poor people constitute the worst form of human proliferation. ... His great fear is the proliferation of the indigent" (364), and what better way to reduce their numbers than through *vibrio cholerae*,[13] easily treated

---

13   As a tribute to Jean Giono's *The Horseman on the Roof*, set in nineteenth-century Provence during a cholera epidemic, Rufin cannot resist adding,

in developed countries with good sanitation and hygiene, but "one of the greatest diseases of the poorest of the poor" (132). The Austrian professor Fritsch, the intellectual inspiration behind Harrow's plot,[14] describes why the poor, not the rich, are the real enemies of the planet:

> [T]he priority of ecology is not to combat our industrial and productivist society, even if it is partially to blame. ... We make constant progress by improving crop yields, recycling, controlling pollution. ... In the end, as long as it is not extended to other civilizations, our industrial model is a lesser evil. The mortal danger comes from poor countries. With their traditional energies and rudimentary technologies, they are primarily responsible for toxic gas emissions. With their immense populations and rudimentary farming methods, they clear the last preserved forests on the globe. They massacre wild animals, poison rivers, traffic in protected species, cut precious woods, and soil hundreds of thousands of kilometers of coastline. (473–74)

Finally, McLeod, the billionaire financier of the cholera plot, explains from his fortified villa outside Geneva that rich countries, through economic and technological progress, ensure the well-being of the earth, while the Third World represents a "demographic catastrophe" (618):

> These bankrupt states are the ones most responsible for the planet's ruin. They do nothing to stop the out-of-control demographic proliferation that transforms their megacities into monsters and their countryside into deserts. ... China, India, Brazil: countries that are developing in great bursts of dirty technology, that maintain monstrous inequalities, that live off the work of children and the *de facto* slavery of two-thirds of their populations. (612–13)

---

through the voice of a French professor at Paris's Pasteur Institute, that cholera is also an important metaphor, a "literary disease": "Cholera," he roars, "is *fear*" (131).
14 The novel can be read as a kind of *roman à clef*. Méryl Pinque considers Professor Fritsch a thinly veiled fictional version of Arne Naess. Also, the ecological groups Greenpeace and Earth First! are incarnated as Greenworld and One Earth.

The plan to poison the waters of the *favela* is eventually thwarted by Paul and Kerry, with the help of Juliette, a young French radical ecologist who is working with the New Predators but ignores their real intentions. When she discovers the horrifying truth of the plot, she informs the agents and helps them prevent it. Then, instead of returning to France, she chooses to stay in Rio and teach the poor children of the *favelas*, those whom she almost unwittingly eradicated. Paul, echoing Rufin's humanism, had convinced her that humans will not survive if they continue, like super predators, to prey upon the poor: "I don't believe that the animal side of man will save him. It will be his human side. The consciousness that he has of himself and his environment, solidarity, justice, love" (682).

Critics greeted *Le Parfum d'Adam* with mostly positive reviews. Reviewers for *L'Express* praised Rufin's "serious documentation," his willingness to refuse political correctness and to suggest that "ecology can also lead to dangerous extremes," especially if its meaning is perverted "to only serve the cause of rich countries." Although some complain about the "interminable" length of the 765-page novel, they appreciate his "fluid writing" and the "beauty of his descriptions" ("Fiches de lecture sur *Le parfum d'Adam*" n. pag.).

Méryl Pinque's article "*Le Parfum d'Adam* ou l'imposture" is a striking exception to the generally favorable reception of the novel. Pinque describes herself as a former spokesperson for PETA (People for Ethical Treatment of Animals) France, and spokesperson for AVF (Vegetarian Association of France). She objects to Rufin's characterization of all radical ecologists as "pathological cases" and "fanatics" (Pinque 2 n. 5, 5). She accuses him of reducing ecology to the excesses of William Aiken—who wrote in *Earthbound* (1984) that 90 percent of the population should be eliminated in order to ensure the planet's survival[15]—and demonizing partisans of animal liberation as part of a "murderous misanthropy" (2). She goes on to write that "sowing confusion in the mind of the public, lying, soiling, and dishonoring under the fallacious pretext of informing, such is the sport of our media-savvy *french doctor*" (2–3). His negative characterization of radical elements of the Animal Liberation Front, persons who, according to

---

15 Rufin quotes Aiken in his postface (*Parfum d'Adam* 756–57), a text described by Pinque as a "monster of partiality" (5).

Pinque, "are armed only with their love, courage, and desire to see justice triumph for all," is nothing short of "slander" ("diffamation," 6).

Pinque concludes her tirade against Rufin by declaring that "by refusing to recognize animals as his equal, in the end he reasons like a barbarian" (9). This "portrait of the artist as a liar" (2) is a bizarrely distorted picture of a writer who has dedicated much of his life to medicine, humanitarian aid, and diplomacy. Indeed, for Pinque, Rufin's greatest sin is that he is a humanist and humanitarian. For humanism, believes Pinque, is but

> a religion that places man, to whom all must be subordinated, at the center of the universe. ... Humanism is narcissism, and Narcissus believes he is eternal. ... Man-God, man sanctified to the point that he has become ontologically innocent of the crimes he commits; that is where this insane humanism, this cult of the self leads. (7)

Pinque is mired in a concept of humanism that Callicott calls "ethical" or "moral" humanism (see Chapter 4 above), the exclusively *human* humanism that Sartre denounces in *Existentialism Is a Humanism* (51–52) as a cult of the human ultimately leading to fascism, and that Lévi-Strauss condemns as the "shameless" precursor of colonialism and the extermination camps ("L'idéologie marxiste" 14). Throughout these pages, and especially in my concluding chapter, I hope to show that an "ecological humanism" (Posthumus, *French Écocritique* 159) is not only possible but essential, if we are to rectify the abject failure of traditional Judeo-Christian humanism which, as Pierre Rabhi notes, has necessitated "humanitarianism as a palliative" (*Manifeste pour la terre et l'humanisme* 53).

In her chapter on "Ecological Politics," Stephanie Posthumus studies *Globalia* and *Le Parfum d'Adam* in the light of Bruno Latour's "renewed" or "redistributed" humanism, which takes into account all entities, living and non-living:

> Latour himself reminds the reader that humanism has always included non-humans, even if we have been blind to their presence as agents in our collective. Redistributing humanism becomes a matter of acknowledging and acting on these previous and currently forming attachments. Instead of searching for the essence of human nature (as involving perfectibility, autonomy,

free will, etc.), Latour's humanism reallocates agency across the board of beings and things, machines and organisms, humans and non-humans. (*French Écocritique* 105)

Unlike Pinque's analysis, Posthumus's reading is nuanced and helpful. She appreciates the value of an author like Rufin who challenges readers to look at all sides of the environmental movement, its potential for bad as well as good:

> These two novels thus illustrate another important element of ecological politics in France, one that remains wary of environmentalism's slippery slope toward misanthropy, racism, and xenophobia. At the same time, both novels open up the question of the collective, reasserting a humanist philosophy deeply concerned with social justice and the devastating effects of Western capitalism. ... They represent the dangers of democracy and globalization. (109–10)

Given his background as a doctor in NGOs such as Doctors Without Borders, Action Against Hunger, and the Red Cross, it is apparent that social justice is at the heart of Rufin's interest in environmental issues. He is all too aware that, as Hervé Kempf, former environmental editor for *Le Monde*, argues in *How the Rich Are Destroying the Earth*, "poverty is linked to environmental degradation ... [I]t is the poor who primarily suffer the impact of the environmental crisis" (41). While maintaining that his novel is "an adventure story and not a lecture course" (*Parfum d'Adam* 759) on the perils of deep ecology, Rufin nonetheless asserts in the postface that he does have a fundamental political concern, and that is the world poverty crisis, not ecology: "[T]rue to the themes of my other novels, it was less a question of analyzing ecological thought than reflecting on how we look at the Third World and poverty" (759). Through fiction he has conveyed his dismay at the lack of "any ethical considerations" (760) governing developed countries' relationships with underdeveloped countries and their "vulnerable, even massacred populations" (760). If deep ecologists are offended by Rufin's perhaps too unnuanced characterization of deep ecology as antihumanist, they must remember that his overriding concern is not ecology, but the devastating effects of globalization on developing countries.

We have seen how, in the non-zones of Globalia, rusty manufactured objects blend with nature to form hybrid objects, whose heterogeneous condition inhabitants of the non-zones accept as completely normal. In *Le Parfum d'Adam*, hybrid objects again play a key role. Gilles Mossière believes that "bridging" is at the core of the novel (169). For example, the plot bridges four continents, and the contrasts between French and American notions of ecology are explored (178–80). Hybrid objects are another sort of bridge. Posthumus observes that in the opening pages, when Juliette breaks into the Polish laboratory, the scientific instruments are contrasted with photos and cartoons attached to the walls; thus "the decor was a mixture of complicated instruments and human intimacies" (*Parfum d'Adam* 17). Human and nonhuman again combine in the cholera bacteria, whose importance is such that it could almost be considered a major character of the novel. After visiting the Pasteur Institute, Paul reflects on the common destinies of humanity and this dreaded disease, which he describes in human terms. The bacteria is "the first true example of globalization"; it has "a perverse familiarity with humans, whom it has always accompanied in their suffering, companion of their wars and poverty"; it is "the hidden face of the human adventure"; finally, "it is the consciousness of our failures, the witness of our weaknesses, the symbol of the earth to which we will always belong, even when our spirit thinks it can fly off towards the sky of ideas, of progress, of immortality" (227).

This "agency of objects," writes Posthumus, "present[s] an interesting contrast to Rufin's insistence on universal humanism as the only foundation for building a politics of human value and worth" (*French Écocritique* 120). If Rufin is more concerned about human than animal rights, about social justice more than the environmental ethics, hybrid beings do nonetheless play an important role in *Globalia* and *Le Parfum d'Adam*, and Rufin, despite his unabashed humanism, can be read as an author who contributes to the closing of the "great divide" between the human and the nonhuman.

This conclusion is justified by the very title of *Le Parfum d'Adam*. "The scent of Adam" refers to a passage on humility from the *Mystic Treatises* of Isaac of Nineveh, a seventh-century Eastern Orthodox saint and ascetic who lived for many years as an anchorite in the wilderness of today's Kurdistan. Rufin quotes Isaac in the novel's epigraph:

> The humble man approaches the beasts of prey and as soon as their eye rests on him, their wildness is tamed and they come to him and accompany him as their master, wagging their tails and

licking his hands and his feet. For they smell from him the smell which spread from Adam before his transgression, when the beasts gathered near him and he gave them names, in Paradise. (Isaac of Nineveh 386)

This then is the image that sets the stage for Rufin's novel about ecological terrorism: an idyllic scene from that mythical golden age before the fall, when human and nonhuman animals lived in peace. Yes, Adam is "master" of the animals, but he is a humble master. Human and nonhuman coexist harmoniously in a symbiotic relationship. This is a far cry from the reality of modern times, in which humans, much like Rufin's fictional "New Predators," have become the super predators of the earth.

As we will see in the concluding chapter, the Adamic humility that Rufin obviously admires also characterizes the philosophy of ecological humanists like Claude Lévi-Strauss, Pierre Rabhi, Edgar Morin, and Michel Maffesoli. The latter reminds us of the etymological link between "humility" and "humus" (*Écosophie* 80): to be humble is to feel affection for the earth. Indeed, Ernest Klein's *Comprehensive Etymological Dictionary*[16] confirms that "humility" derives from the Latin *humilis* (low, humble, on the ground), which in turn comes from the Latin *humus* (earth, ground, soil). Both words can be traced to the Proto-Indo-European root *dhghem* (earth), which gave us, among other words, chthonic, hominid, *Homo sapiens*, human, humane, humble, humiliate, humility, humus, and inhumation (Harper, *Online Etymology Dictionary*).

Finally, the name Adam signifies both "man" and "ground" in Hebrew, since Adam was said to be formed "of the dust of the ground" (Gen. 2.7). That Rufin would begin his novel with Isaac's "scent of Adam" tableau suggests that his humanism does not remotely resemble the narcissism of which Pinque accuses him. Rather, it is truly "grounded" in a humility he shares with other ecological humanists.

---

16 Entries consulted: Adam, human, humble, humus.

Chapter 7

From Ecohumor to Ecohumanism: Iegor Gran's *O.N.G!* and *L'Ecologie en bas de chez moi*

> I know to be suspicious of apocalyptic thinking, my own and everyone else's. Numb denial of global warming will not do, but neither will helpless fear. I worry that among believers and deniers alike, blame is a way of avoiding a deeper problem, the problem of scale: How do we bridge the distance between our own seemingly insignificant lives and actions and the scale of climate change, so global and so slow?
>
> —Kristin Dombek, "Swimming against the Rising Tide"

> The enormity of the diagnosis, the absurd inadequacy of the remedies. Like good boy scouts, the Greens offer us endless home economics advice worthy of our grandmothers. ... Let's be clear: a cosmic calamity is not going to be averted by eating vegetables and sorting our rubbish.
>
> —Pascal Bruckner, *The Fanaticism of the Apocalypse* 32

The list of environmental problems is long and disheartening: climate change, pollution, overpopulation, overfishing, mass extinctions, ocean acidification, lack of drinking water ... it is not the stuff of comedy. Indeed, novels about the environment, typically written by authors who are convinced that an ecological crisis of apocalyptic proportions threatens us, are not known for their humor. There are also etymological reasons for the gravity of ecofiction. For like its sister "economy," "ecology" possesses a somber etymology. Both words derive from the Greek *oikos* (house, dwelling). The primary meaning of "economy" is management of the dwelling place in a local sense, whereas "ecology" manages relationships between living organisms and their dwelling place, in a global sense.

One of the first lessons I learned in economics class is that I probably would not enjoy myself that semester, for the object of my study was "the dismal science." The Scottish historian Thomas Carlyle, a defender of slavery, coined the term in 1849 to criticize economists who claimed that slavery was not profitable, since the law of supply and demand required that workers be free. One could also maintain that economy in its very essence is a dismal science, since its fundamental problem is one of rarity: the impossibility of distributing the earth's finite resources to its people whose needs and desires are infinite.

If economy is a dismal science, so is its etymological sister, ecology, because she is up against the very same problem: the scarcity of resources. And these two sororicidal sisters are caught in a deadly war, like the two ungrateful daughters of King Lear. One could cite many examples of the war between economy and ecology: Economists criticize ecologists when they hinder economic growth by imposing regulations on industry; ecologists in turn accuse economists of sacrificing the environmental health of the planet to an ever-increasing GDP. Let us hope that this war will not be fatal like the one fought by King Lear's daughters; let us hope that the world will come to embrace "ecolonomy" (see Druon, *Écolonomie*)[1] where the two sciences work together. But for the time being the war goes on.

Onto this gloomy stage burst Iegor Gran in 2003 with *O.N.G!*. Gran emigrated to France from the Soviet Union at the age of eight. He is a columnist at *Charlie Hebdo* and in 2014 published his columns under the title *Vilaines pensées* (Evil Thoughts) with *Charlie Hebdo*'s publishing house, Les Échappés. He is the author of 12 humorous novels, all published with P.O.L. Gran is first and foremost a satirist. He ridiculed the literary and intellectual world with *Le Truoc-Nog*[2]

---

1 Emmanuel Druon is an entrepreneur from northern France. His fundamental assertion is that it is more economical to produce goods ecologically.
2 *Le Truoc-Nog* is Goncourt spelled backwards, a reference to France's most prestigious literary prize.

and *La Revanche de Kevin* (Kevin's Revenge), and mocked French anti-Americanism with *Jeanne d'Arc fait tic-tac* (Joan of Arc Goes Tick-tock). *O.N.G!* shocked the *bien pensant* world of environmental fiction with the story of two French NGOs that are forced to share office space in the same building. Unfortunately, La Foulée verte (The Green Stride), which fights pollution and helps endangered species, and Enfance et vaccine (Childhood and Vaccine), which provides vaccines to children in underdeveloped countries, cannot live up to their lofty ideals. Their trivial disagreements about parking spaces and bulletin board space degenerate into a full-scale war: their building is destroyed, and there are numerous victims of injuries and sexual aggression. The action is narrated in a flashback by Julien, an enthusiastic but naïve intern. Before his incarceration for rape during the NGO war, he briefly discovers a meaning to his monotonous existence with La Foulée verte: He hopes that one day he will overcome his addiction to cigarettes and his stuttering, and that he will better the boring life he shares with his despised "mini-bourgeois" parents.

Iegor Gran's humor belongs to the great French tradition of satire. It illustrates the point made by Walter Redfern in *French Laughter* that "French culture is heavily incestuous. Writers cannot simply ignore predecessors or contemporaries. More profoundly, they have a strong sense of tradition, of all being engaged in a common, if superior, enterprise" (4). Gran, while influenced by many Russian writers,[3] is also indebted to the works of two great French humanists: Rabelais (*Gargantua*, 1534) and Voltaire (*Candide*, 1759). Critics have called *O.N.G!* a Rabelaisian story about a "Picrocholine War" that breaks out for nonsensical reasons and is carried out in a brutal manner. The violence is euphemized, however, by the novel's comic form: Like Rabelais, Gran uses wordplay, religious parody, hyperbole, inventive insults, and bawdy scenes to convey the grotesque absurdity of war.

The hostilities commence when, in the elevator that the two NGOs share, Enfance et vaccine tears down a poster belonging to La Foulée verte (a picture of the endangered Arctic penguin)[4] and replaces it with

---

3 In the interview appearing in the Appendix of this book, Gran mentions his admiration for the nineteenth-century dramatist Nikolai Gogol, as well as twentieth-century writers Mikhail Zoshchenko, Mikhail Bulgakov, and the collaborative team of Ilf and Petrov, known for *The Little Golden Calf* (1931).
4 Penguins, of course, are native only to the Southern Hemisphere.

a poster of a sick African child. A minor incident? No! La Foulée verte likens it to a nuclear disaster. Convinced of their moral superiority as defenders of the environment, they prepare for war:

> A nuclear power plant had exploded.
>
> To war! Each man to his station. To war! The efforts of each one for the good [*le bio*][5] of a common prosperity. To war! Defend the just cause. To war! Our ideals will not falter in the face of barbarism. To war! Thoughts clash, the magic word deploys in letters of fire, and we bless the destiny that allowed us to be born at the right moment. (Gran, *O.N.G!* 63)

At the beginning La Foulée verte, inferior in numbers, suffers heavy losses against the warriors of Enfance et vaccine, the majority of whom are women. However, like Gargantua's diabolical troops,[6] our heroes battle valiantly:

> They fought like devils, our comrades, against three times their number, with many wounded among their ranks. But they retreated—it was inevitable—and we could hear through the elevator cage their cries of pain and anguish, and now and again calls for help.
>
> What could we do? Sick and powerless, we tried to encourage them.
>
> "Hold on!" cried Saint-Cyr.
>
> "Aim for the breasts!" advised Celsa. (146–47)

La Foulée verte finally wins the war, but at a horrific cost:

---

5   It is difficult to translate Gran's wordplay. The French noun for "good" is *bien*. Julien manifests his environmental consciousness by always substituting *bio* (organic) for the noun or adverb *bien*, as in *le bio*, *très bio*, or *merci bio*.

6   During the Picrocholine War, Gargantua's troops are so fearsome that the enemy mistakes them for devils. Here Gargantua urges them on against hopeless odds:

> "Comrades, here is an encounter, and in number they are ten times more numerous than we. Shall we charge them?"
>
> "What the devil else should we do then?" said the monk. "Do you value men by their number, not by their valor and boldness?" Then he shouted: "Let's charge the devils, let's charge!"
>
> Hearing which, the enemy thought they surely were real devils, so they began to flee with bridle down. (Rabelais, *Gargantua*, ch. 43, *Complete Works* 99)

What a horrible scene! The violence of the battle had been terrible. Some were limping, others were clutching their bumps and bruises. Broken noses, black eyes. Scratch marks along their cheeks. One volunteer had his nostril ripped off. With blank stares, these broken faces of the war gathered around a hastily organized makeshift infirmary, where they were given bandages and vitamins.

Some were seriously injured. Antony had a double fracture. Palaiseau, a very ugly cut to the thigh. Robinson had been hit on the neck and was seeing stars. Finally, Malabry, a hero among heroes, whose fertile imagination had saved us, had fallen hard on the broken debris of a TV screen. (153–54)[7]

Throughout the novel, Gran—or his characters—manages to offend a great number of people, not just those who work for NGOs. He makes fun of politically correct clichés about sexism and racism, awkwardly pronounced by his *bien pensant* but morally myopic characters. For example, Julien is ashamed of his crush on Celsa, an officer of La Foulée verte: "Telling you that she was beautiful would be at best a euphemism, at worst a sexist reflex that sees only a breeder where a woman stands" (122). He sublimates his desire through smoking, unfortunately forbidden by La Foulée verte. The image on his pack of "Cowboy" cigarettes brings him peace and distracts him from his sexual reveries. Nevertheless during the war he attacks a black woman, whom he pities because her black skin must be "the sad result of pollution … . The oil spill has colored her body" (161). Accused of rape, he maintains his innocence. La Foulée verte would surely support him, because he acted naturally, by instinct: "We are born with it, just like the Arctic penguin. His action did not result from any racial, sexist, religious, or any other prejudice" (160). In effect, his colleagues agree: His act was not rape, but merely a virtuous liberation, for now he is cured of his perverse addiction to cigarettes.

Gran's humor—at times vulgar and shocking—nevertheless earned him the Grand Prix of Black Humor in 2003. This literary prize,

---

7 Commuters on Paris's RER-B train, direction Saint-Rémy-lès-Chevreuse, will recognize the names of the heroes of La Foulée verte. Antony, Palaiseau, Robinson, and Malabry are all communes and train stops not far from Orly. Philippe Lançon, in "Merci bio," suggests that these suburban names reveal the sad "mediocrity" of the characters.

according to the president of the jury, rewards artists who express "desperate thoughts in an amusing way" (Beyern n. pag.). Indeed, only an author with desperate thoughts could find humor in the dismal science of ecology. The term "Black Humor" (*l'humour noir*) was coined by André Breton in 1940; his *Anthology of Black Humor* is a response to the despair and absurdity that he had experienced during the First World War. In memory of his friend Jacques Vaché, who died of an opium overdose soon after the armistice, Breton defines black humor in military terminology. During the war, many soldiers deserted; Vaché, on the other hand, "opted for another kind of insubordination, which we might call desertion within oneself…, a stance of utter indifference, along with a will not to serve any purpose whatsoever, or more precisely to conscientiously *disserve*" (Breton, *Anthology of Black Humor* 293–94). Like desertion during wartime, black humor is a subversive way to escape the misery and absurdity of life. It is Rabelais and Voltaire with a bit of nihilism and existentialism thrown in, reacting to a horrifying situation with derisive indifference. For black humor, writes Breton, "is the mortal enemy of sentimentality, which seems to lie perpetually in wait" (xix). There is a strong bond between war and black humor, which is the defining humor of the ecological crisis, itself a war between humanity and the world, as Michel Serres has noted (*Natural Contract*, pp. 10–11).

We have seen Gran's comic depiction of violence which recalls *Gargantua*. One could also cite *Candide* as an important precursor to Gran's ecohumor. The naïve (and candid) narrator of *O.N.G!* reminds us of Voltaire's hero, gifted with "a profoundly straightforward mind" ("l'esprit le plus simple," *Candide* 1). Voltaire's satire of Leibniz's harmonious universe is ultimately pessimistic, according to some critics, because the protagonists end up experiencing "a gnawing sense of insignificance and futility. … And in the end we see Candide intently cultivating his garden, an automaton immersed in mind-numbing labor" (Pratt, "People Are Equally Wretched Everywhere" 188). At the end of the novel, when Candide declares that "we need to work our fields" (Voltaire, *Candide* 129), his friend Martin responds: "Let us work without thinking. That is the only way to make life bearable" (130).

Gran's critique of NGOs and ecologists trapped in their trivial clichés is equally dispiriting. At the novel's end, the two rival NGOs are dissolved, and Julien is condemned to a long prison term. That Gran finds humor in racism and sexual violence might shock us today, but there are many parallels in *Candide*: Cunégonde was "disemboweled by Bulgar soldiers, after she'd been raped as many times as conceivably possible. They smashed in the Baron's head, because he tried to defend her; the Baroness was chopped into little pieces" (11). An old woman, daughter of the pope, recounts how she was raped by a pirate captain, "a disgusting black man" (33), sold into slavery, had "one buttock cut off," and was "raped a hundred times by Negro pirates" (126). In another passage, Candide describes villagers wounded, raped, and murdered by crazed Bulgars:

> [R]ifle fire removed from this best of all worlds some roughly nine to ten thousand wretches who'd been infecting its surface. ... Here old men beaten black and blue had watched their slaughtered wives die, holding babies to their bloody breasts. There disemboweled girls, having first satisfied the natural needs of numbers of heroes, had shuddered their final breath, and others, half burned, had screamed for someone to come and kill them. Brains were scattered all over the ground, along with severed arms and legs. (7–8)

Alan R. Pratt summarizes *Candide*'s influence on modern practitioners of black humor: Like them, Voltaire works by "juxtaposing—or integrating—comic understatement with gut-wrenching realism" ("People Are Equally Wretched Everywhere" 184). Voltaire's humor has a serious objective: to expose the absurdity of Leibniz's claim that this world, with all its misery, is nevertheless "the best of all possible worlds." *O.N.G!*'s goal is more modest. Employing a lighter form of black humor and caricaturing well-meaning defenders of good causes, Gran merely wants to illustrate the narrow-minded arrogance of some environmentalists and humanitarians, too convinced of the truth of their own ideology to consider other points of view.

With *L'Écologie en bas de chez moi*, Gran continues his satire on what his narrator calls "ecological pruritus" (22). The term pruritus (itch; skin infection; but also, according to the *OED*, "a strong desire or craving") reappears often as a metaphor for the obsessional enthusiasm of some environmentalists. Gran especially targets three characteristics of the ecological itch: opportunism, religiosity, and antihumanism.

The main victim of Gran's biting irony is Yann Arthus-Bertrand, director of the ecological documentary *Home* (2009), which evokes the original beauty of our planet, followed by its tragic destruction through industrialization and the thirst for energy. Gran asks how we can believe in the sincerity of this film, sponsored by a company strongly resembling the enormous Western companies that have played a large part in environmental degradation: Pinault-Printemps-Redoute.[8] Gran reproaches Arthus-Bertrand especially for his opportunism. For example, in celebration of the film, one could buy "ecological pumps," designed by Sergio Rossi (370 euros), or a *Home* tee-shirt by Gucci in "organic cotton" (140 euros). Gran observes that "greenwashing has made immense progress" (*L'Écologie en bas de chez moi* 152) in numerous business sectors, and finds truth in the Marxist claim that "sustainable development is sustainable capitalism in disguise" (69).

Here Gran highlights one of the common criticisms of environmentalism: that it is a luxury reserved for the wealthy classes of rich capitalistic nations, the very countries that environmentalists like Hervé Kempf accuse of destroying the planet. In *How the Rich Are Destroying the Earth*, Kempf denounces the governments of the rich countries of the North—in particular the United States—as a "predatory and rapacious ruling class," "a blind oligarchy" (58) bent on creating even more wealth, "blind to the poisoning of the biosphere that the increase in material wealth produces, poisoning that means deterioration in the conditions for human life" (59). Like Gran, he is critical of the notion of sustainable development, which is merely "a semantic weapon used to shove aside the dirty word, 'ecology'"; its function is "to maintain profits and avoid the (necessary) change in habits by barely changing course" (Kempf 21–22).

---

8 "PPR" manufactures and sells luxury goods, including the Gucci, Bottega Veneta, Saint-Laurent, and Sergio Rossi brands. PPR changed its name to Kering in 2013. The new name derives from the Breton *ker* (home). It is also a homophone of the English word "caring," which evokes a warm and benevolent company. Iegor Gran would undoubtedly have appreciated this excerpt of a company press release entitled "PPR Becomes Kering," published on 22 March 2013:

> Above all, Kering sounds like "caring" in English. Indeed, this is what the company does: it has a unique way of caring for its brands, its employees, its partners, and the environment. The "-ing" ending expresses the company's vitality and its international dimension. Ker, signifying "home" or "place of life" in Breton, is an allusion to our Breton origins.
>
> Kering also has a new emblem. Symbolizing wisdom, protection, and clairvoyance, the owl incarnates the company's visionary character.

Neil Gross, in a December 2018 *New York Times* article titled "Is Environmentalism Just for Rich People?," questions the veracity of the notion that only the rich can afford to be environmentalists, a theory that he traces back to a 1995 essay (*Value Change in Global Perspective*) by the "postmaterialist" sociologist Ronald Inglehart:

> Mr. Inglehart argued that citizens were apt to prioritize environmental concerns only if they were rich enough not to have to fret about more basic things like food and shelter. Environmentalism was part of a larger "postmaterialist" mind-set, focused on human self-realization and quality of life, that was naturally to be found in the world's economically advanced societies—and especially among better-educated, wealthier citizens. (n. pag.)

Inglegart's theory would seem to apply to the massive 2018–19 "Yellow Vest" protests against a planned gasoline tax increase in France. There is a large cultural gap separating President Emmanuel Macron and his privileged, highly educated supporters from the less fortunate protesters whose slogan is that while Macron worries about the end of the world, they worry about getting paid at the end of the month.

Gross, however, identifies an obvious weakness in Inglehart's (and Gran's) claim that it is generally prosperous and well-educated countries—like France and the United States, for example—that are likely to support environmentalism. If this were true, the French and Americans would theoretically hold similar views on environmental issues. Yet studies show that while 79 percent of the French consider climate change to be a serious problem, only 44 percent of Americans feel the same way. Moreover, poor countries facing environmental destruction often take stronger pro-environmental stances than do rich countries. Gross reminds us that "Fiji—which stands to be decimated by global warming, rising sea levels and storms—ratified the Paris climate agreement on a unanimous parliamentary vote before any other nation did" (n. pag.). Gross concludes that for the environmental message to take hold, it must go hand in hand with "a concerted effort to address [the] inequality" (n. pag.) exposed by the Yellow Vest movement. The Greens will never succeed without the support of the Yellows. Kempf comes to a similar conclusion in a chapter titled "Environmental Crisis, Social Crisis": "Overall, poverty and the environmental crisis are inseparable. Just as there is a synergy between different environmental crises, there is a synergy between the global environmental crisis and the social crisis: they respond to one another, influence one another, and deteriorate in tandem" (43).

It is important to note that Gran finds fault less with the content of *Home* than with its form: the paternalistic tone of the narrator who addresses us in the informal *tu*; the unnuanced "binary vision": "man-bad, Earth-pretty. ... Earth-our venerated mother, man-cockroach. Worse than a cockroach-a *roach sapiens*" (*L'Écologie en bas de chez moi* 164). Above all, Gran finds a stylistic resemblance between *Home* and another famous propaganda film, Leni Riefenstahl's *Triumph of the Will* (1935), which documents the 1934 Nazi Party congress in Nuremberg. Aware that he is vulnerable to the accusation of *reductio ad Hitlerum*, Gran insists again that he is comparing not the content, but the form of the two films, such as the use of aerial photography and stirring music: "Because of the form of his discourse, Yann is the worthy successor of Leni Riefenstahl, while greatly lacking her creative boldness" (18). Gran was born in the Soviet Union, and his father spent seven years in prison for his dissident writings. He is thus quite sensitive not only to the opportunism but also to "the shadow of totalitarianism" (30) lurking in the ideology behind the two films.

With an irony not unlike the Voltaire of *L'Ingénu*, Gran also rails against the religiosity of some ecologists. In effect, *Home* illustrates the dogmatic aspect of ecology. The reassuring tone of the narrative voice and the spectacular aerial shots of the earth persuade the audience that the principles of ecology are infallible: "A dogma ... is not debatable ... . It says: start by believing, then we'll see" (30). Like the Crusaders, Arthus-Bertrand's disciples "define themselves as *believers*. From the outset, they gather under the banner of faith" (31). They adore a "new, restrictive, and combative God" (41), and practice a "new religion, exacting and jealous" (158). They recite by heart their Credo, the *Ecological Pact*, in which the prophet Nicolas (Hulot) proclaims that "the enemy does not come from the outside, he sits inside our system and inside our consciences" (45). Their Satan is known by a chemical formula: CO_2.

For this humorist, an annoying trait of the ecological religion is that, like other monotheistic religions, it lacks a sense of humor. The Old Testament prophets were not exactly jokesters, and for centuries the fathers of the Catholic church considered laughter an invention of the devil (see Redfern 52).[9] There is, remarks Gran's narrator, "an appalling

---

9 This is one of the plot lines of Umberto Eco's *The Name of the Rose*. In the labyrinthian library of an Italian monastery, monks have discovered the

absence of humor as soon as one speaks of religion. It's a well-known fact that laughter desacralizes" (48). Laughter frees the narrator from his friend Vincent, an ardent environmentalist: "My irony crashes against Vincent's laconic pose. ... My laughter protects me from his God, allows me the freedom to be a carefree idiot; the man who laughs ignores the Deluge, he is as drunk" (49).

Refusing to believe in the great flood, the narrator also rejects the Apocalypse, a "psychosis" common to "any religion worthy of the name" (32–33), and especially the new secular religion of ecology. Indeed, according to the ecocritic Lawrence Buell, "Apocalypse is the single most powerful master metaphor that the contemporary environmental imagination has at its disposal" (285; qtd. in Garrard, *Ecocriticism* 93). In 2011, the year Gran published *L'Écologie en bas de chez moi*, two French essays appeared that stand as philosophical and scientific complements to Gran's ecological satire: *Le Fanatisme de l'Apocalypse. Sauver la Terre, punir l'Homme* (*The Fanaticism of the Apocalypse: Save the Earth, Punish Human Beings*) by the philosopher Pascal Bruckner, and *L'Apocalypse n'est pas pour demain: Pour en finir avec le catastrophisme* (*The Apocalypse Is a Long Way Off: Putting an End to Catastrophism*) by Bruno Tertrais, Senior Research Fellow at the Fondation pour la recherche stratégique in Paris. Contrary to much of the climate change skepticism coming out of the United States—often born of economic or religious conservatism—the skepticism of these two essayists is very French. Like Gran's, their cynicism is rooted in a Voltairian distrust of all self-righteousness, and an antipathy towards authoritarian ideologies.[10]

---

lost second volume of Aristotle's *Poetics*, considered scandalous because it dealt with comedy. Elie Wiesel, a master of black humor, understands that laughter separates humans from their creator. In *The Gates of the Forest*, his character Gavriel describes laughter as "God's mistake. When God made man in order to bend him to his wishes he carelessly gave him the gift of laughter. Little did he know that later that earthworm would use it as a weapon of vengeance. When he found out, there was nothing he could do; it was too late to take back the gift" (Wiesel 21).

10 Stéphane Foucart, scientific and environmental writer for *Le Monde*, writes in "Haro sur les écolos!" that "American 'ecolophobia' is especially motivated by the defense of economic freedom. Environmental questions are seen as obstacles to free enterprise—an avatar of communism." In France, on the other hand, most ecolophobes are motivated by their attachment to progress and technology. Citing the climatologist Valérie Masson-Delmotte, Foucart writes:

Bruckner's and Tertrais's essays contain many passages disputed by ecologists, fueling the complex and eternal battle between ecolophobes and ecolophiles. Stéphane Foucart accuses Bruckner and Tertrais—and climate change skeptics like Claude Allègre and Luc Ferry—of inaccuracies and a lack of scientific rigor. For example, Bruckner (118), like Tertrais (50–51) asserts that millions of people died because DDT was banned (thanks in large part to the efforts of Rachel Carson), and thus mosquitoes in the tropics were not eradicated. Foucart calls this report an "urban legend" and a "modern fable": DDT was never banned in the fight against malaria. Tertrais (104) claims that global warming is not reducing the population of polar bears. If the population is indeed falling in certain regions, it is a result of hunting. Foucart retorts that Tertrais's source is not scientific: it is an article reflecting the point of view of non-specialists, "explicitly compensated by the petroleum corporation Exxon and the American Petroleum Institute" (n. pag.). Finally, Foucart believes that all ecolophobes are wrong to criticize the IPCC (Intergovernmental Panel on Climate Change), the organization established by the United States to evaluate climate change. The IPCC is often accused of being dominated by "ecological ideologues"; however, according to Foucart, its reports are in fact "as conservative as possible" (n. pag.).

Despite these serious reproaches to their research, I do not consider Bruckner and Tertrais—or Gran—anti-environmentalists. They are, however, ecoskeptics. As humanists, they are wary of the apocalyptic rhetoric of those whose ecocentric world view comes at the price of underestimating the value of human genius, its contributions to our planet's past and its role in the creation of a viable future. Like Gran, Bruckner and Tertrais ridicule the religious discourse of environmentalism, and especially its apocalyptic excesses. Like Catholicism, environmentalism has its version of indulgences: carbon credits allow us to pay someone else to offset our own sins (Tertrais 13). The new religion also has its own original sin—the stain of the carbon footprint—and a "collective credo," which Bruckner actually considers a positive force: "Ecologism, the sole truly original force of the past half-century, has challenged the goals of progress and raised the question of its

"Source of well-being and disalienation, technology has also become a source of difficulties and dangers, even though 'many people cling to the idea that it allows and will allow us to solve all our problems'" (n. pag.).

limits. It has awakened our sensitivity to nature, emphasized the effects of climate change, pointed out the exhaustion of fossil fuels" (*The Fanaticism of the Apocalypse* 2). What Bruckner objects to in this "new secular religion" is "the infantile disease that is eroding and discrediting it: catastrophism" (3), an "apocalyptic scenography" that has already been tried out in Messianism, Gnosticism, and communism (2).[11] In the summary on the back cover of the French edition, Bruckner states that "catastrophism transforms us into panicked children, easy to control." He describes this "vulgate" which covers the human species in guilt as "nonsensical," narrow," and "totalitarian." Bruckner espouses instead a "rational" ecology, broadening and democratic, which seeks not to accuse humanity, but to inform it "about the damage done by industrial civilization" (3). Tertrais asserts that fear sells (Tertrais 10), recalling the opportunism of which Gran accuses Arthus-Bertrand and his sponsors. Fear and radical pessimism are an obstacle to solving environmental problems and negate the "enlightened catastrophism" and the "reasonable fear" expressed, for example, in the environmental philosophy of Hans Jonas (23).

The "nonsensical" ecology decried by Bruckner and Tertrais corresponds to what Greg Garrard describes as tragic apocalyptic rhetoric, whereas "rational" ecology would adhere to the rhetoric of comedy. Garrard cites *Arguing the Apocalypse: A Theory of Millennial Rhetoric* (68), in which Stephen O'Leary differentiates between tragic and comic framing of the apocalypse:

> Tragedy conceives of evil in terms of *guilt*; its mechanism of redemption is *victimage*, its plot moves inexorably toward *sacrifice* and "the cult of the kill". Comedy conceives of evil not as guilt, but as *error*; its mechanism of redemption is *recognition* rather than victimage, and its plot moves not toward sacrifice but to the *exposure of fallibility*. (Garrard, *Ecocriticism* 87; emphasis added)

Thus Rachel Carson's *Silent Spring* (1962) tends towards the tragic mode, because it calls the contamination of the environment by pesticides "irrecoverable"; moreover, "the warning is presented in terms of absolute authority; the material threat is 'evil,' and so, by association,

---

11 According to Greg Garrard, the first apocalyptic narrative of the end of time is likely to be found in the philosophy of the Persian prophet Zoroaster, around 1200 BC (*Ecocriticism* 85).

are the authors of it; the consequences of failure to heed the warning are catastrophic, and the danger is not only imminent, but already well under way" (Garrard, *Ecocriticism* 95). On the contrary, Al Gore's *Earth in the Balance* (1992), while it "flirts with tragic apocalypse" (Garrard, *Ecocriticism* 99), generally follows the "Christian 'stewardship' tradition" (88), "in the name of mainstream Christianity and a comic eschatology that emphasizes human agency" (89), rather than the radical, tragic rhetoric of millenarian Christian movements. Garrard concludes that environmental apocalyptic discourse is a double-edged sword. For example, "doom merchants" adopt a tragic mode that "interpret[s] every drought or ice storm as a 'sign' of catastrophic global warming, while climatologists consistently adopt a comic apocalyptic rhetoric that denies the possibility of linking specific weather events to global climate change" (106). Tragic discourse tends to combine "very varied environmental problems within the concept of a singular, imminent 'environmental crisis'" (106–07). It is more constructive, Garrard maintains, to adopt a comic discourse, and break down this total crisis into more solvable, discrete problems:

> Environmental problems, whilst they should not be seen in isolation, might seem more amenable to solution if they are disaggregated and framed by comic apocalyptic narratives that emphasize the provisionality of knowledge, free will, ongoing struggle and a plurality of social groups with differing responsibilities. In this way, problems are not minimised, but those who describe them become less vulnerable to the embarrassments of failed prophecy and to the threat of millennial enthusiasms. (107)

Bruckner concludes *The Fanaticism of the Apocalypse* with an epilogue entitled "The Remedy Is Found in the Disease" ("Le remède dans le mal"), a reference to the Greek *pharmakon*, which can mean both "poison" and "remedy." The cures to our environmental problems will necessarily be discovered by those who have poisoned the planet: human beings. The apocalypse—"an ecology of accusation"—must give way to a new humanism—"an ecology of admiration" (Bruckner 185). Prophets of doom will not help us; only human scientific and technological genius, the very root of environmental degradation, can someday revitalize the earth: "Only an increase in research, an explosion of creativity, or an unprecedented technological advance will be able to save us" (184–85).

A third target of Gran's humor is the antihumanist current he detects in many ecologists. Humans are largely responsible for the environmental crisis, but Gran insists nonetheless that we give humanity credit for the cultural and artistic marvels it has created. *Home* condemns humans for the destruction of the planet; Gran would rather recall our constructive contributions to the world, such as the scientific progress that has led to the well-being of billions of people, or great art and architecture:

> The most appalling aspect of *Home* is neither the ecolo-marshmallowy clichés, nor the paternalism as subtle as a freight train, but the decision to totally ignore art (in any form) in the appraisal of the 200,000 years that humans have labored on this earth. The Chrysler Building that the helicopter flies over, far from representing one of the world's most beautiful architectural creations, symbolizes instead the frenetic expansion of cities, the monstrous gangrene that we are.
>
> Man soils Nature and culture is complicit. (*L'Écologie en bas de chez moi* 139)

Although it is true that the excesses of scientific progress, especially since the Industrial Revolution, share in the degradation of the earth, only science, according to Gran, can find solutions to the environmental crisis:

> Humans have managed to put a guy on the moon and can't find a way to get past oil? … We conquered smallpox yet would let ourselves be tied to a raw material that *Homo sapiens* ignored for 99.9 percent of their existence? … One must be historically myopic to have no confidence in the genius of human beings. … Oil, like coal, is a step. Neither more nor less than the Bronze Age. (86–87)

Gran evokes the totalitarian specter of an ecology that places primary importance on the collective to the detriment of the individual. Art, he writes, presupposes the effort of an individual, an effort rejected by the "*collective* obligation" (142–43) that is ecology. He cites the 2005 Constitutional Charter of the Environment, which describes the environmental duties of the French in a language replete with collective nouns, such as "the French people," "each person," "international and European action" (143). The propositions of this document are "perfectly calibrated to build a totalitarian utopia" (144), writes Gran.

The possibility of an ecological dictatorship figures among the most worrisome criticisms of deep ecology. We have seen the example of *Globalia* in the preceding chapter. Jean-Christophe Rufin imagines a society in which the entire world is governed by a repressive regime organized according to the principles of deep ecology, formulated by Arne Naess and George Sessions in 1984. Eating animals or using animal products is strictly forbidden in Globalia, which is founded on "respect for the animal, protection of nature, in short, the modern conception of human rights extended to animals" (Rufin, *Globalia* 73). Young people are scorned in this world where human life expectancy is very long but the birth rate approaches zero in order to avoid population growth. Lawrence Buell recognizes that the platform of deep ecology, especially the principle declaring that for nonhuman life to flourish, the human population must decline, invites accusations of utopian or fascist ecologism. Yet Buell reminds us that we must distinguish between deep ecology and "ecocentric thinking generally," which certain "environmental humanists" (*The Future of Environmental Criticism* 102), like Luc Ferry (137), fail to do. As for the humanist Iegor Gran, it is true that one could accuse him of picking an easy target for his satire: ecologism's extremist wing does not represent the vast majority of ecologists or environmentalists.

So what is Iegor Gran's place in French ecoliterature? Underneath their burlesque surface, Gran's satires examine serious problems and force environmentalists to ask themselves important questions, especially regarding the formal aspects of their discourse, which is at times hysterical, at times pedantic and paternalistic. Gran contributes a Voltairian lightness to the dismal science of ecology, and to the equally somber fiction it inspires. Walter Redfern reminds us that, unlike Voltaire, Jean-Jacques Rousseau, the great ancestor of the French ecological movement, was relatively lacking in humor: "A self-chosen martyr like Rousseau not uncommonly has an undernourished sense of humor" (47). On the contrary, "the spirit of Voltaire"—the anti-Rousseau—makes philosophy fun. One Voltaire specialist has praised Voltaire's "attachment to action, ... [which] accounts for his lively, sharp and agile style" (Belaval 153). Another calls his humor "the laugh of aggression" (Favre 43–61), and his anticlerical writings a "battle for justice, tolerance, clarity, and finally, humanity" (61), even if one does not entirely share his views. Gran provides a similar service to environmentalists, most of whom probably do not share many of his opinions. As Voltaire uncovered many of Catholicism's problems, such as mistakes in the Bible or the corruption of the Jesuits, Gran in turn exposes the weaknesses in the new secular religion of ecology. And his service has not gone unnoticed by ecologists. Alice Audouin—journalist, author of an environmental novel (*Écolocash*, 2007), sustainable development consultant—appreciates *L'Écologie en bas de chez moi*. It is a "brilliant and impertinent attack," she writes, "a striking, sincere and funny photograph of the rejection of ecology by the cultural and intellectual elite, or rather its rejection of ecology's discourse judged, at best, to be awkward and moralizing" (Audouin n. pag.).

Conclusion
Environmentalism Is a Humanism

> One cannot be a humanist if one is not an ecologist; ... one cannot be an ecologist if one is not also a humanist.
>
> —Philippe Desbrosses, interviewed by Denis Cheissoux, *CO2 mon amour*, 16 May 2015

> The glory of the human has become the desolation of the Earth ... the desolation of the Earth is becoming the destiny of the human.
>
> —Thomas Berry, "Teilhard in the Ecological Age" 57

The Great Divide

Ecocritics have long been at odds with humanism. In the Introduction to this study I cite Luc Ferry, who accuses environmentalists of likening humanism to "original sin" (*New Ecological Order* 60). Stephanie Posthumus explains that

> [i]n his attack on deep ecology, which lumps together thinkers as diverse as Aldo Leopold and Michel Serres, Ferry calls for a renewal of humanism by going back to the thinking of Jean-Jacques Rousseau and Immanuel Kant. He reasserts the notion of a universal human nature and posits humans as necessarily anti-natural. (*French Écocritique* 3)

She writes of the "Ferry effect" (3), concurring with Catherine Larrère that Ferry's book had a "censoring effect" (4) on environmental philosophy in France in the 1990s. Baptiste Lanaspeze echoes her concern, writing that only a handful of philosophers—such as Catherine Larrère, Edgar Morin, and Michel Serres—study environmental issues. Even the popular French TV magazine *Télérama* got in on the act with this headline in December 2006: "Ecology: The Silence of French Intellectuals" (Lanaspeze n. pag.).

The meaning of humanism has of course changed over time. Renaissance humanism was above all an intellectual movement that encouraged students to rediscover and translate the literature of Greek and Roman antiquity. *Studia humanitatis*, the sciences of the mind, or, as we say today, the humanities—especially classical languages, literature, and culture—were encouraged, as opposed to the sciences of nature. Such an education was considered necessary for one to become fully human.

Most Renaissance humanists were also Christian, and beholden to Church doctrine that devalued nature as it glorified humans. Indeed, in "On the Dignity of Man" (1486) the Italian Renaissance humanist Giovanni Pico della Mirandola has God declare to Adam:

> I have placed thee at the center of the world, that from there thou mayest more conveniently look around and see whatsoever is in the world. Neither heavenly nor earthly, neither mortal nor immortal have We made thee. Thou, like a judge appointed for being honorable, art the molder and maker of thyself; thou mayest sculpt thyself into whatever shape thou dost prefer. Thou canst grow downward into the lower natures which are brutes. Thou canst again grow upward from thy soul's reason into the higher natures which are divine. (qtd. in Richard Norman, *On Humanism* 3)

Humanity thus has God to thank for its preeminent status among creatures. However, each person is "maker of thyself," possessing the free will to rise up with the angels or fall down with the brutes. Clearly, humans are not "earthly," and are thus from the beginning disconnected from nature. Genesis initiates the split between humans and nature: "Made in the image of God, man is cut off from nature" (Larrère and Larrère, *Du bon usage* 57). Thus begins "the great divide" (93) between humanity and nature, which only widens in the seventeenth century with the rise of Cartesian science and philosophy. Humans are the "masters and possessors of nature" (Descartes, *Discourse on the Method*, part 6, p. 119), the sole creatures gifted with a mind and the ability to speak and reason; an animal is but "a machine ... made by the hands of God" (part 5, p. 116), lacking language and "hav[ing] no reason at all" (117).

Ecological Humanism

In recent years, some ecocritics have recognized the importance of healing the fracture between humanism and ecology. Posthumus devotes several pages to "ecological humanism," declaring that her "approach includes the human without resurrecting the universal (white, male) human subject" (*French Écocritique* 159). She quotes Kerry Whiteside, who, convinced that humanism need not be anthropocentric, writes that "humanism becomes ecological when it opens itself to reflecting on how nature and humanity are mutually reflecting" (159; quoting Whiteside 4). Bruno Latour calls for a democracy that includes humans and nonhumans, writes Posthumus, suggesting a "redistributed humanism" that "reallocates agency across the board of beings and things, machines and organisms, humans and non-humans" (*French Écocritique* 105). Finally, Posthumus cites Serenella Iovino as an ecocritic who "is attentive to the staying power of humanistic thought in the European context" (160). Iovino asks the question: "What does 'human' mean for ecocriticism?":

> As a culture of difference and an "evolved" form of humanism, ecocriticism should take into account the difference that the concept of "human" finds *within* itself. This means extending the reflection on the idea of "human" beyond its socially constructed characterizations (as in the "second wave" ecocriticism), at the same time rethinking the concept of "otherness" not exclusively in relationship to non-human nature (as in the "first wave" ecocriticism). By placing the focus not *outside* but *inside* the human being, ecocriticism can contribute to a critical reflection on humanism, in which the category of *radical otherness*, taken as an attribute *of* the human, plays a pivotal role. (Iovino 55; emphasis original)

Ecological humanism must study humanity in all its complexity, especially its "islands of otherness" or "wilderness zones," which include

> Wilderness of the body: deformity, physical disability;
> Wilderness of the mind: madness, altered states of consciousness, mental disability;
> Wilderness of the "more than human": mystical experience. (55)

In the preceding chapters, we have seen several calls for new humanisms. In *Existentialism Is a Humanism* (see Chapter 4 above) Sartre condemns the humanism that considers humans to be "the supreme value" (51), thus erecting a "cult of humanity" (52) that can eventually lead to fascism. He proposes instead an "existentialist humanism," an atheistic humanism by which "we remind man that there is no legislator other than himself and that he must, in his abandoned state, make his own choices" (53). Far from exalting humanity, existentialism believes that each person "is nothing other than what he makes of himself" (22).

Animal ethicists have especially been ill-disposed towards humanism, even Sartre's humbler version. Martin Gibert, the author of *Voir son steak comme un animal mort* (Seeing Your Steak as a Dead Animal), a defense of veganism, considers Sartre's humanism insufficient because it does not extend to animals. In a chapter titled "Veganism is a humanism," Gibert distinguishes between "exclusive" and "inclusive" humanism. The former "consists in limiting moral consideration solely to members of the human species. ... Thus, exclusive humanism is fundamentally speciesist and is indistinguishable from human supremacy" (Gibert 173). The latter

> designates a group of values, norms, and moral virtues that form the basis of a constant extension of the circle of morality. It advocates equality, freedom, and solidarity and shows concern for the most vulnerable. It is inclusive in the sense that it does not set out any a priori limits on the sphere of application of these values. This is the humanism of Voltaire and Rousseau, of Jeremy Bentham and John Stuart Mill, of Martin Luther King and Gandhi. (173)

Gibert considers Sartre's existentialist humanism "exclusive," because Sartre is concerned only with humans, not animals.

In his foreword to Mackenzie and Posthumus's *French Thinking About Animals*, another animal ethicist, Jean-Baptiste Jeangène Vilmer, contends that the reader must

> understand that humanism ... is a way of putting humans at the center of everything, subjugating the environment in order to fulfill the Cartesian project that humans become "as masters and possessors of nature." ... According to the humanist view, humans and animals are like communicating vessels; so giving more consideration to the one means necessarily giving less consideration to the other. (ix)

Four French Ecological Humanists: Lévi-Strauss, Rabhi, Morin, Maffesoli[1]

Lévi-Strauss
Lévi-Strauss denies his reputation as an antihumanist. He insists, however, that humanism as we know it must be rehabilitated. Catastrophes like colonialism, fascism, and the Nazi death camps are not inconsistent with the European humanism inherited from the Judeo-Christian tradition. Rather, they are "its natural extension" ("L'idéologie marxiste" 14). He

---

1 I include Pierre Rabhi, Edgar Morin, and Michel Maffesoli in my analysis of ecological humanists, because they are important ecological thinkers who have not been widely studied in English-language ecocritical texts. Lévi-Strauss must be considered because he "was a key figure in drawing attention to the West's destruction of the natural world" (Posthumus, *French Écocritique* 12). Even though he did not write on ecology, I should also mention Gaston Bachelard, whose essays on the material imagination (the four elements) are key to my analysis of Tournier's *Gemini* in Chapter 1. Mary McAllester Jones has called Bachelard a "subversive humanist," in that his humanism—like that of Lévi-Strauss, Rabhi, Morin, and Maffesoli—is decentered from humans. On the one hand, Bachelard seems to acknowledge humanity's superiority to nature when he writes that "the world is conditioned by man's provocation" (Jones, *Gaston Bachelard, Subversive Humanist* 4; quoting Bachelard, *L'Activité rationaliste de la physique contemporaine* 141). On the other hand, writes Jones, Bachelard's humanism does not stem from Kantian idealism, in which reality is constructed by human ideas. Rather, "Bachelard's humanism ... rests on a conception of man decentered, transcended by something beyond his control. ... Bachelard's is a subversive humanism. In his work both on science and on poetry, he undermines traditional views of the subject every bit as

calls for a humanism decentered from humans and extended beyond humans to all living creatures. We have seen above in the Introduction that in 1973 Lévi-Strauss declared humanism "corrupted at birth" (*Structural Anthropology* 41) by self-interest. A decade later, in a chapter on "Race and Culture" in *The View from Afar*, he again disparages "Western humanism," which has encouraged a hierarchical vision of the world in which the Western human is "lord and master" over other humans, and by extension over all living creatures:

> By isolating man from the rest of creation and defining too narrowly the boundaries separating him from other living beings, the Western humanism inherited from antiquity and the Renaissance has deprived him of a bulwark; and, as the experiences of the nineteenth and twentieth centuries have proved, has allowed him to be exposed and defenseless to attacks stirred up within the stronghold itself. This humanism has allowed ever closer segments of humanity to be cast outside arbitrary frontiers to which it was all the easier to deny the same dignity as the rest of humanity, since man had forgotten that he is worthy of respect more as a living being than as the lord and master of creation—a primary insight that should have induced him to show his respect for all living beings. (23)

A few pages earlier, Lévi-Strauss observes that the "so-called primitive peoples" (13) he has lived among, like the Brazilian Nambikwara, have "vast systems of rites and beliefs that may strike us as ridiculous superstitions but help to keep a human group in harmony with the natural environment" (14). We may look to indigenous

---

effectively as recent thinkers in France. ... Subversively, he reinvents man, against idealism, beyond conventional notions of subject and object" (4). James L. Smith has pointed out the affinity between Bachelard's research on the material imagination and the new materialism that Jane Bennett proposes in *Vibrant Matter*. Smith writes that both thinkers "attempt to correct the notion that Bennett (2010 VII) describes as the parsing of the world into 'dull matter' (the *it* and the category of things) and 'vibrant life' (the *us*, and the category of beings). Bachelard presents the same false dichotomy. For to him 'the duality of subject and object is iridescent, shimmering, unceasingly active in its inversions' (Bachelard 1997: XIX). Bennett proceeds by affirming the inhuman vitality of matter, and Bachelard stresses the complete dependence of human imagination on objects" (J. Smith 159, quoting C. Picart, "Metaphysics in Gaston Bachelard's 'Rêverie,'" *Human Studies*, vol. 20, 1997, pp. 59–73).

peoples as models for a humble, decentered humanism in a horizontal world where humans are not, as Sartre wrote, "the supreme value" (*Existentialism Is a Humanism* 51), but merely one among many species:

> Indigenous philosophy may even contain the idea that human beings, animals, and plants share a common stock of life, so that any human abuse of any species is tantamount to lowering the life expectancies of human beings themselves. All these beliefs may be naïve, yet they are highly effective testimonies to a wisely conceived humanism, which does not center on man but gives him a reasonable place within nature, rather than letting him make himself its master and plunderer, without regard for even the most obvious needs and interests of later generations. (Lévi-Strauss, *The View from Afar* 14)

Rabhi

I briefly mentioned Pierre Rabhi and the need for "reenchantment" in discussing the fairy Mélusine in Chapter 3 above. Rabhi is an organic farmer and ecological activist born in Algeria, who settled in Ardèche when he was in his early twenties. He founded the association Terre et Humanisme[2] (Earth and Humanism), whose mission is to promote agroecology, a philosophy of farming that

---

2 Pierre Rabhi is perhaps better known for one of his more recent organizations: Colibris (Hummingbirds), whose mission is "the construction of an ecological and human society. At the heart of its *raison d'être* is personal change, because the association is convinced that societal change is totally subordinated to human change" (Rabhi, "Notre Mission"). According to the Colibris website, the organization shares many values with Terre et Humanisme, but each association is "independent and autonomous." Colibris owes its name to an Amerindian myth about the hummingbird who attempts to fight a forest fire with the few drops of water he can carry in his beak. When the armadillo mocks him, saying that he would never be able to extinguish the fire, the hummingbird responds: "I know, but I am doing my part." Patrick Chamoiseau dedicated *Les Neuf Consciences du malfini* (The Nine Consciousnesses of the Hawk) to Rabhi. It is the story of a vicious hawk converted to environmentalism by a minuscule hummingbird. These heroic hummingbirds recall the literary valorization of smallness analyzed by Bachelard in *The Poetics of Space* (chapter 7: "Miniature"), and Gilbert Durand's concept of "gulliverisation" (204). See Chapter 1 above on Tournier's discussion of the miniature Japanese gardens in *Gemini*. In 2011 Rabhi published *La Part du colibri*, which Keith Moser analyzes in "The Decentered, Ecocentric Humanism of Pierre Rabhi in

considers all the elements of the ecosystem and social system, assuring the quality of their interrelations. Agroecology is thus a harmonious balance combining agriculture and ecology, quantity and quality, human activities and biodiversity, philosophy and techniques. (Rabhi, "Notre définition de l'agroécologie")

In 2008 Rabhi published a manifesto for his association, entitled *Manifeste pour la terre et l'humanisme* (Manifesto for the Earth and Humanism). In his preface, Nicolas Hulot writes that agricultural reform goes beyond economics: It "must start with man" (9). Each individual must "be conscious of the unconscious," and adopt "values of soberness [*sobriété*] and moderation" (9) if agricultural catastrophe is to be avoided. Rabhi's mission is local, featuring farms, gardens, and research in Ardèche and in other regions. It is also international, with centers in West and North Africa fighting against desertification. Rabhi believes that a "planetary" (*Manifeste* 14) and "universal humanism" (61), along with a respect for the earth that has given us life, are necessary for "the survival of the human species" (14). We must begin by freeing ourselves from the idea that humans are outside of and rule over nature. Echoing Jane Bennett's concept of *Vibrant Matter*, Rabhi's ecology "is on the scale of the cosmos, the universe. Interactivity includes solar, lunar, and planetary influences ..., in an infinite energetic and vibratory bath. ... Everything is in everything and nothing is unconnected with anything" (61).

Like Jean-Christophe Rufin, Rabhi links humanism and humanitarianism. The global exploitation of the South by the North gave birth to humanitarian movements, based chiefly in the North, like Rufin's Doctors Without Borders and Action Against Hunger. Humanitarianism, which attempts to palliate the immense misery of the South, is only necessary because humanism has failed; that is, a

La Part du Colibri." Moser concludes his essay with this appreciation of Rabhi's non-anthropocentric humanism:

> In *La Part du Colibri* and throughout his œuvre, Rabhi outlines a radically different sort of ecological humanism which more accurately represents the material realities of living in an interconnected and interdependent cosmos in comparison to classical humanism and the "engagement" of earlier twentieth-century writers. Rabhi strives to create a committed army of mobilized "hummingbirds" all doing their small part to end the war that humanity has been waging for far too long and to preserve the fragile equilibrium that sustains life. (65–66)

"true humanism" (53) is still to be created. As Lévi-Strauss proposes a humanism based on "indigenous philosophy" in *The View from Afar*, so Rabhi feels that pure rationality is no basis for true humanism. The industrial, rational North can learn a lesson from a farmer and his tiny grain of wheat: "We can understand the mechanisms of germination and growth, but the intelligence at the origin of this impulsion is hidden behind a mystery that simple reason cannot access" (*Manifeste* 46).

What Rabhi calls the "world food tragedy" (17) has many causes: soil erosion due to deforestation; accelerated salinization of some soils; chemical fertilizers, pesticides and herbicides; genetically selected seeds; monoculture; loss of plant and animal biodiversity; loss of small farms; overconsumption of animal proteins; mistreatment of animals, which are nothing more than "protein-producing machines" (20); destruction of bees; and the various ramifications of climate change, such as drought, flooding, and abnormal temperature changes (19–21). These are all very concrete problems that agroecology is working to overcome. But at the heart of Rabhi's mission is an aesthetic quest: "Can beauty save the world?" (105) he asks.[3] Yes, he answers, but then clarifies what he means by beauty and which world he is talking about. The farmer becomes a poet as he describes the splendors of the universe: "a canopy of heaven" dominated by the sun and the moon; "faraway constellations petrified in an infinite silence"; "the lightness of the breeze"; "the enchantment of colors, perfumes, and birdsongs [that] already existed long before us" (105). Beauty does not care about humans. We are contingent creatures; our existence is pure chance. Beauty exists "by itself and for itself," and would continue to exist if we were to become extinct (106).

Rabhi's insistence on "the immense beauty of nature" (100) brings to mind another Franco-Algerian philosopher: Albert Camus. In Chapter 4, I referred to Camus's "Human Crisis" lecture at Columbia University in 1946. Camus's message then was much like Rabhi's today: we need to foster human dignity, to reconstruct the world according to a just humanism where "might makes right" is not the ruling creed. In 1948 Camus published an essay titled "Helen's Exile," lamenting the disappearance of beauty from the modern world. The

---

3 Rabhi has said that his question was inspired by Dostoevsky, whose Prince Myshkin in *The Idiot* maintained that "beauty would save the world."

ancient Greeks, he writes, expressed their despair through art and beauty. Theirs was a tragedy bathed in sun. The despair of Europe, by contrast, struggling to emerge from the fog of war, "fed on ugliness and upheavals" (Camus, "Helen's Exile" 148). Greek philosophers like Heraclitus—whose Fragment 94 states that even "[t]he sun will not go beyond its bounds"—extolled the virtue of moderation or measure.[4] "But the Europe we know, eager for the conquest of totality, is the daughter of excess [*démesure*]. We deny beauty" (149). The Greeks went to war to save Helen from Paris's Troy, but "[w]e have exiled beauty" (148).

Camus, like Rabhi, mourns a world in the process of destroying itself. For Camus, ugliness takes the shape of misuse of power and ideologies through which humans lose their humanity and become abstractions, resulting in the calamity of war. For Rabhi, it is the environmental crisis—and particularly the agricultural tragedy—that threatens the world, as "destructive ugliness and constructive beauty" (*Manifeste* 109) wage war inside each one of us, and the human race continues—as Michel Serres put it—its "objective war" (*Natural Contract* 38) against nature. For Camus, two opposing forces are out to remake the world: history (power), whose goal is tyranny, and art, whose struggle is for freedom and beauty ("Helen's Exile" 152).

Camus is not writing an ecological essay; his concerns are purely human.[5] We have lost the Greeks' respect for measure and limits, as

---

4 In his *Carnets*, Camus divides his works into three cycles, the absurd, revolt, and moderation (*mesure*), sometimes translated as "measure" or "judgment." Each cycle is symbolized by a divinity from Greek mythology: Sisyphus for the absurd, Prometheus for revolt, and Nemesis for moderation. Nemesis punished those who, ignorant of limits, were guilty of hubris or lack of moderation.

5 Keith Moser points out that Rabhi's environmental activism differentiates him from twentieth-century French humanists like Camus: "Not only does Rabhi's humanism compel us to act on behalf of the collective good in human societies, but it also urges us to protect the sanctity of life itself. In this regard, he is different from both classical humanists and twentieth-century humanistic thinkers like Sartre, Camus, and Malraux. His strand of humanism is inseparable from the field of environmental ethics" (65). That is not to say that Camus is indifferent to the beauty of nature, as many lyrical passages on the Mediterranean sun, sea, and stars in *The Stranger* attest. In "Helen's Exile," Camus again exalts the beauty of the Mediterranean sun and regrets that "[w]e turn our backs on nature, we are ashamed of beauty" (150), a beauty nonetheless personified by a human: Helen of Troy.

"we are now witnessing the Messianic forces confronting one another, their clamors merging in the shock of empires" (151). Reason knows no boundaries and has become deadly. The world reels from the scourge of totalitarianism and the threat of nuclear war, when "the atom too bursts into flame, and history ends in the triumph of reason and the death agony of the species" (152). The human crisis will only be alleviated when Helen is freed:

> [M]an cannot do without beauty, and this is what our time seems to want to forget. We tense ourselves to achieve empires and the absolute, seek to transfigure the world before having exhausted it, to set it to rights before having understood it. Whatever we may say, we are turning our backs on this world. (152)

We have seen that, unlike Camus, Rabhi espouses a humanism very much decentered from humans. He stresses the contingency of humankind, whereas the beauty of nature is timeless, has existed before us and will exist after we disappear. The human being has from the beginning been "sensitive to nature" not just because it provided food, shelter, and clothing, "but also, through myths and symbols, because it stirred something in his psyche, in his most private emotions ... that inscribed him in the great mystery of life" (*Manifeste* 106). We are surrounded by man-made beauty, too: treasures of music, art, and architecture. But these artifacts are not the beauty that will "save the world." That can only be done by the "constructive beauty" that—through our interconnectedness to nature—each one of us holds in ourselves: "compassion, sharing, moderation, fair-mindedness, generosity, and respect for all forms of life. This is the only beauty capable of saving the world. For it is nourished by this mysterious fluid of constructive power that nothing can equal, and that we name Love" (109). Rabhi calls his love for the world a "symphony of the Earth" (59),[6] in which he—much like the hummingbird who inspired *Colibris*—strives to be a "little instrument" (59) for change.

Morin

Edgar Morin shares the guarded optimism of Pierre Rabhi as he looks into the abyss of the countless ecological crises the world

---

[6] See Chapter 3 above on the relevance of Rabhi's "symphony of the Earth" to *Mélusine des détritus*.

faces—Chernobyl, Fukushima, and many others—as a result of "science without conscience" (19). Unlike Rabhi, who came to ecology and philosophy via farming, Morin has had a long career in academia as a teacher and researcher in sociology, philosophy, and ecology, and is one of the foremost intellectuals of his time. As a young man in 1943, he joined the French resistance because, according to his biographer, "he could no longer abstract himself from a worldwide struggle between life and death" (Lemieux 7), and some 70 years later he feels that once again he must try "to save the world from itself" (7). Morin's ecological humanism is evident from the title of his 2016 book, *Écologiser l'homme* (Ecologize Man), which traces his ecological thought through ten essays dating from 1972, when he first began publishing on ecology, to 2016.

Morin's fundamental task is to overturn the Cartesian humanism that elevates humanity to a place of dominance over the rest of the universe, a subject among objects: "It is the ideology of man as an insular unit, a sealed monad in the universe" (26). He considers colonialism the great evil of European humanism and values the courage of those who have dared speak out against the supposed superiority of Western civilization, like Montaigne (in "Of Cannibals," for example), and ethnologists like Lévi-Strauss. Today's globalization is just the last step in what Morin calls the "planetary era" (77), which, in the Cartesian "chimera of the total mastery of the world" (76), began with Columbus's voyages to America at the end of the fifteenth century, and was characterized by "predation, slavery, colonization," and the exchange of deadly germs between Europe and the Americas (77). This was the disgraceful consequence of European humanism, but Morin points out this paradox: it was also humanistic ideals ("rights of man, rights of women, rights of people, rights of nations") that led to "emancipation of the oppressed and the colonized" (79).

Humans and the ecosystem are interdependent, and we must use our "ecological conscience" to act "like shepherds of nucleoproteins—living beings—and not like the Genghis Khan of the solar suburbs" (26–27). The relative insignificance of our solar system (Morin refers to the sun as "our little suburban star") makes the Cartesian project of the "conquest and possession of nature" even more "ridiculous" (45), given the infinite dimensions of the universe. The myth of progress symbolized by Prometheus "leads to the ruin of the biosphere, and thus to humanity's suicide" (45). Morin sums up his ecological humanism by stating: "The deification of man in the world must stop. Of course, we must respect man, but we know today that we can only do this by also respecting life: a deep esteem for man comes after a deep esteem for life" (45).

On the question of humanity's place in nature, Morin finds a paradox. On the one hand, he insists that we are "supermammals" or "superprimates," not "extra-mammals" or "extra-primates." In other words, as Serres and Latour have stressed, we are "not detached" (41) from nature, meaning that "biological organization ... is outside of us, in nature, but also inside of us, in our nature" (41). We are "children of the cosmos" (42), of the stardust of carbon and helium formed in the first few seconds of the universe. In a sense, however, we have been "wrenched" from nature, as Vercors wrote in *You Shall Know Them*. Morin explains: "Indeed, we are fully children of the cosmos. But through evolution, through the particular way in which our brain developed, through language, culture, and society, we have become strangers to the cosmos, we have distanced and marginalized ourselves from it" (42). We are thus at the same time one with and distinct from nature.

Morin envisions the earth like a spaceship with four motors: "science, technology, industry, and economy" (86). Each motor has positive and negative poles, but unfortunately "the evil, perilous, even fatal aspects have dominated." Spaceship Earth "has no pilot," and to make matters worse, "the passengers are fighting among themselves" (86). In a final chapter Morin proposes three possible solutions to our predicament, "three principles of hope in hopelessness" (123). The first is the principle of the "improbable" (123–25). In 1941, for example, Hitler's domination of Europe was probable. But an improbable series of events (the failed German attack on Moscow due in part to the brutal Russian winter, the Japanese attack on Pearl Harbor that brought the United States into the war, etc.) led to the improbable Allied victory. We can hope that such improbable good fortune may help us avoid an ecological disaster. The second principle of hope stems from untapped human potential in the form of creative solutions to problems. This creativity, says Morin, "often needs a violent shock in order to manifest itself, as was the case in France in 1789" (126). Perhaps it will take a calamity to inspire human beings to find unprecedented solutions to the environmental crisis.[7] The third principle of hope comes from the possibility of a social metamorphosis: "Today the planet can no longer solve its deadly problems nor take care of its vital needs. Now a system that can't meet its basic needs either falls apart or manages to metamorphose into a richer and more complex metasystem, capable of solving these problems" (128). The world is in its dying agony, and since agony means a battle between the forces of life and death, "that which brings death can bring new life" (128). The closer we get to a catastrophe, the closer we come to a possible metamorphosis. Morin quotes the beginning of Hölderlin's poem "Patmos": "But where danger is, grows / The saving power also" (128).[8] Only humans, the root of the environmental crisis, can invent solutions to it. "Promethean man" must metamorphose into "promising man" (112). Morin's conclusion ends with a plea for humanity to change its path, to choose "the path of hope" and perhaps find a glimmer of hope in the midst of a desperate environmental crisis.

Maffesoli
We have already seen how Michel Maffesoli's ideas on the need for "reenchantment" are pertinent to the disenchanted fairy in *Mélusine des détritus* (see Chapter 3 above). Maffesoli is a professor emeritus of Paris Descartes University (Paris V), where he held the Durkheim Chair of Sociology, and his work has been deeply influenced by Gilbert Durand's theories on myth, symbols, and the imaginary.

---

7 Stéphane Audeguy makes the same point at the end of his interview (see the Appendix below): "I don't think that radical change can come without a major calamity." I can't help but wonder if, as this book goes into production, the calamity of which Morin and Audeguy speak is raging across the planet in the form of the COVID-19 pandemic.
8 Heidegger quotes these lines of Hölderlin in "The Question Concerning Technology," which I briefly refer to in Chapter 2. Heidegger's essay inspired Stéphane Audeguy's remark that, through technology, we have commandeered (*arraisonné*) nature in the name of our endless pursuit of progress. In Heidegger's words, science "entraps nature" (303), reducing it to a "storehouse of the standing energy reserve" (302). We are "chained to technology" (287); it is a menace. However, as Hölderlin writes in "Patmos": "But where danger is, grows / The saving power also" (310). Heidegger maintains that in technology's very essence may hide what protects us from it: "in technology's essence roots and thrives the saving power" (310).

He has written on many subjects, including violence, the Dionysian spirit, nomadism, modern tribalism, and postmodernity. In 2017 he published *Écosophie. Une écologie pour notre temps* (Ecosophy: An Ecology for our Time). In this section we will define the term "ecosophy," and develop some of *Écosophie*'s key concepts, already introduced in Chapter 3: Promethean "progressism" versus Dionysian "progressivism," "correspondences" between humans and their environment, and the "return to the Real."

In an interview, Maffesoli explains that he borrowed the concept of "ecosophy" from Raimon Pannikar, a Spanish theologian who published an essay entitled *Ecosofía* in 1994 (interview by Alexandre Devecchio n. pag.). Most ecocritics, however, would associate the term with Félix Guattari or Arne Naess, the founder of deep ecology, who coined the word in *Ecology, Community, and Lifestyle* (1976). Stephanie Posthumus explains the difference between Naess's ecosophy and the concept developed by Guattari in *Qu'est-ce que l'écosophie?* (2013):

> Naess's ecosophy rejects the notion of humans as separate from nature. ... Naess argues that the ecological Self emerges when the human subject goes beyond narrow human concerns and recognizes itself as part of an ecospheric whole. Through the realization of this greater Self, humans relinquish their place as above or outside of nature. (Posthumus, *French Écocritique* 34)

> For Guattari, ecosophy is first and foremost a philosophy according to which there exist three overlapping and heterogeneous ecologies: social, mental, and environmental. ... Ecosophy represents, he explains, "a political-ethical choice for diversity, creative dissensus, responsibility with respect to difference and alterity." (33–34; quoting Guattari 33, translated by Posthumus)

Maffesoli's ecosophy is closely aligned with Naess's, in that both men stress that we share the earth's biosphere with all creatures; we are not the crown of creation. In the Devecchio interview, Maffesoli implies that some ecologists believe that humans are to be distinguished from nature. But "[i]n ecosophy, man is not separate from nature, he is an element of it. ... To take an example, ecosophy considers that we humans are an animal species. Refusing this animality leads us to bestiality." In *Écosophie*, Maffesoli writes that, unlike modernity's unbridled race to some uncertain future, ecosophy involves respect for the past and the "ancient wisdom (*sophia*)[9] of our common house (*oikos*), this earth" (10, 132); "What passes for reality (in economics, in politics, in the media) is but appearance" (10).

Like all ecological humanists, Maffesoli condemns the exploitation of nature that stems from Genesis and from Descartes's *Discourse*. Modernity (which for Maffesoli extends roughly from the Industrial Revolution through the 1950s) has run its course: "A number of the values of modernity—individualism, the social contract, and in a certain measure representative democracy—are saturated" (interview by Devecchio). Dominated by the myth of progress, modernity's philosophy is one of "progressism" ("progressisme"), symbolized by Prometheus. Postmodernity (beginning for Maffesoli earlier than for most, in the 1950s) is slowly moving towards "progressivism" ("progressivité"), symbolized by Dionysus.

Prometheus symbolizes for environmentalists the hubris and destructiveness of modern technological progress. For Camus, on the contrary, the titan is a positive figure, personifying revolt, the second cycle of Camus's *œuvre*, which features the novel *The Plague* (1947) and the essay *The Rebel* (1951). In "Prometheus in the Underworld," composed shortly after the end of World War II, Camus writes that Prometheus, "this victim of persecution is still among us and ... we are still deaf to the great cry of human revolt of which he gives the solitary signal" (138). People have betrayed the great rebel in the way they have faced history: "instead of mastering it, they agree a little more each day to be its slave" (140). Prometheus gave us many gifts: "fire and liberty, technology and art" (138–39). Sadly, humanity only cares about technological progress: "We rebel through our machines, holding art and what art implies as an obstacle and a symbol of slavery" (139).

In *Le Crépuscule de Prométhée*,[10] François Flahault, like Maffesoli, urges the "formulation of a post-Promethean thought" (back cover). The modern Prometheus, writes Flahault, is not the same as the Greek Prometheus who inspired Camus's *The Rebel*: he has been changed by

---

9 Cf. the last chapter of Michel Tournier's *The Wind Spirit*, "Sophia's Misfortunes," discussed above in Chapter 1.
10 See Chapter 2, where I reference Flahault in the discussion of Stéphane Audeguy's passages on Hiroshima.

his "meeting with monotheism" (26). For the Greeks, he symbolized emancipation and justice; under the influence of Christian humanism and the subsequent elevation of humans above all other creatures, emancipation became destruction and justice became excess (40).

So it is Dionysus, always a key figure for Maffesoli,[11] who is called to replace Prometheus. Dionysus is the anti-Prometheus: frenetic, wild, drunken, chaotic, even cannibalistic.[12] How exactly can such characteristics benefit society? Maffesoli emphasizes Dionysus's closeness to the earth: He is a "chthonic, autochthonous god, that is, an inhabitant of this earth" (*Écosophie* 12); he does not soar above the earth, as do humans in the myth of progress. Dionysus symbolizes a "progressive philosophy which, without negating the advancements of technology, can enrich them with more spiritual values, banking on the reversibility and the interaction between nature and society" (13). Maffesoli uses the metaphor of the heartbeat to differentiate between the two divine symbols of modernism and postmodernism. Modernism is diastolic, that is, "Promethean, where extension, the projective, in short, economics dominate." The ecosophic postmodern is systolic, "more Dionysian, withdrawn, focused on this world, this nature; thus we become autochthons, members of the earth (*chtonos*) and, in some way, responsible for it" (28).

Exchange between nature and culture is key to Maffesoli's ecosophy. This interaction is based on Gilbert Durand's declaration that in order to understand the imagination,

> we must deliberately position ourselves in the perspective of what we shall call the *anthropological dialectic* [*trajet anthropologique*], that is, *the ceaseless exchange taking place on the level of the imaginary between subjective assimilatory drives and objective pressures emanating from the cosmic and social milieu* ... we shall postulate that there is

---

11 In 1985, Maffesoli published *The Shadow of Dionysus: A Contribution to the Sociology of the Orgy*, where he argues that Dionysian excess is a necessary and constructive aspect of society. Dionysus parties in an eternal present, while hardworking Prometheus is concerned with the future fruits of his labor.
12 Marcel Detienne writes that Dionysus represents the bestial side of humans: "Humanity and bestiality interpenetrate and are confounded. ... Dionysus the savage hunter is not simply the 'eater of raw flesh' ...; the omophagy [eating raw flesh] he requires of his devotees leads them, like true wild beasts, to indulge in the most cruel allelophagy [eating human flesh]" (62).

a *reciprocal genesis* which alternates between the drive-motivated gesture and the material and social environment, and vice versa. (41–42; emphasis original)

As Baudelaire sensed in "Correspondances" that nature and humans exchange "confused words" in "forests of symbols," so Maffesoli sees "correspondences" (*Écosophie* 31) and even "reversibility" between us and our environment, ceaselessly repeated: "Repetitions showing the shift from the Promethean obsession—which considers nature an exploitable object—to "correspondence," a holistic reversibility, by which nature is culturalized and culture is naturalized" (31).

Ecosophy is a "return to the Real. ... A Real rich in dreams, myths, and fantasies" (13). The Real, which Maffesoli also calls "ecosophical sensibility" (14–15), recalls the "close connection between a territory and the people who live there" (14). Maffesoli is thus practicing a kind of cultural ecology, studying the relationship between land and people, habitat and inhabitants. Spatial, rather than temporal relationships, are at the core of his analysis: "Obsession with temporality was the mark of modern philosophy; naturalism, attached to roots, is substituting another concept, spatiality" (153–54). The return to the Real then is a return to nature, reminding us of our animality; a *radical* change from modernity, it recalls our roots in the earth: "with *humility*, recognize that the *human* is molded from *humus*" (80).

Humility, modesty, and respect characterize Maffesoli's ecosophy. He describes his version of ecological humanism as "a humanism that does not just concern the human, but respects nature in its entirety. Respect consisting of restraint and decency, modesty as well. Respect with discretion, consideration, and reserve *vis-à-vis* the strange strangeness of the natural thing" (73). These same values characterize the humanism of Lévi-Strauss, Rabhi, and Morin. Lévi-Strauss explains how imperialism, colonialism, slavery, and the Nazi death camps were the logical result of an arrogant European humanism that elevated humans over nonhumans, and then European humans over other ethnicities. Like Maffesoli, Lévi-Strauss insists on the need for a humanism based on "humility." Respect for others must be founded on the principle of "[h]umility before life, because life represents the rarest and most surprising creations that we can witness in the universe" (Lévi-Strauss, "L'idéologie marxiste" 14). As for Rabhi, respect for the earth is a constant refrain in his *Manifeste*. Like Pascal, in *Pensée*

72, "Man's Disproportion," he is humbled by the infinitely great—the vast night sky above the Cévennes mountains—and the infinitely small—the complexity of the tiniest seed (66). A twenty-first-century humanism requires "simple values such as benevolence towards those around us, a sober life, so that others may live; compassion, solidarity, respect, and the protection of Life in all its forms" (Rabhi, *Manifeste* 93). Morin too believes that we must lead "sober" lives if we are to be "ecologized." We must seek a cure for the various "intoxications" that contribute to ecological degradation, such as "automobile intoxication" (Morin 70) and "consumerist intoxication" (71). Moderation is the key to the ecologized human: "The problem is complex because mental and emotional discontent comes with our material well-being. We must rediscover that life's purpose has to do with living well, not having all; in quality—notably in human relations—and not quantity. We must ... become conscious of our dependence on the biosphere" (76).

Thomas Berry and "The New Story"

Lévi-Strauss, Rabhi, Morin, and Maffesoli advocate a new humanism that is compatible with environmentalism. They are part of the "New Story" told by Thomas Berry, who warns us in the epigraph to this chapter that hubris has led to the earth's desolation. This destruction will be our destiny, unless we reverse modernity's idea of "progress" and turn our "imperialist attitude to nature ... toward sustaining an integral Earth community in which the human becomes a functional component and not an oppressive destroyer" (Berry, "Teilhard" 62). Berry, an ecotheologian and Catholic priest, is nonetheless quite critical of the Christian model of humanism. He links the Western world's failure to respect the earth to a suppression of "pagan attitudes that were never assimilated into the tradition. ... A certain fear of these natural forces seems to exist in both religious and humanist traditions, fear lest established beliefs be weakened or some dark power from a realm of evil pervade the human order" (64). Maffesoli makes the same point when he declares that Christianity's struggle "against naturalism is essentially fought against the implacable enemy that is paganism" (*Écosophie* 40). He reminds us of the history of the Latin word *paganus*, which meant a person living in a rural area. Thus "*paganus* is the peasant [*paysan*] attached to this world, even in love with the land he comes from. That is the struggle against 'Darkness'" (40).

Berry proposes a "New Story" to explain the creation of the cosmos and the earth, and to determine our place in it. The "Old Story" has been dysfunctional since the fourteenth century, when the Black Death wiped out about half the population of Europe. Neither the religious nor the scientific community could offer adequate responses to this terrifying upheaval, and ever since, our society has lacked a working creation myth:

> It's all a question of story. We are in trouble just now because we do not have a good story. We are in between stories. The Old Story—the account of how the world came to be and how we fit into it—is not functioning properly, and we have not learned the New Story. (Berry, "The New Story" 77)

The "New Story" is a story of ongoing creation and continual transformation, an understanding of nature as process—*natura naturans* (see Larrère and Larrère, *Du bon usage* 71–81)—where the most important values are differentiation (the earth process produces variety in all things; there is an "inherent indestructible value of the individual" [Berry, "The New Story" 85]), subjectivity ("Every being has its own interior, its self, its mystery, its numinous aspect" [85]), and communion ("Each atomic particle is in communion with every other atom in the vast web of the universe" [86]). The restriction of subjectivity to solely the human race has resulted in what Berry calls the "savage plundering of the entire earth" ("The Viable Human" 176), with the following consequences:

> The vast mythic, visionary, symbolic world with its all-pervasive numinous qualities was lost. Because of this loss human beings made their terrifying assault upon the Earth with an irrationality that is stunning in its enormity, while we were being assured that this was the way to a better, more humane, more reasonable world.
>
> Such treatment of the external physical world deprived of subjectivity could not long avoid encompassing the human also. ("The New Story" 86)

According to Berry, humanity has passed through three stages in its history: from "tribal" to "civilizational" to "technological." His

"New Story" of the "cosmic-Earth-human" process, based on the three values of individual differentiation, extension of subjectivity to all beings, and "intercommunion of the universe within itself and of each part with the whole" (86–87) hopes to introduce a fourth historical stage, and restore the lost numinous aspect of our relationship with nature. Berry's "New Story" is a new account of the mystery of human existence—its past, present, and future— similar to the idea that Gauguin was trying to express in his famous Tahitian painting *Where Do We Come From? What Are We? Where Are We Going?* (*D'où venons nous? Que sommes nous? Où allons nous?*). Like Lévi-Strauss, Rabhi, Morin, and Maffesoli, he rejects the humanism of the Christian tradition, calling for an ecological humanism to include "the feeling for an interdependent biological community of the human with the natural world as the functional context for earthly existence" ("Teilhard" 59).

Berry's ambitious "New Story" of creation is being built on the more modest creations of novelists like the ones who have been the subjects of the preceding chapters, writers for whom the environment is, if not the protagonist, at least an important character. In *Gemini*, we have seen how meteorological phenomena like the tides structure the plot. At the end of the novel, Paul's human subjectivity dissolves, and his porous body joins the elements in an ecological subjectivity. It is said that future events are often predicted by works of fiction.[13] Tournier's *Gemini* raised awareness of landfill and incineration pollution well before serious steps were taken to address it. His ragpicker characters represent the lost practice of recycling, forgotten during the throw-away era of the "Trente Glorieuses," during the final years of which *Gemini* was published. In Chapter 2, we briefly examined Tournier's most ecological novel, *Friday*, which features a Crusoe who eventually rejects the imperialist humanism of Defoe's *Robinson Crusoe*; he comes to see the black man Friday as his equal, and learns to enjoy a symbiotic rather than parasitic relationship with nature.

---

13 Jules Verne and other science fiction writers are of course known for their uncanny predictions. But Tournier is also such an author. His *Ogre* raised the issue of French collaboration almost two decades before the French began to recognize their responsibility in the Holocaust, a painful process that has been dubbed the "Vichy Syndrome" (see J. Krell, *The Ogre's Progress* 129–31; Golsan 182).

In *The Theory of Clouds*, Stéphane Audeguy explores our ambiguous relationship to nature. He considers himself an ecological humanist (see his interview in the Appendix), and thus believes humans to be attached to nature; however, Promethean technology has detached us from nature and turned us into nature's predators. Audeguy's story of clouds reflects an important value of Berry's "New Story": communion between nature and humans, macrocosm and microcosm. For Audeguy, however, this communion is essentially erotic, an encounter between two infinitudes: human desire and boundless nature (*Opera mundi* 39).

Chantal Chawaf's *Mélusine des détritus* also demonstrates the close bond between humans and nature. Both the protagonist and the planet are sick from pollution and terrified of nuclear power and its endless containers of radioactive waste; both are victims of the Promethean age of progress, suffering in the present and facing a bleak future.

Vercors's and Rosenthal's novels question the prevailing ideas on the boundary between human and nonhuman animals. They are also versions of Berry's "New Story" and its values that include "an increasing differentiation [and] a deepening subjectivity" ("The New Story" 84). Both novelists convey the idea that animals are individuals: they are differentiated "animals," not the undifferentiated "animal." Rosenthal's marginalized narrator identifies closely with the animals she encounters in films and hears about during her conversations with various animal professionals. Her subjectivity extends to the animal world: "Your desire for humanity is more or less equivalent to your desire for animality. In reality, it is absolutely impossible to distinguish them" (Rosenthal, *Que font les rennes après Noël?* 164).

Finally, J.-C. Rufin and Iegor Gran contribute a healthy skepticism to environmental literature. Rufin's career as a doctor for humanitarian organizations, and later as a diplomat, provides him with a unique perspective on the connection between social and environmental problems. Like Rabhi, he understands that the need for humanitarian aid is proof of the failure of traditional humanism. As the rich countries of the North exploit the poorer countries of the South in the real world, so the fictional Globalia exploits, pollutes, and attacks the inhabitants of the non-zones, and then showers them with humanitarian aid. Both *Globalia* and *Le Parfum d'Adam* warn of the potential adverse consequences of an environmentalism devoid of humanism, when, as Posthumus writes, "'save nature' or 'save the planet' modes of intervention take on unsettling proportions, becoming an instrument used to keep people in line" (*French Écocritique* 109).

Iegor Gran is a Voltaire for our age, an intelligent satirist who exposes the excesses of environmentalism: hyperbolic apocalypticism, humorless dogmatism, paternalism, the shameless opportunism of greenwashing, and above all an antihumanism that reduces human beings to a single dimension: perpetrators of the environmental crisis. Gran does not dispute human responsibility, but he accentuates the obvious fact that only humans can find solutions to the crisis. We are the *pharmakon* that is both poison and cure, the inventors of a Promethean technology that, as Morin hopes, holds the promise of a remedy, for the "Promethean man" is also the "promising man" (112). Gran suggests that science, culture, and civilization can save us from our crisis like it saved Noah from his: "Noah saved himself by using engineering science, not by lamentations or self-flagellation, shutting himself in a cave, nor by doing a little something each day to save the planet" (*L'Écologie en bas de chez moi* 63 n. 1). Gran ends his novel with a plea for humanism, which for him means "seeing in each human being a gift to the world, not a mouth to feed, nor a CO_2-emitting apparatus, nor an intestinal parasite of nature" (161). In his uniquely entertaining way, Gran sends the same message to ecocritics as do the editors of *Ecocritical Approaches to Literature in French*. They "are more convinced than ever that the contributions to ecocriticism by scholars of French-language literature will foster an inclusive, sustainable, and humanist environmentalism that is truly global" (Boudreau and Sullivan 190), because "environmentalism [is] a manifestation of humanism" (195).

Appendix
Interviews with Stéphane Audeguy and Iegor Gran

Interview with Stéphane Audeguy on *The Theory of Clouds*
Paris, 24 June 2016

JK: Why did you decide to write a novel about clouds?

SA: I wonder in fact if the project itself didn't resemble a cloud, that is, a cluster of very different things: themes, personal passions, and ideas. As for ideas—and in my opinion the ideas do not come first—it's important to say that I don't think one can describe how one had an idea of something; it is in fact an *a posteriori* reconstitution that one is trying to do. It is exactly as if I were to ask you how a cloud appears. You couldn't answer, because it's quite difficult to witness the formation.

For the formation of my novel about clouds, there were important ideas. For example, one idea was to write a novel about globalization. About the global, let's say. Not on globalization in the journalistic sense, but on the world becoming, knowing that in my opinion this is the work of the human species, which is a globalizing species. So, there's a first idea. And next, meteorology was interesting because it is the science of a system, the science of the global. And I would say that a novel about meteorology involves understanding a system. For modern meteorology to exist, people must believe that the world is finite. For example, I remember that the French national meteorology service was founded because a storm had damaged Napoleon III's ships. France was at war with Crimea at the time, and a meteorologist said to Napoleon III: "But if you had just given me meteorological stations, I could have predicted this catastrophe." And thus meteorology is linked to a military issue, a global issue. Weather reports exist to make war, to amend the famous expression of a famous geographer, Yves Lacoste, who said that geography exists to make war. So meteorology, then, is a second idea in *The Theory of Clouds*.

Next, I would say that besides ideas there are loves or passions, and my particular passion was for John Constable and J. M. W. Turner, two great painters of clouds. And then I could add one of Baudelaire's *Little Prose Poems*, "The Stranger," in which an isolated, lonely, and mysterious man is asked what he likes, and he responds that he likes neither family nor friends nor gold nor anything in fact on which normal human values are founded. (I am certain that Camus was thinking of this poem when he wrote his novel, but I've rarely seen it cited as a source.) Anyway, as you know, at the end of this poem, Baudelaire writes: "I love the clouds—the clouds that pass—yonder—the marvelous clouds." And so, I had in mind a number of ideas, texts, and a passion for certain painters. And these little droplets ended up coming together to form a sort of nebula: references, ideas, and sensations that became the novel. It's a novel about clouds that grew and then appeared like a cloud.

JK: On its famous red band, Gallimard described *The Theory of Clouds* as a *Theory of Bodies*. Was this your idea? For you, what is the connection between nature and the human body, this "confrontation between the limitlessness of desire and the unthinkable infinity of nature" that you describe in *Opera mundi* (39)? Did Courbet's *L'Origine du monde* inspire your invention of the "Abercrombie Protocol"?

SA: The advertising band wasn't my idea, but I wasn't against it. Why not? For me, Courbet has always been an important reference. He is a painter of the female body: this famous painting that still makes American women shriek when they encounter it at the Orsay Museum. They see it and cry, "Oh my God!" … it's great! This painting is intense, violent, and obviously very well known. But Courbet is also an interesting painter of sea clouds. And what people sometimes forget is that Courbet often painted the Loue, a small river in his region, not far from Besançon. I remember seeing Courbet's paintings of the Loue, where you can see a sort of dark valley with a little hill and a thicket of trees above it. Everyone says that Courbet finds the same eroticism in nature as in bodies. I think that it's through the body that the civilized human being stays in contact with nature. Even if he is no longer a farmer, no longer this, no longer that; what remains of a consubstantial connection between nature and us is, on the one hand, our own body, and on the other hand, naturally, the sky. That is, even in a city I can still see the sky. Clouds are what remains when there is nothing else. Even in the center of São Paulo, with its 12 million people, you gaze upward, and you can still catch a glimpse of nature. Furthermore, I think that eroticism is also a way to become depersonalized, and to touch that ocean of pleasure, the body, the body's humors and drives. In that way indeed *The Theory of Clouds* is Courbetian. One of the characters in my novel begins to photograph female genitalia, and of course this is a nod to that particular time in the nineteenth century. As soon as photography is invented, people start taking photos of female genitalia, Courbetian photographs. I have a book by Auguste Belloc, a photographer who took stereoscopic pictures of naked women. He was arrested and sentenced in 1860. Photography was invented around 1839, and pornographic photographs have existed since the beginning.

JK: Richard Abercrombie was partially based on Ralph Abercromby, the author of *Seas and Skies in Many Latitudes* (1889). How do these two men resemble one another?

SA: Writers are often asked about the source of their characters. But if I try to respond scrupulously to the question of how Richard and Ralph are alike, I would say "not at all" in a sense, because one is a paper character, fictitious, invented by me, and the other is a historical person, a traveler named Ralph Abercromby who went around the world twice taking photographs of clouds. I must insist on their essential difference. Even if I were to write my self-portrait—God forbid—and made myself a character, there would be an *essential* difference between the character and me. But obviously I can't pretend there is no connection between them.

What struck me about the character of Ralph Abercromby was that he was English in all the potential horror of that word: that is, someone who could twice circle the globe without in any way being moved by the world that he moves through, without being modified by it. Abercromby is a tourist, if you will, in the worst sense of the term. One can be a tourist and be deeply moved by a journey, of course. But here was this fascinating person who, fundamentally, was the typical Westerner. Now, he is traveling at a time when atypical Westerners—like Arthur Rimbaud, Paul Gauguin, Robert Louis Stevenson, D. H. Lawrence—are traveling to unknown lands in search of something new. Also, there is the whole tradition of peripatetic writers. All these people travel to heal themselves. Stevenson and others, for example, go to warm countries because they think it's better for their health. In a sense, they will also heal something of the Western sickness. We can recall Gauguin who, at first, works in the bank and paints on Sundays; but his bourgeois marriage was rather boring, it seems, and he escaped.

And so, I imagined that Abercrombie—mine—would resemble Ralph, but he would be capable of change. Now that I think of it, I realize that I changed the spelling of the name a bit in order to point out this difference, which is not phonetic, but written. Moreover, my Abercrombie is more feminine in French—because his name ends in "e"—than Ralph Abercromby. It's as if the feminine is an access road to a kind of deconstruction of Western masculine identity.

JK: In *The Forge and the Crucible*, Mircea Eliade recalls how the world has always been sexualized, and that nature has always been feminized. And Carolyn Merchant's first chapter of *The Death of Nature* is titled "Nature as Female." At the end of *The Theory of Clouds*, would you say that your character Virginie, by her association with clouds, assumes her independence and frees herself from feminine stereotypes?

SA: Indeed, it all ties together. It's funny, I realize all that when I discuss it with you. But I don't ask myself this kind of question when I work. One can say that in *The Theory of Clouds* there is a female character named Virginie, and I notice, for the first time in my life, that her name ends in "ie," like Abercrombie. Thus, we are once again in the feminine. So, if I were a psychoanalyst, I would point out to you that my name ends in a "y." But as a child, the first thing that fascinated me about my name was that I thought my last name was made up of two first names, one feminine—Aude—and the other masculine—Guy. However, etymologically, that is completely false, because the "Aude" is a peasant name that means *alt*/"old." Audeguy means "old guy"; there is nothing feminine about it!

Now we come to the question of the feminine. In fact, the novel's protagonist, in some ways, is a woman, since Virginie is the main character of the frame narrative. I wanted to invent a character who did not seem very intelligent in the beginning. She says herself that she is not intelligent, which is not false. I also wanted to imagine a character who changes and who, in her relations with others, in her relations with alterity, by way of clouds, experiences an initiation and a metamorphosis. She is someone who changes and frees herself from a certain stereotypical identity, through how she relates to clouds.

JK: Not through men, but through clouds.

SA: Well, through men as well, except that I wanted to avoid the cliché—always annoying—of the woman initiated to the truth by a man. Most notably, she has a relationship with the Japanese fashion designer who is the novel's hero. Now this relationship is not sexual, and I insisted that it not be. The older man initiating a younger woman is a grotesque stereotype. Thus, indeed the character evolves through her relationships with men, but also beyond men; her evolving sexuality is closely linked to nature. The storms of sensuality correspond to nature's storms. This kind of reverie was behind the novel. It is a *Bildungsroman*, strangely enough, in the sense that the character is educated, opens up to something, and changes. I have written other novels like this: *The Only Son* (*Fils unique*) is a *Bildungsroman*. I am very interested in this question of emancipation.

JK: You once said in an interview that humans "have seized [*arraisonné*] nature, like a ship: we board and search it, we believe we own it" ("De la nature de quelques choses" 244; see Chapter 2 above). How does *The Theory of Clouds* demonstrate this boarding, searching, and seizing (*arraisonnement*)?

SA: Here again we touch on the question of sources. I was quite struck by the text in which Heidegger employs this particular term: "The Question Concerning Technology" (see Chapter 2 above). Now I am neither a Germanist nor a philosopher, so I don't guarantee the Heideggerian orthodoxy of my ideas. But what was it about Heidegger's term—usually translated in French as *arraisonner, arraisonnement*[1]—that struck me? Heidegger considers how humans, especially since the scientific revolution of the Renaissance, have been attempting to seize control of nature. And then he gives a very striking example. Of course, people had always tried to control or establish a connection with nature, but they had never taken possession of it. If I recall, Heidegger differentiates between a mill and a dam. Obviously, they are quite different. A mill diverts the energy of a river in order to activate the mill mechanically. You don't change the nature of the energy, and you barely change the course of the river. You have a small reach of water, a little canal that sends the water towards your wheel. You "plug into" nature, but you are not, as Descartes would say, master and possessor of nature. (By the way, a French writer named Vincent Message recently published a novel called *Défaite des maîtres et possesseurs* (Defeat of the Masters and Possessors). He studied philosophy and codirects with Olivia Rosenthal the master's program of creative writing at Paris VIII.) But let's get back to Heidegger. In contrast to the mill, the hydroelectric dam completely modifies the landscape and the ecosystem; moreover, it transforms the water's energy into something other than mechanical energy. It produces electricity, and this electricity has no particular destination. It is no longer purely mechanical; its nature changes. And that is one of the elements of *arraisonnement*. Therefore, when I read that, and when I think about clouds, as I always think by association, I immediately think of Hiroshima. For Hiroshima is a denaturing of matter itself. Energy comes from matter; 6 August 1945 is a sinister and crucial date in this history of *arraisonnement*.

Moreover, to board, search, and seize a ship (*arraisonner un navire*) means to take ownership of it, inspect and inventory what is inside. Legally, one takes ownership. It is thus an aggression; we take something over, we believe that we possess it. The Cartesian formula is that we are "*as it were*, masters and possessors of nature." Obviously, *arraisonnement* removes the "as it were."

I think my novel moves as it does towards Hiroshima because it considers Hiroshima the absolute founding date of a fury: an uncontrollable technological fury, a weapon of a type unparalleled in history. With Hiroshima we enter an outrageous period of excess.

---

1 The German term is *Ge-stell*, usually translated in English as "enframing."

And, of course, this catastrophe is also our entrance into the second part of the twentieth century. In May 2016 Barack Obama became the first American president to visit the site of Hiroshima. John Kerry, the Secretary of State, had gone there a month or so earlier. Two years before their visits, I was in Hiroshima on 6 August and there was not a large American contingent.

Two more remarks. The first is that *The Theory of Clouds* is not a *roman à these*. The novel does not attempt to prove or teach anything. On the other hand—and this is the second remark—the novel ends on a storm that was not forecast. And I am always struck, obviously, by the ridiculous nature of the claim that we can master nature. It reveals a human hubris, a human immoderation, pride, pretentiousness, and—to use a word that I love—*outrecuidance* (overconfidence, self-importance; literally "to believe beyond"), a Western *outrecuidance* that is unbelievable. I was one of the people who laughed when in 2010 an Icelandic volcano grounded all European airplanes. It was alright to laugh, because no one died. But there was something very remarkable about this eruption: I was told (but I never verified) that the energy generated by the volcano was greater than that of Hiroshima. It's fascinating, of course, because it shows us that there is an immoderation even greater than our own.

JK: Are you an ecologist?

SA: I am not a fundamentalist ecologist. I don't think that things were better in the past; I don't think that we must "go back" to something. I am quite struck by the extraordinary ingenuity of the human species. An anecdote: I was invited two weeks ago to a Sunday program on *France Culture* to speak about the catastrophic flooding that recently hit l'Île-de-France. My first remark was very simple. The flooding destroyed an enormous number of houses. The death toll from this catastrophe, in a region of 12 million people: four. Cost of the damage: more than a billion euros. That is to say that catastrophes in the world that we have in the West have little effect on humans. The species is not threatened; individual humans themselves are barely threatened. No one dies! Who is the main victim? The consumer society. What we see on television are houses ripped apart, broken freezers, spoiled frozen food, and the people are desperate. I understand them; I'm not saying they are wrong. But it's remarkable to see a civilization of *things* like this; one capable of sustaining a billion-euro catastrophe that is not a human catastrophe. Because if this happens in certain parts of India or Africa, the result will not be the same. People will lose nothing because they have nothing, but they will die. This is a measure of the extraordinary efficiency of Western civilization.

JK: Would you then call yourself an ecological humanist?

SA: Yes. Radical ecologists at least have the merit of having drawn attention to important problems. I do not always agree with them, nor with the speciesists, nor with the deep ecologists. Take, for example, the demographic growth rate, an intrinsically ecological problem. I am not in favor of starting a war in order to solve this kind of issue, but nevertheless overpopulation is obviously a problem. But behind demographics lurk Malthusian questions that no one wants to ask. And I am rather pessimistic because it seems to me that the consumer system requires an enormous population. The system, the Moloch of consumerism, needs consumers. And without changing that mentality, nothing will be solved. We seem indeed to be headed towards a catastrophe. However, I am not a catastrophist, and I fervently hope we will not get there.

JK: In June 2015 Pope Francis published his encyclical *Laudato si'*, in which he criticizes countries for deeming the environmental crisis secondary "to technology and finance"; instead, we must "redefin[e] our notion of progress." Isn't that the fundamental theme of *The Theory of Clouds* as well as *Nous Autres* (2009)?

SA: We are in a situation so serious that even I, a non-papist, non-Christian, non-believer—I am completely atheistic—pay close attention to the pope's declarations, because he represents a community. I am happy that Catholics seem to be on this side now and are concerned about the environment. We need all people of good will, just as it says in the Bible! But that said, I am still struck by something. Your question implies another question, a political one: In what sense can the Church actually commit to the pope's statements? Does the Church have power enough to achieve the conversion called for by the pope? Personally, I doubt it. I think, however, that this pope is unique. I strongly doubt that his encyclical was received by all the cardinals with great enthusiasm. This pope's point of view is quite emancipated in many ways. And also—very unusual in the history of Catholicism—he is revisiting the declarations of Pope Pius XII's encyclical *Miranda Prorsus* (1957, on the modern media), which state that television and radio can be tools of evangelization. Thus, at one time the Church was a force of modernity, not at all hostile towards it.

I think that in the message of Pope Francis there are a certain number of "returns to." The text says: "return to … simplicity." But that raises a very very simple problem: there is never a "return" in history. I don't know of any. New "kinds of" may be invented, but I have never seen any "returns to." Return to the plow, return to the candle? No. I don't think that this is good positioning, if I may say so. Besides the pope, I think that some ecologists present their theses in an extremely anxiety-provoking way, and not creatively or positively enough. As for Pope Francis, he can't ignore that the roots of this technological civilization—which succeeded in dominating nature like none other—are profoundly Christian. Perhaps Christianity, as the philosopher Marcel Gauchet said, is the religion that allows one to leave religion. That is, it's the religion that produces atheism, while perhaps other religions don't produce atheists with as much enthusiasm. And it is clear that *incarnation* is the divine in the human, the possibility to give a certain dignity to objects of nature, contrary to a very common myth in France that the Church was a uniquely antiscientific force. On the contrary, the incarnation gave a theological dignity to the material world, so that it is not by chance that the sciences developed in the Judeo-Christian context. And America is an offshoot—not Catholic, but Christian—of this civilization. The whole Western world is a Christian world, and it is this Christian world that has shaped, I would say, our way of approaching the notion of *progress*, to take an example other than incarnation. I think that the incarnation is closely linked to the development of the sciences, but, on the other hand, the notion of progress assumes a conception of history—the one in which we are living—where history has and must have a meaning: that is, a direction. There must be progress. And I would also say that a good part of the ecological movement is still Christian in the way that it is announcing an apocalypse: "Repent, the end is near." And there are also ecological fantasies of "a life after": a world—after the end of the world—that will be better.

JK: *Laudato si'* doesn't condemn progress. At the end of his text, the pope writes that he wants to redefine progress in terms other than GDP growth. Do you believe that this too is a fantasy?

SA: There seems to be a tendency among French economists to reject the traditional criteria that define progress. Some believe that aggregates like GDP are merely quantitative criteria of economic success and as such they are insufficient. Certain economists oppose the Chicago school of economics, declaring that to truly measure the success of a country, GDP is not enough; we must use the Human Development Index (HDI), which includes not only GDP, but also education and life expectancy. If this is what the pope is saying, I agree.

Anyway, the true paradox here is that, indeed, perhaps a good part of Christianity could today become a force of resistance to capitalism, even if it also gave birth to it. That is well-known: after all, the Marxists did not emerge from the ranks of the proletariat.

JK: Pope Francis is a revolutionary, is he not? He doesn't represent the majority.

SA: Yes, yes it's strange. I thought he would be assassinated … poisoned …

JK: A Dan Brown novel become a reality.

SA: Yes, unfortunately. Alas! But I am actually fairly sensitive to these attempts to redefine progress. For there are others. There are the alter-globalists.[2] Then there are atheistic forms of this movement, and personally I prefer those to the religious variety for the reasons I just mentioned. Because I think that to redefine progress is to challenge capitalism … completely. And if the pope wants to do that, I don't think his cardinals will support him. He seems very isolated; it's very strange. It's like a revolutionary saint at the head of an ultra-reactionary college. All you have to do is compare him politically to his predecessor, Benedict XVI. The difference is incredible. And Francis is a Jesuit!

---

2 The alter-globalization movement protests against the injustices inherent in economic globalization.

Everyone works in his own way. I don't do politics; I would never write an essay on ecology because that's not my temperament: I write novels. Therefore, I try to work in my own way to redefine certain cultural terms such as "progress." For me it's clear that my characters who progress are people who take a different path from the capitalistic society in which they live. Even Abercrombie in *The Theory of Clouds* is a rebellious man. In this way, I like contradiction; I am glad that the pope is like that. It makes me happy because I think people should be contradictory. We have to be attached to our memories—we must remember everything that this civilization offers us—before saying we have to throw it all out. Thus, I am not a radical in that sense. Unfortunately, I wonder too how we can impose this new definition of progress. I don't think it will come from us, by the way. It might only come if there is a war. I don't think that radical change can come without a major calamity. Anyway, I write novels, I don't set off bombs, thus I participate in politics in my way, by writing books, by teaching.

Culture and education: it's a bit of a banal conclusion, but I think that each time I write a book, it's a way of redefining. Writing is, as Mallarmé said, "to give a purer meaning to the words of the tribe" ("The Tomb of Edgar Poe"). Thus, writing is an attempt to modify the meaning of words. For example, when someone baptizes a novel *The Theory of Clouds*, it is an endeavor to attract people's attention to the fact that "theory" means "parade," "procession," but also "science" or "contemplation." The Greek meaning is "to observe," "to contemplate"; the modern sense is "hard science." I found the third meaning, "procession," in Diderot and d'Alembert's *Encyclopédie*. Thus, the clouds that pass are at the same time objects of a scientific theory and objects of contemplation, and not just of consumption … let alone something to take a selfie in front of!

Interview with Iegor Gran on *O.N.G!* and *L'Écologie en bas de chez moi*
Paris, 4 July 2016

We are sitting in the Café Rostand, facing the Luxembourg Gardens, their black fence covered with enormous photographs.

JK: Your novels on ecology—*O.N.G!* and *L'Écologie en bas de chez moi*—are the opposite of "politically correct." Were the reactions of the press and your readers mostly positive or negative?

IG: The press reacted rather positively. I had negative reactions for both books, but mostly during radio or television interviews. For example, I was on *France Culture* radio for *O.N.G!* There were several of us on the set discussing film and literature, including a young columnist who wrote on cinema. During a musical break, he turned to me and, off-mic, said, "I really wanted to tell you that what you have written there is an obnoxious book, because you, sir, are here in Paris, taking it easy, while I have a friend who is saving people in Africa." He spoke very seriously and was quite aggressive. Then he got up and walked off because he had finished his commentary. There are several very interesting things about this anecdote. First of all, he was not the one in Africa, but by proxy of his friend who was, he considered himself above us. He allowed himself this moral right to judge me, which is frightening, but interesting. And so I said to myself, it's true, in fact, those who are saving people in Africa are a moral guarantor for the rest of us who are saving no one, who are here in Paris, who read newspapers, who write columns about movies. And we are reassured by the fact that there are people in Africa who save people. Thus, in reality we are in a medieval system of the monastery where those who want to pray, pray for salvation—not for themselves but for the salvation of the world. They pray for people who live in sin—greed, fornication, whatever you like. They cut themselves off from the world and pray for the salvation of the rest of humanity, and we are very happy that they are there. I thought that there was something fairly important in what that columnist had said.

For *O.N.G!*, I was on the set of LCI (La Chaîne Info). I was invited with Bruno Rebelle, then a director of Greenpeace France.

The journalist asked us a question about my book. Rebelle said, yes, this book is funny, but it's not very serious. And then the cameras go off for a commercial, and he picks up my book and throws it at me, saying, "Your book is shit!" And I said, "What a shame, you are an absolute coward. You waited until the cameras cut off before saying that. I would have loved to hear you say it on live TV. But you know, as I do, that you are a communications professional, and thus you have to pretend to be pleasant when you are on TV." (He is much more professional than I, by the way. I'm very bad on television, but he is excessively good because communication is his job: he sells his stuff.) So that was a second aggressive reaction against *O.N.G!*

There was also violent criticism of *L'Écologie en bas de chez moi*. For example, on a Canal+ show called *La Matinale*, there was a literary columnist who had liked my book. She was speaking about it in very positive terms. The journalist organizing the program cuts her off and says, "Yes, but what if everyone started writing things like that? Where would that lead? Humanity is condemned! The planet is condemned! This book is absolutely irresponsible! I don't want to hear another word!" So we were cut off. It was pretty funny.

And then of course there are a lot of negative reactions when I give readings in the provinces. There is always an ecologist in the crowd who stands up and gives me a lecture on my total irresponsibility: because of me, the planet is in danger! It's pretty crazy. There are superheroes, the ones who save you, who sort your garbage and recycling, who do lots of things to help save the planet. But I am a supervillain. We live in a cartoon world, a DC Comics world, where it is truly good versus evil, every day. That is one of the ideas I was obsessed with while writing *L'Écologie en bas de chez moi*. They say to people: You little, insignificant, ordinary creature; you can save the planet! Superman isn't going to save the planet, you will! Because you are going to take fewer showers, you are going to put a catalytic converter on your car, you are going to separate waste, you are going to do all kinds of little acts to help the planet (it's these "little acts" that get on my nerves); you are going to become a superhero. Now in my opinion, this is a sin of pride, impossibly vain. Humans take themselves for demigods, when they are no better than mollusks! On the one hand, I find that very funny, and on the other hand, frightening. And I detect there a certain assault on individual freedom, since the second logical mechanism is that, all alone, you can take as many short showers as you like, stop flushing the toilet, and avoid polluting. However, all alone you won't save the planet, of course. It will only work if we all work together. Obviously, this idea contains a grain of totalitarian coercion, because if just *one* person doesn't try to save the planet, doesn't sort garbage, then the planet is threatened.

Last March I was on Laurent Ruquier's show, *On n'est pas couché*.[1] We were discussing my novel *La Revanche de Kevin* (Kevin's Revenge, 2015). We were also talking about other books I had written, when all of a sudden, while we were speaking about literature, one of the columnists—a man who is extremely aggressive and unpleasant with everyone—said to me, "Do you sort your recycling?" It came out of nowhere, an absolutely surreal question, a bit like saying, "Do you have syphilis?" or "Do you like to look at little girls, while imagining things?" So my response was, "Who cares?" (*bof*). He was indignant because I didn't say right away: "Of course, I separate my garbage like everyone, like you. I think constantly about my garbage." Today's human being is someone who must, day and night, think about his garbage. All day long, we must think about our garbage, whereas it was so simple before: you put everything in the same bin, and it was sorted by workers who knew what they were doing. By the way, recently a Danish friend sent me an article about separating garbage and recycling in Denmark, which is much more advanced than we are in this matter. A serious study just came out, which concluded that sorting was not worth it, because more often than not all the containers are mixed together when they arrive at the center. Even the hyper-disciplined Danes sometimes make mistakes. Or else, perhaps a Danish grandmother who is not all there puts a bottle in the wrong bin, and they are forced to sort everything again. So essentially, separating recyclables and garbage seems not to work so well.[2]

Another question that I wonder about, since we're talking about recycling, is the real cost for the global economy. No one ever talks

---

1   *On n'est pas couché* (We Are Not Asleep) is a late-night talk show on the France 2 television network.
2   Recent news articles confirm Gran's suspicions that recycling may not be working so well. As part of its 2017 antipollution campaign, China began refusing to accept foreign recycling: "In particular, exports of scrap plastic to China, valued at more than $300 million in 2015, totaled just $7.6 million in the first quarter of this year [2018], down 90 percent from a year earlier" (Albeck-Ripka n. pag.). Many recyclable materials are now ending up in landfills.

about this. What does that mean, the fact that there is not one, but five containers? What does it mean in terms of lost time for the people who separate their recyclables? There is of course a cost. They say that time is money, and truly, citizens are spending time on recycling. But their time is worth nothing, because it is understood that they are losers. I'm not the one saying it; it's governments who are imposing this sorting, who *de facto* are telling their citizens that their free time has no value. You are better off sorting recyclables in your free time rather than reading a book, going to a movie, going for a walk, etc. My question is: When will there be an objective study of the costs of recycling centers in terms of energy, time, taxpayers' money, etc.? But this study will never be done, not because I'm a conspiracy theorist, but because it is not in anyone's interest today to produce such a study. Neither the government nor the citizens want it. Everyone is very happy, very enthusiastic about the idea of spending their time sorting recyclables, because it is a little act to help save the planet: "I too am doing something. I am not passive in the face of global warming."

JK: Are you familiar with Pascal Bruckner's *The Fanaticism of the Apocalypse* (2011)? He also believes that all these "little acts for the planet" are laughable because of the sheer scale of a potential environmental disaster: "a cosmic calamity is not going to be averted by eating vegetables and sorting our rubbish" (32).

IG: This book is very serious. What is the "little act" a sign of? When I walk past a church, I make the sign of the cross, because you never know. There was a time, even at the beginning of the twentieth century, that when you came across a hearse in the street, you made the sign of the cross. Why? It was the "little act," and it reassured everyone. Today we are happy to do our "little act." It's not that there is an evil government or evil ecologists who have imposed this by totalitarian pressure. Absolutely not. We are living in Dostoevsky's *Grand Inquisitor*: humans want to be told what to do, to have someone explain to them in simple terms what is useful.

JK: That's why we invented gods.

IG: Yes, but today there are no more gods. Especially in France we live in a secular world. The only god in France is the Republic, a goddess whose profile you see everywhere. You can see "Liberty, Equality, Fraternity" even on certain French churches: this dates from the time of the Revolution.

JK: How did people react to the violence against women in *O.N.G!*? There are similar scenes in *Candide* (Cunégonde's story, for example), but we are no longer in the eighteenth century. Were you criticized for including a rape scene in a comic novel?

IG: To my great regret, I assume that, since the scene appears at the end of the book, many readers never got that far! And many who got there didn't necessarily understand what was happening. That surprised me, because the scene seemed clear to me. *O.N.G!* did well in France, but it seems as if many readers didn't understand, and thought that the man and the woman were merely fighting. This reaction is very interesting. So I said to myself that they probably don't want to understand what is happening. I do it on purpose—I am a wicked writer, as you have understood—I don't dot my i's, I don't give the technical details of this scene. Thus, readers cannot admit that it is a rape scene, because that would be outrageous. I've discovered that the French reader—perhaps because the teaching of literature in school is catastrophically mishandled—often reads too literally. I've been in literature for 18 years. I've met with high school students, seniors, all sorts of people, and I conclude that the average French reader—perhaps because of his rational, deterministic, and logical heritage from the Age of Enlightenment—does not understand when one only suggests things. To be understood you must be very clear. Those who read my novel and understand that it is a rape apparently belong to the educated elite. They've read *Lolita*, Sade, Henry Miller, etc., a myriad of extremely provocative and shocking books, and therefore a rape scene doesn't bother them. Some people are easily shocked. But I didn't write this scene to shock readers. I wrote it because it was the *summum* of what my character could do. And I find it rather funny that he cannot see what he has done; he makes up excuses; he believes he is a noble warrior even when he does these horrible things.

JK: And if someone told you that rape was not a subject suited to a funny novel?

IG: Then nothing is a subject. We would have to forbid *Candide*, we would have to forbid Rabelais, where there are scenes that are hilarious but not at all proper. I adore the unpredictability of Rabelais. You begin reading a chapter, and you have no idea where it will lead. Do you remember the chapter of *Gargantua* where soldiers are trampling the monks' vines? Frère Jean is watching from the monastery window, and he says, "What, the holy vines that I cultivate to make our good wine are being trampled!" So, he takes a cross, and he goes out and starts killing the soldiers, beating them with his cross, and then he administers extreme unction. He kills them, then he blesses them. You have a great number of hysterical scenes that are absolutely not politically correct. Rabelais is phenomenal, but unfortunately today's France is not at all Rabelaisian. Elitist France loves to quote Rabelais, but in reality, fundamentally, it is much more Montaigne, Montesquieu, or Pascal; rather cold and logical. And so, people like to pretend to mix with the riff-raff and quote Rabelais, but in reality France is much sadder than that, unfortunately.

JK: Your novels are obviously influenced by Rabelais. Critics have explicitly compared the war between La Foulée verte and Enfance et vaccine in *O.N.G!* to the Picrocholine War in *Gargantua*. Which other authors have inspired you?

IG: There are many very funny Russian authors who are not well-known in France. Such as Mikhail Zoshchenko, a great twentieth-century author who has not been widely translated. Or Ilf and Petrov, known especially for *The Little Golden Calf* (1931). There are also Mikhail Bulgakov and Nikolai Gogol. But I can't say that they are my only models. I have others who are less funny but who have also inspired me. Louis-Ferdinand Céline is not necessarily funny, but I am an enthusiastic admirer of his writing. And not only *Journey to the End of the Night*. Even his anti-Semitic writings are worth reading, from a literary point of view, because they are in fact written in a language that is absolutely astonishing. They are interesting too in order to understand what is happening in his brain, what the period was like, and how one could ever become like that. We should read all of Céline, as we should watch Leni Riefenstahl's films. But in France, public screenings of *Triumph of the Will*, which I refer to in *L'Écologie en bas de chez moi*, are still forbidden. Thanks to the internet, one can see it, but it will never be seen here on television. In France, when you go to the flea market, you cannot sell or buy—in theory—Nazi objects. If there is a swastika on something, it cannot be sold. So, what does the antique dealer do? He tapes a little piece of paper over it—don't ask, don't tell—and the customer can buy it. Denial is the height of hypocrisy and it makes us extremely vulnerable. Instead of teaching sex education in school, I think it is imperative to show *Triumph of the Will*, so students understand how the mechanics of Nazism work, and how indoctrination works.

JK: In *L'Écologie en bas de chez moi*, you compare Arthus-Bertrand's film *Home* to *Triumph of the Will*. I would never have thought of comparing these two documentaries, but it is true that from a formal point of view the resemblance is there. Was your first reaction to *Home* negative, or were you, like so many others, at first charmed by the beautiful images seen from the sky?

IG: When one is born and grows up in the Soviet Union, surrounded by propaganda every day, one knows full well that there is always something behind a beautiful image. Look across the street: the beautiful images hanging on the fence of the Luxembourg Gardens. What's funny is that these photos are absolutely without meaning: a beautiful mountain, a beautiful landscape, a beautiful lake. They have no value, no message. But watch the people who pass by: they cannot not look at them. They study, voluntarily, an insignificant image. It's really funny. The question is: Why is this image here? It's because the Senate, which is adjacent to the gardens, has money to spend, and since it would like to be seen as cool and nice, it organizes the exhibition of these meaningless pictures. You'll see for yourself when you leave the café. It's rather funny: there is not one photo that is interesting. They are the most insipid postcards possible. And they hang them on this fence that is so pretty in itself. Why am I saying this? Because when you display a beautiful image, no one will yell at you. Showing a beautiful image is safe. When you hang up a beautiful image, you are sure to achieve consensus. Look at how delighted the people are to look at these photos. It's surprising. Whereas there are images that are much more interesting to look at—even non-controversial pictures—images of scientific exploits, bizarre images, photos by great photographers, etc. But those ones on the fence, no! And people are enthusiastically looking at them, anyway. We are witnessing here the attraction of vacuous beauty.

Getting back to Yann Arthus-Bertrand: he was not unknown to me when I went to see *Home*. He had published a book, *Earth From Above* (1999), an incredible bestseller that was on everyone's coffee table. For years, you went into a bookstore and there it was, on display next to the entrance. It was everyone's Christmas present. And what is this book? Pretty—but trivial—images of the earth. There is no meaning in these images, except, perhaps, an ecological meaning: "Look how pretty our earth is." I should say egotistical, rather than ecological: "I am an inhabitant of this pretty world and I am looking at myself. I am looking at this pretty world in which I live." Thus, when I saw *Home*, of course I expected to see pretty images! What shocked me the most about this film was the voice-over: infuriating! I found it poorly done. We are in the land of Big Brother without being able to distance ourselves; we are being crudely manipulated. A beautiful voice accompanied by dreamy and absolutely idiotic music! And then there is the fact that it was being shown everywhere for free. One can never be too suspicious of something free. What's free is never free. There's always something behind it. Anyone who like me grew up in the Soviet Union would react exactly in the same way. We are highly sensitive to manipulation. We are capable of seeing what is behind the image. We don't listen to the news, we decode it. I think that Russians who are younger than me—the post-Soviet Union generation—are duped by Russian news. They don't have this decoding skill like the people of my generation do, who understand what is happening. Therefore, indeed I fell off my chair—and I understood what I had to write—when I saw *Home*. In any case, these ideas are in the article on *Home* that I wrote for *Libération* (4 June 2009).

JK: Here is the last sentence of that article: "I shudder, and I feel a bit alone." Are you really alone? Aren't there other writers who share your ideas?

IG: My problem—and I mention it in *L'Écologie en bas de chez moi*—is that there are a bunch of idiots who are climate change skeptics for all the wrong reasons, like my character the dentist. I don't understand his arguments: they are false. If I am skeptical, it's for reasons more intelligent and subtler than his bogus arguments. To respond to your question: Yes, I feel totally alone. That is, my "friends" say to me, "Oh! Your book is great! You really gave it to them, those stupid greens!" In reality, they are not my friends at all. I am more benevolent towards the guy who told me that my book was "irresponsible." My response is yes, I claim the right to be irresponsible; it is a basic human right. And then we can talk. But when a guy tells me, "Your book strengthens my anti-environmentalism and climate skepticism," I feel a little sick.

Recently I read an article in *The New York Times* about some scientists, defending the official line that climate change is anthropic and irreversible, who do not want the skeptics to express their opinion. An American professor declared that skeptics should not be given as much media coverage as anti-skeptics (if I may call them that!). There is an official party line, proven by scientists, which says that global warming exists. 97 percent of scientists are convinced, the other three percent must not be allowed to exist. The reason the professor criticizes the media is that often, a scientist from the IPCC (Intergovernmental Panel on Climate Change) is invited to speak about climate change, and a skeptic is invited to present an opposing opinion. That makes it 50-50, as if the scientific community were evenly divided. However, she says that scientists are not divided: 97 percent believe in climate change. And since the skeptics make up only three percent, they should not have the right to express their point of view in the media. For her, it is a crucial issue. To justify her opinion, she says that these skeptics are not innocent: they are financed by Exxon, they are right-wing extremists, creationists, etc. This is why, when people say that Iegor Gran is a skeptic, I feel bad. I don't like this label of "skeptic."

JK: At the end of an interview on the website of your publisher, P.O.L., you said, in referring to Nietzsche, that heretics are the best part of religion, and that you are more of a heretic than a skeptic. Could you please explain?

IG: Yes, I admit it. I'm a heretic. Why? Because being a heretic assumes that there is a belief, a faith. This is one of the themes of *L'Écologie en bas de chez moi*. I try to show that much of ecology—or ecologism—is based on a belief. People need to believe in something. They can't just eat, work, and die. No, they need to believe. Even if you take away their religious beliefs, you have to give meaning to their lives. Thus, ecology is not just scientific reasoning, it also has an element of belief. The proof is Pope Francis's *Laudato si'*, the encyclical on the environment that appeared four years after *L'Écologie en bas de chez moi*. That makes me laugh out loud, and in a way legitimizes my discourse. It validates what I say in the book, that ecology is a faith, and faced with his flock losing its bearings, the pope calls on ecology. There you are, we've come full circle. Yes, I'm okay with being a heretic. The heretic is Giordano Bruno, it's the guy who is burned, it's the annoying clown. *C'est moi*! I love to annoy. So heretic, yes; but skeptic, no, except in the metaphysical sense. If it's skeptic in the Fox News sense, no.

We have the same problem with evolution. For example, perhaps there are certain things that Darwin did not actually prove. The famous biologist Stephen Jay Gould was a Darwinian but, even so, he didn't always agree with Darwin. But he found that disagreeing with Darwin was practically impossible, just like earlier it was unacceptable to criticize Freud. Applying a sort of all-or-nothing reasoning, anyone who criticizes Darwin is automatically categorized as an anti-evolutionary evangelist. You are not allowed to say anything, though there are many things to discuss when it comes to Darwin. But that is perhaps another adventure …

Bibliography

"1912–2012: la décharge d'Entressen ou d'Arles?" *Camargue Insolite*, 28 June 2012, www.camargue-insolite.com/article-1912-2012-la-decharge-d-entressen-104616897.html.

Adorno, Theodor. *Minima Moralia: Reflections on a Damaged Life*. Translated by E. F. N. Jephcott, Verso, 2005. Translation of *Minima Moralia*, Suhrkamp Verlag, 1951.

Aeschylus (disputed). *Prometheus Bound*. 5th century BC. Translated by David Grene, edited and introduction by David Grene and Richard Lattimore, Washington Square Press, 1973.

Albeck-Ripka, Livia. "Your Recycling Gets Recycled, Right? Maybe, or Maybe Not." *The New York Times*, 29 May 2018, www.nytimes.com/2018/05/29/climate/recycling-landfills-plastic-papers.html.

Amanieux, Laureline. "La théorie des nuages (et des corps)." *Agora Vox*, 30 Sep. 2009.

Arendt, Hannah. "French Existentialism." *The Nation*, vol. 162, 1946, pp. 226–28.

———. *The Origins of Totalitarianism*. 1951. Harcourt, Brace & World, 1966.

Aristotle. *Meteorology*. 4th century BC. Translated by E. W. Webster, Generic NL Freebook Publisher, 2000.

Armbruster, Karla, and Kathleen R. Wallace. *Beyond Nature Writing: Expanding the Boundaries of Ecocriticism*. University Press of Virginia, 2001.

Attenborough, David. "Zoos Should Use Peepholes to Respect Gorillas' Privacy." *Guardian*, 18 Oct. 2016, www.theguardian.com/world/2016/oct/18/david-attenborough-zoos-respect-gorillas-privacy-peepholes.

Audeguy, Stéphane. "De la nature de quelques choses." *Les Assises Internationales du Roman 2009. Le Roman: hors frontières*. Christian Bourgois, 2009, pp. 241–48.

———. *In Memoriam*. Gallimard, 2009.

———. *Opera mundi*. Créaphis, 2012.

———. *The Theory of Clouds*. Translated by Timothy Bent, Harcourt, 2007. Translation of *La Théorie des nuages*, Gallimard, 2005.

Audier, Serge. *La société écologique et ses ennemis. Pour une histoire alternative de l'émancipation*. La Découverte, 2017.
Audouin, Alice. "Iegor Gran: un iceberg jeté dans la marmite écolo, qui éclabousse le GIEC." 14 Feb. 2011, www.aliceaudouin.com.
Bachelard, Gaston. *Earth and Reveries of Repose: An Essay on Images of Interiority*. Translated by Mary McAllester Jones, Dallas Institute Publications, 2011. Translation of *La Terre et les rêveries du repos. Essai sur les images de l'intimité*. José Corti, 1948.
——. *The Poetics of Space*. Translated by Maria Jolas, Beacon Press, 1969. Translation of *La Poétique de l'espace*. PUF, 1957.
——. *Water and Dreams: An Essay on the Imagination of Water*. Translated by Edith R. Farrell, The Pegasus Foundation, 1983. Translation of *L'Eau et les rêves. Essai sur l'imagination de la matière*. José Corti, 1942.
Bailly, Jean-Christophe. *The Animal Side*. Translated by Catherine Porter, Fordham University Press, 2011. Translation of *Le Versant animal*. Bayard, 2007.
Bakhtin, M. M. *Rabelais and his World*. MIT Press, 1965. Translated by Hélène Iswolsky, Indiana University Press, 1984.
Barsam, Richard Meran. *Nonfiction Film: A Critical History*. Indiana University Press, 1992.
Baudelaire, Charles. *Œuvres complètes*. Seuil, 1968.
Becket, Fiona, and Terry Gifford, editors. *Culture, Creativity and Environment: New Environmentalist Criticism*. Rodopi, 2007.
Belaval, Yvon. "L'esprit de Voltaire." *Studies on Voltaire and the Eighteenth Century*, vol. 24, 1963, pp. 139–54.
Benjamin, Walter. *Illuminations*. Edited by Hannah Arendt, translated by Harry Zohn, Schocken, 1969. Translation of *Illuminationen*. Suhrkamp Verlag, 1955.
——. "The Storyteller." *Illuminations*, pp. 83–109.
——. "The Work of Art in the Age of Mechanical Reproduction." *Illuminations*, pp. 217–51.
Bennett, Jane. *Vibrant Matter: A Political Ecology of Things*. Duke University Press, 2010.
Bentham, Jeremy. *An Introduction to the Principles of Morals and Legislation*. 1789, 2010–15, www.earlymoderntexts.com/assets/pdfs/bentham1780.pdf.
Berry, Thomas. "The New Story: Comments on the Origin, Identification and Transmission of Values." Fabel and St. John, pp. 77–88.
——. "Teilhard in the Ecological Age." Fabel and St. John, pp. 57–73.
——. "The Viable Human." Zimmerman, pp. 175–84.
Bertolini, Gérard. "Dis-moi ce que tu jettes: un état des lieux." Chevallier and Tastevin, pp. 49–61.
Beuve-Méry, Alain. "Stéphane Audeguy: 'Nous avons arraisonné la nature'." *Le Monde des livres*, 21 May 2009.
Beyern, Bertrand. *Grands Prix de l'humour noir*, bertrandbeyern.fr/spip.php?rubrique60.
The Bible. Authorized King James Version, www.kingjamesbibleonline.org/.

Bingham, Alfred J. "Voltaire and the New Testament." *Studies on Voltaire and the Eighteenth Century*, vol. 24, 1963, pp. 183–218.
Birnbaum, Jean, editor. *Qui sont les animaux?* Gallimard, 2010.
Bitoun, Olivier. "Critique de film: *La Fête sauvage*." *DVDClassik*, 5 Mar. 2015, www.dvdclassik.com/critique/la-fete-sauvage-rossif.
Blanc, Nathalie, et al. "Littérature et écologie: vers une écopoétique." *Ecologie et Politique*, vol. 36, no. 2, 2008, pp. 17–28.
Boudreau, Douglas L., and Marnie M. Sullivan, editors. *Ecocritical Approaches to Literature in French*. Lexington Books, 2015.
Bouloumié, Arlette. "*Les Météores*, Notice." Michel Tournier, *Romans, suivis de Le Vent Paraclet*. Gallimard, 2017, pp. 1610–31.
———. "Michel Tournier, un écrivain écologiste?" *Modernité de Michel Tournier*. Edited by Arlette Bouloumié. Presses Universitaires de Rennes, 2016, pp. 91–101.
Boyd, Brian. *On the Origin of Stories: Evolution, Cognition, and Fiction*. Belknap Press of Harvard University Press, 2009.
Bradsher, Greg. "The Nuremberg Laws: Archives Receives Original Nazi Documents That 'Legalized' Persecution of Jews." *Prologue*, vol. 42, no. 4, 2010, www.archives.gov/publications/prologue/2010/winter/nuremberg.html.
Brendlé, Chloé. "Dossier Olivia Rosenthal." *Le Matricule des Anges*, vol. 171, 2016, pp. 14–23.
Breton, André. *Anthology of Black Humor*. Translated by Mark Polizzotti, City Lights Books, 1997. Translation of *Anthologie de l'humour noir*, 1940. J.-J. Pauvert, 1972.
———. *Arcanum 17*. Translated by Zack Rogow, Sun & Moon Press, 1994. Translation of *Arcane 17*, 1945. J.-J. Pauvert, 1971.
Brooks, Peter. *Body Work: Objects of Desire in Modern Narrative*. Harvard University Press, 1993.
Broqua, Aliette de. "Fermeture d'une des plus grandes décharges de France." *LeFigaro.fr*, 1 Apr. 2010, www.lefigaro.fr/actualite-france/2010/04/01/01016-20100401ARTFIG00384-fermeture-d-une-des-plus-grandes-decharges-de-france-.php.
Bruckner, Pascal. *The Fanaticism of the Apocalypse: Save the Earth, Punish Human Beings*. Translated by Steven Rendall, Polity, 2013. Translation of *Le Fanatisme de l'Apocalypse. Sauver la Terre, punir l'Homme*. Grasset et Fasquelle, 2011.
Buell, Lawrence. "Ecocriticism: Some Emerging Trends." *Qui Parle: Critical Humanities and Social Sciences*, vol. 19, no. 2, 2011, pp. 87–115.
———. *The Environmental Imagination*. Princeton University Press, 1995.
———. *The Future of Environmental Criticism: Environmental Crisis and Literary Imagination*. Blackwell, 2005.
Bureau, Luc. *Terra erotica*. Fides, 2009.
Butnariu, Monica. "The Oxygen Paradox." *Journal of Pharmacogenomics & Pharmacoproteomics*, 14 Jan. 2012, www.omicsonline.org/the-oxygen-paradox-2153-0645.1000e104.php?aid=3762.

Cabestan, Philippe. "Lévi-Strauss, Claude." *Dictionnaire Sartre*. Edited by François Noudelmann and Gilles Philippe. Honoré Champion, 2004, pp. 286–87.

Calarco, Matthew. *Zoographies: The Question of the Animal from Heidegger to Derrida*. Columbia University Press, 2008.

Calarco, Matthew, and Peter Atterton, editors. *Animal Philosophy: Essential Readings in Continental Thought*. Continuum, 2004.

Call, Laura. "Waste Treatment: Resource Recovery in *Les Glaneurs et la glaneuse* and *La Clôture*." Boudreau and Sullivan, pp. 145–68.

Callicott, J. Baird. "Animal Liberation: A Triangular Affair." *Environmental Ethics*, vol. 2, 1980, pp. 311–38.

———. "Animal Liberation and Environmental Ethics: Back Together Again." Zimmerman, pp. 147–56.

———. "La Nature est Morte, vive la nature!" *The Hastings Center Report*, vol. 22, no. 5, 1992, pp. 16–23.

———. "The Role of Technology in the Evolving Concept of Nature." *Ethics and Environmental Policy: Theory Meets Practice*. Edited by Frederick Ferré and Peter Hartel. University of Georgia Press, 1994, pp. 58–83.

Callicott, J. Baird, and Robert Frodeman, editors. *Encyclopedia of Environmental Ethics and Philosophy*. MacMillan Reference USA, 2009. 2 vols.

Camus, Albert. "Helen's Exile." 1948. *Lyrical and Critical Essays*. Edited by Philip Thody, translated by Ellen Conroy Kennedy, Knopf, 1968, pp. 148–53. Translation of "L'exil d'Hélène," *Noces, suivi de L'été*. Gallimard-Folio 1959, pp. 133–40.

———. "The Human Crisis." *Twice a Year: A Book of Literature, the Arts, and Civil Liberties*, vols. 14–15, 1946–47. Edited by Dorothy Norman, translated by Lionel Abel, Kraus Reprint Corporation, 1967, pp. 19–33. Translation of "La Crise de l'homme," rpt. in Albert Camus, *Conférences et discours (1936–1958)*. Gallimard, 2017, pp. 34–58.

———. *The Myth of Sisyphus and Other Essays*. 1955. Translated by Justin O'Brien, Vintage, 1991. Translation of six essays, including *Le Mythe de Sisyphe. Essai sur l'absurde*. Gallimard, 1942.

———. *The Plague*. Translated by Robin Buss, Penguin Classics, 2002. Translation of *La Peste*. Gallimard, 1947.

———. "Prometheus in the Underworld." 1947. *Lyrical and Critical Essays*. Edited by Philip Thody, translated by Ellen Conroy Kennedy, Knopf, 1968, pp. 138–42. Translation of "Prométhée aux Enfers," *Noces, suivi de L'été*. Gallimard-Folio 1959, pp. 119–24.

———. *Resistance, Rebellion, and Death: Essays*. Translated by Justin O'Brien, Vintage International, 1995.

Cesbron, Georges. "Introduction." Cesbron and Jacquin, pp. 7–11.

Cesbron, Georges, and Gérard Jacquin, editors. *Vercors (Jean Bruller) et son œuvre*. L'Harmattan, 1999.

Chawaf, Chantal. *Le Corps et le verbe: la langue en sens inverse*. Presses de la Renaissance, 1992.

——— [Marie de la Montluel]. *Mélusine des détritus*. Rocher, 2002.

Chawaf, Chantal, and Régine Deforges. *L'Érotique des mots*. Rocher, 2004.
Cheissoux, Denis. *CO2 mon amour*. Podcast, France-Inter, 16 May 2015.
Chevallier, Denis, and Yann-Philippe Tastevin, editors. *Vies d'ordures: De l'économie des déchets*. Mucem, 2017.
Clark, Timothy. *The Cambridge Introduction to Literature and the Environment*. Cambridge University Press, 2011.
Clarke, Baptiste. "Décharge d'Entressen: la blessure peine à cicatriser." *Actu-Environnement.com*, 30 May 2016, www.actu-environnement.com/ae/news/pollution-nappe-phratique-decharge-entressen-26885.php4.
Cocula, Barnard. "*Les Animaux dénaturés*, fable anthropologique." Cesbron and Jacquin, pp. 147–57.
Coetzee, J. M. *The Lives of Animals*. Princeton University Press, 1999.
Cohen, Jeffrey Jerome, and Lowell Duckert, editors. *Elemental Ecocriticism: Thinking with Earth, Air, Water, and Fire*. University of Minnesota Press, 2015.
Compagnon, Antoine. "La boue des villes." Chevallier and Tastevin, pp. 145–47.
———. "Le moment du chiffon." Chevallier and Tastevin, pp. 79–81.
Conley, Verena. "Manly Values: Luc Ferry's Ethical Philosophy." Calarco and Atterton, pp. 157–63.
Corbin, Alain. *Le Ciel et la mer*. 2005. Flammarion, 2014.
———. *The Lure of the Sea: The Discovery of the Seaside in the Western World, 1750–1840*. Translated by Jocelyn Phelps, University of California Press, 1994. Translation of *Le Territoire du vide. L'Occident et le désir du rivage, 1750–1840*. Aubier, 1988.
Coudrette. *Le Roman de Mélusine*. 1401. Translated by Laurence Harf-Lancner, Flammarion, 1993.
Craige, Betty Jean. *Laying the Ladder Down: The Emergence of Cultural Holism*. University of Massachusetts Press, 1992.
Cuomo, Chris. Review of *The New Ecological Order*, by Luc Ferry. *Isis*, vol. 87, no. 4, 1996, pp. 768–69.
Cyrulnik, Boris. "Les animaux révélés." Matignon and Rosane, pp. 193–265.
Deleuze, Gilles. "Postface: Michel Tournier et le monde sans autrui." *Vendredi ou les limbes du Pacifique*, by Michel Tournier. Gallimard, 1967, pp. 295–325.
Derrida, Jacques. *The Animal that Therefore I Am*. Edited by Marie-Louise Mallet, translated by David Wills, Fordham University Press, 2008. Translation of *L'Animal que donc je suis*. Galilée, 2006.
———. "No Apocalypse, Not Now (Full Speed Ahead, Seven Missiles, Seven Missives)." *Nuclear Criticism*, special issue of *Diacritics*, vol. 14, no. 2, 1984, pp. 20–31.
———. "Plato's Pharmacy." *Dissemination*. Translated by Barbara Johnson, Continuum, 2004, pp. 67–186. Translation of *La Dissémination*. Seuil, 1972.
———. *Séminaire. La Bête et le souverain*. Galilée, 2008–10. 2 vols.
Desblache, Lucile. "Introduction: profil d'une écolittérature." *L'Esprit Créateur*, vol. 46, no. 2, 2006, pp. 1–4.
———. *La Plume des bêtes. Les animaux dans le roman*. L'Harmattan, 2011.

Descartes, René. *Discourse on the Method of Rightly Conducting the Reason and Seeking for Truth in the Sciences. The Philosophical Works of Descartes*, pp. 81–130. Translation of *Discours de la méthode Pour bien conduire sa raison, et chercher la vérité dans les sciences*. Jan Maire, 1637.

———. *Meditations on First Philosophy: The Philosophical Works of Descartes*, pp. 144–97. Translation of *Méditations métaphysiques*. Michael Soly, 1641.

———. *The Passions of the Soul: The Philosophical Works of Descartes*, pp. 331–427. Translation of *Les Passions de l'âme*. Henry Le Gras, 1649.

———. *Philosophical Letters*. Translated and edited by Anthony Kenny, Oxford University Press, 1970.

———. *The Philosophical Works of Descartes*, vol. 1. Translated by Elizabeth Haldane and G. R. T. Ross, Cambridge University Press, 1967.

Detienne, Marcel. *Dionysos Slain*. Translated by Mireille Muellner and Leonard Muellner, Johns Hopkins University Press, 1979. Translation of *Dionysos mis à mort*. Gallimard, 1977.

Dombek, Kristin. "Swimming against the Rising Tide," *The New York Times*, 10 Aug. 2014, www.nytimes.com/2014/08/10/opinion/sunday/secular-climate-change-activists-can-learn-from-evangelical-christians.html.

Drolet, Marie-Josée. Review of *Voir son steak comme un animal mort*, by Martin Gibert. *Bioéthique Online*, 18 Oct. 2016, bioethiqueonline.ca/docs/5/36.pdf.

Druon, Emmanuel. *Écolonomie*. Actes Sud, 2016.

Dunlany, Melissa. *The Aesthetics of Waste: Michel Tournier, Agnes Varda, Sabine Macher*. 2017. University of Pennsylvania, PhD dissertation.

Durand, Gilbert. *The Anthropological Structures of the Imaginary*. Translated by Margaret Sankey and Judith Hatten, Boombana Publications, 1999. Translation of *Les Structures anthropologiques de l'imaginaire*, 11th ed. Dunod, 1992.

Dutheil, Marie-Charlotte. "Saint-Escobille: après 15 ans de lutte, les opposants à la décharge géante célèbrent leur victoire." *Leparisien.fr*, 30 May 2018, www.leparisien.fr/essonne-91/saint-escobille-apres-15-ans-de-lutte-les-opposants-a-la-decharge-geante-celebrent-leur-victoire-30-05-2018-7744119.php.

Eliade, Mircea. *The Forge and the Crucible*. Translated by Stephen Corrin, University of Chicago Press, 1978. Translation of *Forgerons et alchimistes*. Flammarion, 1956.

———. *Mythes, rêves et mystères*. Gallimard, 1957.

Fabel, Arthur, and Donald St. John, editors. *Teilhard in the 21st Century: The Emerging Spirit of Earth*. Orbis Books, 2003.

Favre, Robert. *Le Rire dans tous ses éclats*. Presses Universitaires de Lyon, 1995.

Ferry, Luc. *The New Ecological Order*. Translated by Carol Volk, University of Chicago Press, 1995. Translation of *Le Nouvel Ordre écologique. L'arbre, l'animal et l'homme*. 1992. LGF, 2002.

"Fiches de lecture sur *Le parfum d'Adam.*" *L'Express*, 21 June 2007, www.lexpress.fr/culture/livre/fiches-de-lecture-sur-italique-le-parfum-d-adam-italique_822219.html.

Finch-Race, Daniel A., and Stephanie Posthumus, editors. *French Ecocriticism: From the Early Modern Period to the Twenty-First Century.* Peter Lang, 2017.

Flahault, François. *Le Crépuscule de Prométhée. Contribution à une histoire de la démesure humaine.* Mille et une Nuits, 2008.

Fontenay, Élisabeth de. "Les animaux considérés." Matignon and Rosane, pp. 97–191.

———. *Le Silence des bêtes. La philosophie à l'épreuve de l'animalité.* Fayard, 1998.

———. *Without Offending Humans: A Critique of Animal Rights.* Translated by Will Bishop, University of Minnesota Press, 2012. Translation of *Sans offenser le genre humain: Réflexions sur la cause animale.* Albin Michel, 2008.

Foucart, Stéphane. "Haro sur les écolos!" *Le Monde*, 5 Nov. 2011. *Culture et idées* 1, LexisNexis Academic, www.lemonde.fr/culture/article/2011/11/03/haro-sur-les-ecolos_1598585_3246.html.

Foucault, Michel. *Discipline and Punish: The Birth of the Prison.* Translated by Alan Sheridan, Vintage, 1979. Translation of *Surveiller et punir: naissance de la prison.* Gallimard, 1975.

Foundation for Deep Ecology. "The Deep Ecology Platform," 2012, www.deepecology.org/platform.htm.

Frazer, Sir James George. *The New Golden Bough: A New Abridgement of the Classic Work.* Edited by Theodor H. Gaster. Criterion Books, 1959.

Gaillard, Françoise. "Allégorie d'un fantasme fin de siècle, Courbet: *L'Origine du monde.*" *Mimesis et Semiosis: Littérature et représentation. Miscellanées offertes à Henri Mitterand.* Edited by Philippe Hamon and Jean-Pierre Leduc-Adine. Nathan, 1992, pp. 427–34.

Garcia, Tristan. *Nous, animaux et humains. Actualité de Jeremy Bentham.* François Bourin, 2011.

Garrard, Greg. *Ecocriticism.* Routledge, 2004.

———, editor. *The Oxford Handbook of Ecocriticism.* Oxford University Press, 2016.

Garric, Audrey. "L'industrie alimentaire se détourne en masse des œufs de poules en cage." *Le Monde*, 10 Jan. 2017, www.lemonde.fr/biodiversite/article/2017/01/09/l-industrie-alimentaire-se-detourne-massivement-des-ufs-de-poules-en-cage_5059785_1652692.html.

Gibert, Martin. *Voir son steak comme un animal mort. Véganisme et psychologie morale.* Lux Éditeur, 2015.

Gibert-Joly, Nathalie. "Jean Bruller-Vercors: la rébellion comme spécificité humaine." Birnbaum, pp. 210–24.

Giraudoux, Jean. *Ondine.* Bernard Grasset, 1939.

Gobineau, Arthur de. *The Inequality of Human Races.* Translated by Adrian Collins, G. P. Putnam's Sons, 1915. Translation of *Essai sur l'inégalité des races humaines.* Firmin-Didot Frères, 1855.

Golsan, Richard J. "History and Responsibility of Memory: *Vichy: Un passé qui ne passe pas* and the Trial of Paul Touvier." *Fascism's Return: Scandal, Revision, and Ideology since 1980*. Edited by Richard J. Golsan. University of Nebraska Press, 1998, pp. 182–99.

Goodbody, Axel, and Kate Rigby. *Ecocritical Theory: New European Approaches*. University of Virginia Press, 2011.

Gran, Iegor. *L'Écologie en bas de chez moi*. P.O.L.-Folio, 2011.

———. Interview by Raphaëlle Rérolle. "L'actualité est un morceau de papier alu qui brille." *Le Monde des Livres*, 20 May 2011, www.lemonde.fr/livres/article/2011/05/19/l-actualite-est-un-morceau-de-papier-alu-qui-brille_1524227.

———. *O.N.G!* P.O.L.-Folio, 2003.

Gross, Neil. "Is Environmentalism Just for Rich People?" *The New York Times*, 14 Dec. 2018, www.nytimes.com/2018/12/14/opinion/sunday/yellow-vest-protests-climate.html.

Guattari, Félix. *Qu'est-ce que l'écosophie*. Lignes, 2013.

Guichard, Thierry. "Le monde réapproprié: Dossier Stéphane Audeguy." *Le Matricule des Anges*, vol. 101, 2009, pp. 18–27.

Harf-Lancner, Laurence. *Les Fées au Moyen Age*. Honoré Champion, 1984.

Harper, Douglas. *Online Etymology Dictionary*, www.etymonline.com/.

Harrison, Sarah. *Waste Matters: Urban Margins in Contemporary Literature*. Routledge, 2017.

Hawes, Elizabeth. *Camus, A Romance*. Grove Press, 2009.

Heidegger, Martin. "The Question Concerning Technology." 1953. *Basic Writings*. Edited by David Farrell Krell. Routledge and Kegan Paul, 1978, pp. 287–317.

Hiltner, Ken, editor. *Ecocriticism: The Essential Reader*. Routledge, 2015.

Houssin, Xavier. "Olivia Rosenthal: 'Flirter avec les limites'." *Le Monde des Livres*, 4 Sep. 2014, www.lemonde.fr/livres/article/2014/09/04/olivia-rosenthal-flirter-avec-les-limites_4481678_3260.html.

Huggan, Graham, and Helen Tiffin. *Postcolonial Ecocriticism: Literature, Animals, Environment*. Routledge, 2010.

Hugo, Victor. *Les Misérables*. Translated by Isabel F. Hapgood, First Avenue Editions, 2015. Translation of *Les Misérables*. Albert Laroix et Cie, 1862.

Hulot, Nicolas. "Préface." Rabhi, *Manifeste*, pp. 7–16.

Hutin, Reha, and Jean-Pierre Marguénaud. "Les animaux officiellement 'doués de sensibilité': un point de départ ambitieux." *Le Nouvel Observateur*, 2 Feb. 2015, leplus.nouvelobs.com/contribution/1317634-statut-juridique-de-l-animal-un-point-de-depart-ambitieux-les-mentalites-vont-evoluer.html.

Huysmans, J.-K. *Against Nature*. Translated by Brendan King, Dedalus, 2008. Translation of *À rebours*. G. Charpentier et Cie, 1884.

Ingram, Annie Merrill et al., editors. *Coming into Contact: Explorations in Ecocritical Theory and Practice*. University of Georgia Press, 2007.

Iovino, Serenella. "The Human Alien: Otherness, Humanism, and the Future of Ecocriticism." *Ecozon@*, vol. 1, no. 1, 2010, pp. 53–61.

"The Influence of the Nuremberg Trial on International Criminal Law." Robert H. Jackson Center, www.roberthjackson.org/speech-and-writing/the-influence-of-the-nuremberg-trial-on-international-criminal-law/.

Irigaray, Luce. "A Chance for Life: Limits to the Concept of the Neuter and the Universal in Science and Other Disciplines." *Sexes and Genealogies*, pp. 183–206. Translated by Gillian C. Gill, Columbia University Press, 1993, pp. 183–206. Translation of "Une chance de vivre. Limites au concept de neutre et d'universel dans les sciences et les savoirs." *Sexes et parentés*. Minuit, 1987.

Isaac of Nineveh. *Mystic Treatises by Isaac of Nineveh*. Translated by A. J. Wensinck, Koninklijke Nederlandse Akademie van Wetenschappen, 1923.

Jean d'Arras. *A Bilingual Edition of Jean d'Arras's Mélusine, or, L'histoire de Lusignan*. Edited by Matthew W. Morris, Edwin Mellen Press, 2007. Translation of *Le Roman de Mélusine, ou l'Histoire des Lusignan*, 1393.

"Justinian." *Humanistic Texts*, www.humanistictexts.org/justinian.htm#_Toc483882739.

Kanegsberg, Barbara, and Ed Kanegsberg. "Must it Rust? Causes, Consequences, and Control of Corrosion." *Controlled Environments*, 1 May 2007, www.cemag.us/article/2007/05/must-it-rust-causesconsequencesand-control-corrosion.

Kant, Immanuel. *Critique of Pure Reason*. Translated by F. Max Müller, Anchor Books, 1996. Translation of *Kritik der reinen Vernunft*. Hartknoch, 1781.

Kaplan, Robert D. *Balkan Ghosts: A Journey through History*. Picador, 2005.

Kempf, Hervé. *How the Rich Are Destroying the Earth*. Translated by Leslie Thatcher, Chelsea Green Publishing, 2008. Translation of *Comment les riches détruisent la planète*. Seuil, 2007.

Kerridge, Richard. *Writing the Environment: Ecocriticism and Literature*. Zed Books, 1998.

Klein, Ernest. *A Comprehensive Etymological Dictionary of the English Language: Dealing With the Origin of Words and Their Sense Development Thus Illustrating the History of Civilization and Culture*. Elsevier, 1971.

Klein, Richard. "Knowledge of the Future: Future Fables." *Derrida and Democracy*, special issue of *Diacritics*, vol. 38, no. 1–2, 2008, pp. 173–79.

King, Ynestra. "The Ecology of Feminism and the Feminism of Ecology." Plant, pp. 18–28.

Kolodny, Annette. "Unearthing Herstory: An Introduction." *The Ecocriticism Reader: Landmarks in Literary Ecology*. Edited by Cheryll Glotfelty and Harold Fromm, University of Georgia Press, 1996, pp. 170–81.

Krell, David Farrell. *Contagion: Sexuality, Disease, and Death in German Idealism and Romanticism*. Indiana University Press, 1998.

———. *Derrida and our Animal Others: Derrida's Final Seminar, "The Beast and the Sovereign."* Indiana University Press, 2013.

——. "Introduction to the Question Concerning Technology." *Basic Writings*, by Martin Heidegger, edited by David Farrell Krell, Routledge and Kegan Paul, 1978, pp. 284–86.

——. *The Tragic Absolute: German Idealism and the Languishing of God*. Indiana University Press, 2005.

Krell, Jonathan. "Between Demon and Divinity: Mélusine Revisited." *Mythosphere: A Journal for Image, Myth, and Symbol*, vol. 2, no. 4, 2000, pp. 375–96.

——. "Michel Tournier's 'Degenerate' Art." *Art and Contemporary Prose*, special issue of *Dalhousie French Studies*, vol. 31, 1995, pp. 139–56.

——. *The Ogre's Progress*. University of Delaware Press, 2009.

——. *Tournier élémentaire*. Purdue University Press, 1994.

Lanaspeze, Baptiste. "L'écologie profonde est-elle un humanisme?" *La Bibliothèque résistante*, www.la-bibliotheque-resistante.org/mes_textes/ecologie_profonde.

Lançon, Philippe. "Merci bio." *Libération* (Livres), 16 Jan. 2003, www.liberation.fr/livres/2003/01/16/merci-bio_427994.

——. "Russe dessous." *Libération*, 23 Mar. 2005, www.liberation.fr/portrait/2005/03/23/russe-dessous_513837.

Larrère, Catherine, and Raphaël Larrère. *Du bon usage de la nature: pour une philosophie de l'environnement*. 1997. Flammarion, 2009.

——. *Penser et agir avec la nature: une enquête philosophique*. La Découverte, 2015.

Latour, Bruno. "Arrachement ou attachement à la nature?" *Ecologie politique*, vol. 5, 1993, pp. 15–26.

——. "Comment redistribuer le grand partage?" *Revue de Synthèse*, vol. 110, 1983, pp. 203–36.

——. *Nous n'avons jamais été modernes: essai d'anthropologie symétrique*. 1991. La Découverte/Poche, 1997.

Lemieux, Emmanuel. "Préface." Morin, pp. 7–16.

Leopold, Aldo. "The Land Ethic." *A Sand County Almanac*, 1949. Oxford University Press, 1987, pp. 201–26.

Lévi-Strauss, Claude. Interview by Jean-Marie Benoist. "Lidéologie marxiste, communiste et totalitaire n'est qu'une ruse de l'histoire." *Le Monde*, 21–22 Jan. 1979, pp. 1, 14.

——. *The Savage Mind*. Translated by anonymous, University of Chicago Press, 1966. Translation of *La Pensée sauvage*. Plon, 1962.

——. *Structural Anthropology Volume 2*. Translated by Monique Layton, University of Chicago Press, 1983. Translation of *Anthropologie structurale deux*, 1973. Plon, 1996.

——. *The View from Afar*. Translated by Joachim Neugroschel and Phoebe Hoss, University of Chicago Press, 1992. Translation of *Le Regard éloigné*. Plon, 1983.

Levy, David M., and Sandra J. Peart. "The Secret History of the Dismal Science. Part I. Economics, Religion and Race in the 19th Century." *Library of Economics and Liberty*, 22 Jan. 2001, www.econlib.org/library/Columns/LevyPeartdismal.html.

Lindgaard, Jade. "Nous sommes déchets." Chevallier and Tastevin, pp. 37–44.
Lovelock, James. *Gaia: A New Look at Life on Earth*, 1979. Oxford University Press, 1987.
Lucretius Carus, Titus. *On the Nature of Things*. Translation, introduction, and notes by Martin Ferguson Smith, Hackett, 2001. Translation of *De Rerum Natura*, 1st century BC.
Macauley, David. *Elemental Philosophy: Earth, Air, Fire, and Water as Environmental Ideas*. SUNY Press, 2010.
Macé, Gérard. *Le Goût de l'homme*. Gallimard, 2002.
Mackenzie, Louisa, and Stephanie Posthumus, editors. *French Thinking about Animals*. Michigan State University Press, 2015.
Maffesoli, Michel. *Écosophie. Une écologie pour notre temps*. Les Éditions du Cerf, 2017.
———. Interview by Alexandre Devecchio. "Michel Maffesoli: 'La fin d'un monde n'est pas la fin du monde'." *Le Figaro*, 17 Mar. 2017, www.lefigaro.fr/vox/societe/2017/03/17/31003-20170317ARTFIG00307-michel-maffesoli-la-fin-d-un-monde-n-est-pas-la-fin-du-monde.php.
Mai, Joseph. "'Un tissu de mots': Writing Human and Animal Life in Olivia Rosenthal's *Que font les rennes après Noël?*" *Mosaic*, vol. 49, no. 3, 2016, pp. 55–70.
Markale, Jean. *Mélusine*, 1983. Albin Michel, 1993.
Martinoir, Francine de. "Le discours aux animaux." Review of *Que font les rennes après Noël?*, by Olivia Rosenthal, *La Croix*, 29 Sep. 2010, www.la-croix.com/Culture/Livres-Idees/Livres/Le-discours-aux-animaux-_NG_-2010-09-29-579621.
Matignon, Karine Lou, and David Rosane, editors. *Les Animaux aussi ont des droits*. Seuil, 2013.
McAllester Jones, Mary. *Gaston Bachelard, Subversive Humanist: Texts and Readings*. University of Wisconsin Press, 1991.
Merchant, Carolyn. "Nature as Female." Hiltner, pp. 10–34. Rpt. of Chapter 1 of *The Death of Nature: Women, Ecology, and the Scientific Revolution*. Harper & Row, 1980, pp. 1–41.
Mieder, Wolfgang. *The Pied Piper: A Handbook*. Greenwood Press, 2007.
Mill, John Stuart. *The Subjection of Women*. Longmans, Green, Reader, and Dyer, 1869.
Monsaingeon, Baptiste. *Homo detritus. Critique de la société du déchet*. Seuil, 2017.
Moraru, Christian. Review of *Globalia*, by Jean-Christophe Rufin. *Utopian Studies*, vol. 17, no. 1, 2006, pp. 248–54.
Morin, Edgar. *Écologiser l'homme*. Lemieux Editeur, 2016.
Moser, Keith. "The Decentered, Ecocentric Humanism of Pierre Rabhi in *La Part du Colibri*." *Rocky Mountain Review*, vol. 70, no. 1, 2016, pp. 59–70.
Mossière, Gilles. "An Ecocritical Reading of Jean-Christophe Rufin's *Le Parfum d'Adam*." Boudreau and Sullivan, pp. 169–87.
Neupert, Richard. *A History of the French New Wave Cinema*. University of Wisconsin Press, 2007.

Nietzsche, Friedrich. *Human, All Too Human: A Book for Free Spirits*. Translated by R. J. Hollingdale, Cambridge University Press, 1996. Translation of *Menschliches, Allzumenschliches: Ein Buch für freie Geister*. Verlag von Ernst Schmeltzner, 1878–80.

———. *The Twilight of the Idols and The Anti-Christ*. Translated by R. J. Hollingdale. Penguin, 1990.

Nochlin, Linda. "Courbet's *L'Origine du monde*: The Origin Without an Original." *October*, vol. 37, 1986, pp. 76–86.

Norman, Richard. *On Humanism*. Routledge, 2004.

Novalis [Friedrich von Hardenberg]. *Werke, Tagebücher und Briefe*. Edited by Hans-Joachim Mähl and Richard Samuel, Carl Hanser Verlag, 1987. 3 vols.

The Oxford English Dictionary, www.oed.com.

Palmer, Clare. "Madness and Animality in Michel Foucault's *Madness and Civilization*." Calarco and Atterton, pp. 72–84.

Patterson, Charles. *Eternal Treblinka: Our Treatment of Animals and the Holocaust*. Lantern Books, 2002.

Pearson, Lizz. "On the Trail of the Real Pied Piper." *BBC News*, 18 Feb. 2005, news.bbc.co.uk/2/hi/uk_news/magazine/4277707.stm.

Perrin, Christophe. "Sartre ou la fausse question de l'humanisme." *Archives de Philosophie*, vol. 73, no. 2, 2010, pp. 297–319.

Petit, Susan. *Michel Tournier's Metaphysical Fictions*. John Benjamins, 1991.

Pezechkian-Weinberg, Pary. *Michel Tournier: marginalité et creation*. Lang, 1998.

Phillips, Dana, and Heather I. Sullivan. "Material Ecocriticism: Dirt, Waste, Bodies, Food, and Other Matter." *Interdisciplinary Studies in Literature and Environment*, vol. 19, no. 3, 2012, pp. 445–47.

Pinque, Méryl. "*Le Parfum d'Adam* ou l'imposture: une critique antispéciste du best-seller de Jean-Christophe Rufin et quelques orientations sur ce que sont les droits des animaux." *Revue Jibrile*, June 2007, www.revuejibrile.com/JIBRILE/PAGES/INDEX.htm.

Plant, Judith, editor. *Healing the Wounds: The Promise of Ecofeminism*. New Society, 1989.

Posthumus, Stephanie. *French Écocritique: Reading French Theory and Fiction Ecologically*. University of Toronto Press, 2017.

———. "L'exception écologiste française: *Globalia* de Jean-Christophe Rufin." *Contemporary French and Francophone Studies*, vol. 12, no. 4, 2008, pp. 445–53.

———. "Vers une écocritique française: le contrat naturel de Michel Serres." *Mosaic*, vol. 44, no. 2, 2011, pp. 85–100.

"PPR devient Kering," 22 Mar. 2013, www.kering.com/fr/communiques-de-presse/ppr_devient_kering.

Pratt, Alan R. "Introduction." *Black Humor: Critical Essays*, edited by Alan R. Pratt, Garland, 1993, pp. xvii–xxv.

———. "'People Are Equally Wretched Everywhere': *Candide*, Black Humor and the Existential Absurd." *Black Humor: Critical Essays*. Edited by Alan R. Pratt, Garland, 1993, pp. 181–93.

Proust, Marcel. *Remembrance of Things Past*, vol. 1. Translated by C. K. Scott Moncrieff and Terence Kilmartin, Vintage Books, 1982. Translation of *À la Recherche du temps perdu*. Gallimard, 1954.
Rabelais, François. *The Complete Works of François Rabelais*. Translated by Donald M. Frame, University of California Press, 1991.
Rabhi, Pierre. *Manifeste pour la terre et l'humanisme: pour une insurrection des consciences*. Actes Sud, 2008.
———. "Notre définition de l'agroécologie." *Terre et humanism: l'agroécologie à taille humaine*, terre-humanisme.org.
———. "Notre Mission." Colibris, www.colibris-lemouvement.org/mouvement/notre-mission.
Redfern, Walter. *French Laughter: Literary Humour from Diderot to Tournier*. Oxford University Press, 2008.
Rosenthal, Olivia. Interview by Frédéric Fiolof. 3 Oct. 2010, la-marche-aux-pages.blogspot.fr/2010/10/entretien-avec-olivia-rosenthal.html.
———. *Que font les rennes après Noël?* Gallimard, 2010.
Rousseau, Jean-Jacques. *Discourse on the Origin and Foundations of Inequality Among Men (Second Discourse)*. Edited by Roger D. Masters and Christopher Kelly, translated by Judith R. Bush, et al. *The Collected Writings of Rousseau*, vol. 3. University Press of New England, 1990, pp. 1–95. Translation of *Discours sur l'origine et les fondements de l'inégalité parmi les hommes*. Marc-Michel Rey, 1755.
———. *Œuvres politiques*. Bordas, 1989.
———. *The Social Contract*. Edited by Roger D. Masters and Christopher Kelly, translated by Judith R. Bush, et al. *The Collected Writings of Rousseau*, vol. 4. University Press of New England, 1990, pp. 127–267. Translation of *Du contrat social*. Michel Rey, 1762.
Rufin, Jean-Christophe. *La Dictature libérale. Le secret de la toute-puissance des démocraties au 20e siècle*. J.-C. Lattès, 1994.
———. *Globalia*. Gallimard, 2004.
———. *Le Parfum d'Adam*. Gallimard, 2007.
———. "Rencontre avec Jean-Christophe Rufin, à l'occasion de la parution de *Globalia*." 2002. www.gallimard.fr/catalog/entretiens/01050269.htm.
Saigal, Monique. Compte rendu de *Mélusine des détritus*, par Chantal Chawaf [Marie de la Montluel]. *The French Review*, vol. 77, no. 1, 2003, pp. 190–91.
Sarrazin, Bernard. *Le Rire et le sacré: histoire de la dérision*. Desclée de Brouwer, 1991.
Sartre, Jean-Paul. *Existentialism Is a Humanism*. Edited by John Kulka, translated by Carol Macomber, Yale University Press, 2007. Translation of *L'Existentialisme est un humanism*. Nagel, 1946.
———. *Nausea*. Translated by Lloyd Alexander, New Directions, 1964. Translation of *La Nausée*. Gallimard, 1938.
Sax, Joseph L. "Environmental Law." Callicott and Frodeman, pp. 348–54.
Schuessler, Jennifer. "Albert Camus, Stranger in a Strange Land: New York." *The New York Times*, 24 Mar. 2016, www.nytimes.com/2016/03/25/books/albert-camus-stranger-in-a-strange-land-new-york.html?_r=0.

Serres, Michel. *Malfeasance: Appropriation through Pollution?* Translated by Anne-Marie Feenberg-Dibon, Stanford University Press, 2011. Translation of *Le Mal propre. Polluer pour s'approprier?* Éditions le Pommier, 2008.

———. *The Natural Contract.* Translated by Elizabeth MacArthur and William Paulson, University of Michigan Press, 1995. Translation of *Le Contrat naturel.* François Bourin, 1990.

———. "Revisiting the Natural Contract." Translated by Anne-Marie Feenberg-Dibon, Mara-Stream, Goldsmiths, University of London, 2011, www.mara-stream.org/think-tank/michel-serres-revisiting-the-natural-contract/. Translation of "Retour au 'Contrat naturel'," *CTheory.net*.

Serres, Michel, and Bruno Latour. *Conversations on Science, Culture, and Time.* Translated by Roxanne Lapidus, University of Michigan Press, 1995. Translation of *Éclaircissements.* François Bourin, 1990.

Singer, Peter. "All Animals Are Equal." Zimmerman, pp. 26–40.

———. "Les animaux libérés." Matignon and Rosane, pp. 13–95.

Smith, David Livingstone. *Less than Human: Why We Demean, Enslave, and Exterminate Others.* St. Martin's Press, 2011.

Smith, James L. "New Bachelards? Reveries, Elements and Twenty-First Century Materialism." *Altre Modernità*, 2012, pp. 156–67.

Sokal, Alan, and Jean Bricmont. *Fashionable Nonsense: Postmodern Intellectuals' Abuse of Science.* Picador, 1998. Translation of *Impostures intellectuelles.* Éditions Odile Jacob, 1997.

Stokes, Lawrence D. "Historical Introduction." *The Silence of the Sea*, by Vercors, pp. 1–23.

Stone, Christopher D. "Defending the Global Commons." *Greening International Law.* Edited by Philippe Sands, The New Press, 1994, pp. 34–49.

———. *The Gnat Is Older than Man: Global Environment and Human Agenda.* Princeton University Press, 1993.

———. "Should Trees Have Standing?—Toward Legal Rights for Natural Objects." *Southern California Law Review*, vol. 45, 1972, pp. 450–57. Rpt. in Callicott and Frodeman, pp. 458–84.

Tertrais, Bruno. *L'Apocalypse n'est pas pour demain: pour en finir avec le catastrophisme.* Denoël, 2011.

Tocqueville, Alexis de. *Democracy in America.* Translated by Arthur Goldhammer, Library of America, 2004. 2 vols. Translation of *De la démocratie en Amérique.* C. Gosselin, 1835, 1840.

Tournier, Michel. *Célébrations.* Gallimard, 2000.

———. "Douceurs et colères des éléments." *Petites Proses.* Gallimard, 1986, pp. 204–06.

———. *Friday.* Translated by Norman Denny, Johns Hopkins University Press, 1997. Translation of *Vendredi ou les limbes du Pacifique.* Gallimard, 1967.

———. *Gemini.* Translated by Anne Carter, Doubleday, 1981. Translation of *Les Météores.* Gallimard, 1975.

———. *The Midnight Love Feast.* Translated by Barbara Wright, Collins, 1991. Translation of *Le Médianoche amoureux.* Gallimard, 1989.

———. *The Mirror of Ideas*. Translated by Jonathan F. Krell, University of Nebraska Press, 1998. Translation of *Le Miroir des idées*. Mercure de France, 1996.
———. *The Ogre*. Translated by Barbara Bray, Johns Hopkins University Press, 1997. Translation of *Le Roi des Aulnes*. Gallimard, 1970.
———. "Patricio Lagos ou le passage de la Ligne." *Le Crépuscule des masques*. Hoëbeke, 1992, pp. 160–67.
———. *Romans, suivis de Le Vent Paraclet*. Edited by Arlette Bouloumié et al., Gallimard, 2017.
———. "Tom Thumb Runs Away." *The Fetishist*. Translated by Barbara Wright, Doubleday, 1984. Translation of "La fugue du Petit Poucet," *Le Coq de Bruyère*. Gallimard, 1978.
———. *The Wind Spirit*. Translated by Arthur Goldhammer, Beacon, 1988. Translation of *Le Vent Paraclet*. Gallimard, 1977.
Vercors. "La Sédition humaine." *Plus ou moins Homme*. Albin Michel, 1950, pp. 13–54.
———. *The Silence of the Sea/Le Silence de la mer*. Edited by James W. Brown and Lawrence D. Stokes, translated by Cyril Connolly, Berg, 1991.
———. *You Shall Know Them*. Translated by Rita Barisse, Little, Brown and Company, 1953. Translation of *Les Animaux dénaturés*. Albin Michel, 1952.
Vilmer, Jean-Baptiste Jeangène. "Foreword." Mackenzie and Posthumus, pp. vii–xiii.
Voltaire. *Candide, or, Optimism*. 1759. Translated by Burton Raffel, Yale University Press, 2005.
Waldman, Jonathan. *Rust: The Longest War*. Simon & Schuster, 2015.
Whiteside, Kerry. *Divided Natures: French Contributions to Political Ecology*. MIT, 2002.
Wiesel, Elie. *The Gates of the Forest*. Translated by Frances Frenaye, Holt, Rinehart and Winston, 1966. Translation of *Les Portes de la forêt*. Seuil, 1964.
Wolfe, Cary. *What Is Posthumanism?* University of Minnesota Press, 2009.
Yaeger, Patricia. "Editor's Column: The Death of Nature and the Apotheosis of Trash; or, Rubbish Ecology." *PMLA*, vol. 123, no. 2, 2008, 321–38.
Zeldin, Theodore. "The Prophet of Unisex." *Observer*, 30 Jan. 1983, p. 43.
Zimmerman, Michael E., editor. *Environmental Philosophy: From Animal Rights to Radical Ecology*, 3rd ed. Prentice-Hall, 2001.
"Zoochosis: Abnormal and Stereotypic Behaviour in Captive Animals." *Born Free Foundation*, www.bornfree.org.uk/campaigns/zoo-check/captive-wildlife-issues/abnormal-behaviours/.
Zupančič, Metka. "Chantal Chawaf: la déchirure originelle." *Des Femmes écrivent la guerre*. Edited by Frédérique Chevillot et Anna Norris, Éditions Complicités, 2007, pp. 219–32.

Index

absolute, the 15, 33, 37–38, 45–46, 48, 50, 52, 86, 110, 155, 203
Adorno, Theodor 123, 146
Aeschylus 61
agroecology 20, 89, 199–200, 201
Aiken, William 19, 169
Albeck-Ripka 230n2
animal ethics 132–33, 196, 197
animal studies 96n2, 98, 119
animals
    abattoirs 18, 100, 138–40, 143–47
    animal/human borderline 13, 17, 19, 95–98, 100, 103, 108–10, 113–21, 123–47, 214
    euthanasia 135–37
    imprinting 134–35, 137
    medical experiments 14, 135–37
antihumanism 6, 18, 19, 110, 114, 115, 119, 120, 171, 181, 189, 197, 215
apocalypse (apocalyptic) 7, 14, 60, 83–84, 164–66, 175, 185–88, 215, 225, 231
Arendt, Hannah 100–02, 103–06, 111, 112, 117n28, 119, 144, 145, 146
    see also law of the strongest
Aristotle 16, 23, 114, 185n9
Arthus-Bertrand, Yann 19, 181–82, 184, 187, 234–35
Attenborough, David 131–32
Atterton, Peter 96n2, 115n26

Audeguy, Stéphane 20, 206n7
    "De la nature de quelques choses" 58, 65, 74, 221
    Histoire du lion Personne 130n4
    Nous autres 224
    The Only Son (*Fils unique*) 221
    Opera mundi 70–72, 214
    The Theory of Clouds (*La Théorie des nuages*) 16, 53–75, 214, 217–27
Audouin, Alice 191

Bachelard, Gaston 28–29, 33, 36–37, 197–98n1, 199n2
Bailly, Jean-Christophe 95, 96n2
Barsam, Richard Meran 143
Baudelaire, Charles 71, 133, 210, 218
beauty 3, 20, 27, 43, 45, 54, 82, 109, 162–63, 182, 201–03, 235
Benjamin, Walter 44n16, 53
Bennett, Jane 16, 48–49, 158n5, 198n1, 200
Bentham, Jeremy 196
    animal ethics 97, 132–33
    panopticon 131–32
Berry, Thomas 4, 193, 211–14
Beuve-Méry, Alain 74
Birnbaum, Jean 96n2
black humor 19, 179–81, 185n9
Boudreau, Douglas L., and Marnie M. Sullivan 215

ecological (ecohumanism) 19, 20, 170, 173, 195–215, 224
ethical (moral) 97, 98, 170
European (Christian, Western) 19, 20, 117, 120n30, 170, 197, 198, 200n2, 204, 209, 210, 211, 213
exclusive vs. inclusive 19, 196
existentialist 109–21, 196
redistributed 170–71, 195
Renaissance 194, 198
see also antihumanism; posthumanism
humanitarianism (humanitarian) 18, 151, 161, 170, 181, 200, 214
Hume, David 132–33
Huysmans, J.-K. 44

Inglehart, Ronald 183
inversion (benign and malignant) 41, 50, 162, 163
see also Tournier, Michel
Iovino, Serenella 195
Irigaray, Luce 85
Isaac of Nineveh 172–73

Jackson, Robert H. 107
Jean d'Arras 77, 79, 92

Kaplan, Robert D. 145n17
Kant, Immanuel (Kantian) 7, 37, 55n3, 193, 197n1
Kempf, Hervé 171, 182–83
King, Ynestra 68
Klein, Richard 83–84
Kolodny, Annette 68
Krell, David Farrell 37n10, 65n13, 96n2, 115n26, 155

Lanaspeze, Baptiste 194
landfills (dumps) 16, 22, 24, 27, 38–52, 213, 230n2
Larrère, Catherine and Raphaël 17, 87, 157, 194, 212
  hybrid nature 18, 114–15, 153n3, 158

Latour, Bruno 7, 10n8, 17, 115, 157, 170–71, 195, 205
law of the first occupant 104–05n13, 129
law of the strongest 17, 102–06, 112–13, 118, 129n4, 140, 144
see also might-right doctrine
Leopold, Aldo *see* environmental ethics
Lévi-Strauss, Claude 19, 108n17, 110–11, 117, 119, 121, 170, 173, 197–99, 201, 204, 210, 211, 213
Lindgaard, Jade 41n12, 42
Lovelock, James 13n13
Lucretius 65n10, 74–75
Luxemburg, Rosa 104

Macé, Gérard 143n15
Maffesoli, Michel 20, 32n7, 87–88, 89, 90, 173, 197, 206–10, 211, 212
Mai, Joseph 124, 128, 129n3
Markale, Jean 86
Martinoir, Francine de 128, 133
Mauss, Marcel 45
McAllester Jones, Mary 197
Mélusine 16, 77–79, 86–87, 88–89, 90–92
  Mélusine des détritus see Chawaf, Chantal
Merchant, Carolyn 67–68, 220
meteorology (meteorological, meteorologist) 16, 24, 29, 30, 31, 54, 55, 56, 58, 63, 65n9, 66, 68, 71, 213, 217–18
Mieder, Wolfgang 142
might-right doctrine 103–05, 107, 144, 201
  see also law of the strongest
Mill, John Stuart 102, 103, 196
Monsaingeon, Baptiste 16, 39, 40–41n12, 46–47
Montaigne, Michel de 132, 133, 144, 204, 233
Montluel, Marie de la 79n3
  see also Chawaf, Chantal

Moraru, Christian 161, 162, 163
Morin, Edgar 20, 165n10, 173, 194, 197, 203–06, 210, 211, 213, 215
Moser, Keith 199–200n2, 202n5
Mossière, Gilles 172

Naess, Arne 6n3, 163, 167, 168n14, 190, 207
  see also deep ecology
natura naturans 158, 212
Nazi death (concentration) camps 18, 43n14, 51, 60, 99–102, 112, 117, 119, 120, 142, 144–47
  Auschwitz 41n13, 58, 65, 74, 141, 144
  Treblinka 143–44, 146–47
  see also Holocaust
Nazism (Hitlerism, National Socialism, Nazi, Third Reich) 7–8, 17, 18, 19, 24, 41n13, 43n14, 44–45n16, 60, 91, 99, 100, 101n9, 103, 106, 107, 112, 115, 119, 120, 135n9, 141, 142, 144–47, 184, 234
Neupert, Richard 99n5
Nietzsche, Friedrich 10n8, 37n10, 110, 236
Nochlin, Linda 70, 71
Norman, Richard 194
Novalis (Friedrich von Hardenberg) 155–56
nuclear power 17, 61, 63, 80, 81, 82–84, 86, 88, 178, 214
Nuremberg
  1934 Nazi Party Congress 19, 184
  Laws 107
  Principles 107–08
  Trials 107

Oedipus complex 137
oikos 176, 208

Palmer, Clare 101n10
Patterson, Charles 18, 143–47, 157
Pearson, Lizz 142
Perrin, Christophe 117n27

Petit, Susan 39n11
pharmakon 166, 188, 215
Phillips, Dana, and Heather I. Sullivan 153
Pico della Mirandola, Giovanni 194
"The Pied Piper of Hamelin" 140–43
Pinque, Méryl 168n14, 169–70, 171, 173
posthumanism (posthuman, posthumanist) 11, 19–20, 35, 42
Posthumus, Stephanie 32n8, 156, 170–72, 193, 195, 197, 207, 214
Pratt, Alan R. 180, 181
Prometheus (Promethean) 20, 61–62, 64, 65, 77, 79, 84, 88, 164, 202n4, 204, 206, 207, 208–10, 214, 215
Proust, Marcel (Proustian) 86, 140–41n12

Rabelais, François 19, 177, 178n6, 180, 233
Rabhi, Pierre 20, 87, 89, 170, 173, 197, 199–203, 204, 210–11, 213, 214
ragpickers (rag and bone men) 40–41, 48, 213
Redfern, Walter 177, 184, 190
Riefenstahl, Leni
  Triumph of the Will 19, 184, 233
Rosenthal, Olivia 222
  Que font les rennes après Noël? 17, 94, 123–46, 214
Rousseau, Jean-Jacques 1, 2, 5, 6, 8, 8–9n6, 10n8, 12, 19, 37, 74, 102n11, 103, 104, 105–06, 110, 112, 129n2, 190, 193, 196
Rufin, Jean-Christophe 19, 166n12
  La Dictature libérale 14, 18, 151, 152n2, 164–66
  Globalia 18, 150, 152–64, 166–67, 172
  Le Parfum d'Adam 8n4, 18–19, 167–73
rust (rusted, rusty) 153–59, 161, 171

Sade, D. A. F., marquis de 71, 252
Sartre, Jean-Paul 97, 109, 110, 111, 115, 118, 119n30, 120, 202n5
  Existentialism is a Humanism (*L'Existentialisme est un humanisme*) 110, 116–18, 170, 196, 199
  The Flies (*Les Mouches*) 109, 166–67
  Nausea (*La Nausée*) 111, 117n27
Sax, Joseph L. 12–13
Schuessler, Jennifer 111n20
Serres, Michel 7, 10n8, 12, 13, 14, 17, 166, 193, 194, 205
  Malfeasance: Appropriation Through Pollution? (*Le Mal propre: Polluer pour s'approprier?*) 4, 5
  The Natural Contract (*Le Contrat naturel*) 1–6, 8–9n6, 9, 13n13, 57–58, 180, 202
  "Revisiting the Natural Contract" ("Retour au 'Contrat naturel'") 1, 12, 157
  world-objects 157
Singer, Isaac Bashevis 143, 145
Singer, Peter 12n11, 18, 98, 120n31, 129, 132–33, 135, 136
  humane moralism 97
Smith, David Livingstone 139
Smith, James L. 198n1
Smith, Martin Ferguson 75n19
Sokal, Alan, and Jean Bricmont 85n6
sophia (wisdom) 37–38, 208
Spinoza, Baruch 48
Stokes, Lawrence D. 99
Stone, Christopher D. 10–12, 13n12
Sullivan, Robert 49

technology (technological) 4, 61–65, 75, 85, 86, 87, 96, 115, 131, 146, 158–59, 161, 165–66, 168, 185–86n10, 188, 205, 206n8, 208–09, 212, 214, 215, 221–22, 224–25
technonature 115, 158

temps (time/weather)
  in Audeguy's *The Theory of Clouds* 54–57
  in Tournier's *Gemini* 16, 24–26, 29, 30–33
Tertrais, Bruno 185–87
Thoreau, Henry David 49, 74, 164
tides 16, 23, 24–29, 30, 49, 175, 213
Tocqueville, Alexis de 18, 151, 159–61
totalitarianism (totalitarian) 8–9n6, 14, 64, 100, 103–04, 105n14, 106n12, 117n28, 119, 144, 152, 159, 161, 184, 187, 189, 190, 203, 230, 231
  see also tyranny
Tournier, Michel
  Célébrations 15, 26
  Le Crépuscule des masques 24, 26
  "Douceurs et colères des éléments" 23
  The Fetishist (*Le Coq de bruyère*) 36n10
  Friday (*Vendredi ou les limbes du Pacifique*) 15, 24, 38, 41n13, 45–46, 51, 72–74, 213
  Gemini (*Les Météores*) 15–16, 22, 23–52, 74, 197n1, 199n2, 213
  The Midnight Love Feast (*Le Médianoche amoureux*) 24, 26
  The Mirror of Ideas (*Le Miroir des idées*) 2–3, 24, 28n2, 55, 58
  The Ogre (*Le Roi des Aulnes*) 15, 24, 41n13, 44n16, 142n13, 213n13
  "Tom Thumb Runs Away" ("La fugue du Petit Poucet") 15, 36–37n10
  The Wind Spirit (*Le Vent Paraclet*) 15, 30, 31, 32n8, 37–38, 41, 45, 48n19, 50n22, 55, 162, 208n9
tyranny (tyrannical) 9, 18, 102n11, 152n1, 153, 159–62, 164, 165, 166, 202
  see also totalitarianism

Vercors (Jean Bruller) 111, 112
  "La Sédition humaine" 118
  The Silence of the Sea (*Le Silence de la mer*) 99
  You Shall Know Them (*Les Animaux dénaturés*) 17, 65, 95–121, 124, 205, 214
Verne, Jules 2, 16, 30, 55, 65n12, 213n13
Vilmer, Jean-Baptiste Jeangène 197
Voltaire (Arouet, François-Marie) (Voltairian) 19, 117n28, 177, 180–81, 184, 185, 190–91, 196, 215, 232–33

Waldman, Jonathan 154
Wiesel, Elie 185n9
Wolfe, Cary 19–20

Yaeger, Patricia 77
yellow vest movement 183

Zeldin, Theodore 37n10
Zupančič, Metka 91n10